'Dignity of Labour' for African Leaders:
The Formation of Education Policy in the British Colonial Office and Achimota School on the Gold Coast

Shoko Yamada

Langaa Research & Publishing CIG
Mankon, Bamenda

Publisher:
Langaa RPCIG
Langaa Research & Publishing Common Initiative Group
P.O. Box 902 Mankon
Bamenda
North West Region
Cameroon
Langaagrp@gmail.com
www.langaa-rpcig.net

Distributed in and outside N. America by African Books Collective
orders@africanbookscollective.com
www.africanbookscollective.com

ISBN-10: 9956-550-00-0

ISBN-13: 978-9956-550-00-5

© Shoko Yamada 2018

All rights reserved.
No part of this book may be reproduced or transmitted in any form or by any means, mechanical or electronic, including photocopying and recording, or be stored in any information storage or retrieval system, without written permission from the publisher

Table of contents

List of tables and figures ix
List of pictures xi
Acknowledgments xiii

Part I: Framework of the study 1

Chapter 1: Introduction 3
1-1 Framework of analysis: actors, structure,
   norms, and context 4
1-2 Attention to education in the colonial and
   post-colonial Africa 10
1-3 Data used for the analysis 14
   1-3-1 Documentary research 15
   1-3-2 Interviews 19
1-4 Structure of the book 21

Chapter 2: Literature review 27
2-1 History of colonial education and education in Africa 27
   2-1-1 Chronology of education in British West Africa 27
   2-1-2 Reflection on the British policies and
       planning on colonial education 29
   2-1-3 Studies on the American influence on colonial education 31
   2-1-4 Local politics of education in Africa 34
   2-1-5 Educational practice and experience of schooling 39
2-2 Perspectives on global discourse and transfer
   of educational models 43
   2-2-1 Theories on borrowing and adaptation of educational ideas 43
   2-2-2 Motivations for transferring educational ideas 45
   2-2-3 Global mechanism for developing a
       common policy framework 47
   2-2-4 Limitations of conventional analytical framework 48
2-3 Perennial debate over vocational versus
   literary education 50
   2-3-1 Justifications for vocational education 52

2-3-2 Criticism of tracking and the vocationalization
of the general secondary curriculum... 57
2-3-3 Implication of vocationalism in Africa 60

Part II: Global discourse on the colonial education in Africa and its constructs... 65

Chapter 3: The context which conditioned the discourse... 69
3-1 Political economy of inter-war period in Europe 69
3-2 Interventionist government and scientific planning................ 72
3-3 Education in the systemic web of colonialism 74
3-4 Pan-Africanism and inspirations for
nationalism in Africa.. 78
3-5 Overlapping spaces of global influence.. 83

Chapter 4: Genesis of British colonial education policies... 85
4-1 Convergence of interests 88
    4-1-1 Formulating the Alliance of Mission Societies 88
    4-1-2 Inviting the American Expert... 89
    4-1-3 Jointly moulding the global policy framework 93
4-2 Agencies of the key individuals: 'good'
mediators of interests... 97
    4-2-1 Thomas Jesse Jones: salesperson of
the American model.. 98
    4-2-2 J.H. Oldham: the spider of the missionary web 102
    4-2-3 James Aggrey: a black mediator 107
4-3 Educational transfer and politics of discourse 111

Chapter 5: Philosophical sources of inspiration for African education 119
5-1 Progressive education philosophies:
'learning by doing' 120
5-2 Vocational education in Britain and America........................ 123
5-3 British Victorian moralism in education 129
    5-3-1 'Public school': masculinity in elite education 129

5-3-2 Boy Scout movement: elitist moralism
translated to a mass programme... 133
5-3-3 Girls education: wives of the classed men............................ 134
5-4 Mélange of fashionable ideas to legitimise
colonial education.. 136
5-4-1 Interchangeable concepts for educational adaptation.............. 136
5-4-2 The mixed model for the African colonies............................ 138

Part III: National discourse on education and struggle over the hegemony 145

Chapter 6: Political context on the Gold Coast.................... 149
6-1 Prehistory: education until early 20th Century........................ 149
6-1-1 Castle schools.. 149
6-1-2 Mission schools: a root of vocational versus
literary education controversy.. 149
6-1-3 Involvement of the colonial government in education............ 152
6-2 Issues of political debates and actors
in the early 20th century... 155
6-2-1 Civilising mission and rising criticism of
mission schools.. 156
6-2-2 Saturating the labour market and
scepticism of mission education... 159
6-2-3 Struggle for political representation................................. 161
6-3 Political rivalry and accusation for 'denationalisation'............ 167

Chapter 7: Educational discourse and Guggisberg's administration............................ 171
7-1 Development of the colonial education system
during the governorship of Guggisberg (1918–27)................ 172
7-2 Mission societies' dilemma... 176
7-2-1 Government–mission relationship: forces for alignment......... 177
7-3 African demands for more and better education..................... 182
7-3-1 Demands from the general public.................................... 182
7-3-2 Nationalists' demands for higher education..................... 184
7-4 Secondary schools as the sites for producing
African leaders 187

  7-4-1 Prince of Wales College and School at Achimota 187
  7-4-2. Other secondary schools (Mfantsipim and Adisadel) 190
7-5 Ambivalence among actors 192

Chapter 8: Achimota School as an experiment   199
8-1 Type of character to be developed at school 201
  8-1-1 Efficient workmanship 203
  8-1-2 Leadership 205
  8-1-3 Christian character 207
  8-1-4 Holder of a sense of citizenship 209
  8-1-5 Follower of African traditions and customs 211
8-2 Definition of African Tradition 213
8-3 A Public School in Africa 218
  8-3-1 Social Services 221
  8-3-2 'Adaptation' to African 'tradition' 222
  8-3-3 'Dignity of labour' – handwork 223
  8-3-4 Co-education 225
8-4 Experiencing Achimota education 229
  8-4-1 Social mobility 229
  8-4-2 Boarding school life 231
  8-4-3 Co-education 233
  8-4-4 Cultural production under the name of 'adaptation' 235

Part IV: Post-history and conclusion 243

Chapter 9: Educational adaptation and
public response in Ghana after independence 245
9-1 External influences on the vocational
  secondary education policies 246
  9-1-1 The 1950s and 1960s 246
  9-1-2 From the 1970s to early 1980s 248
  9-1-3 The 1980s: the age of structural adjustment 249
  9-1-4 From the 1990s to the mid-2000s: the dominance
    of 'education for all' 250
  9-1-5 Recent revival of vocationalism and promotion
    of competency-based training 253
  9-1-6 Longitudinal patterns of debates on vocational education 254

9-2 Education policies in the post-colonial Ghana
   and the changing focus on vocational education....................257
   9-2-1 System development in the 1960s 257
   9-2-2 Turmoils in the 1970s 258
   9-2-3 1987 Education reform: socio-moralist vocationalism 259
   9-2-4 Popularisation of basic education:
       sidelined (vocational and general) secondary education........... 261
   9-2-5 2007 New education reform.......................................262
9-3 Dialectics between the global and the national......................263
   9-3-1 Convergences and divergences of Ghanaian
       policies and global trends 263
   9-3-2 Practices of secondary education in Ghana:
       persistent distrust in the vocational track.................266

Chapter 10: Conclusion **271**
10-1. Framework of policy analysis 276
10-2. Educational philosophies in colonial Africa........................279

Bibliography... **281**

Appendix: List of interviewees... **309**

Index **315**

List of tables and figures

Figure 3-1: Cocoa Export Price, 1900–1940 70

Figure 3-2: Trend of Cocoa Export, 1900–1940 71

Table 6-1: Educational Statistics of the
Gold Coast: 1880–1945 154

Table 8-1: Ethnic Backgrounds of
Achimota Students (1932) 214

Table 8-2: Composition of Achimota
Teaching Staff (1932) 220

Table 8-3: Core Curriculum of Achimota
Middle and Secondary Schools 224

Table 8-4: Achimota College and School –
Number of Students 228

Figure 8-1: Parental Occupation of
Achimota Students (1932) 231

Table 9-1: Distribution of Project Investments
by Education Sub-sector, FY 1963–90 251

Figure 9-1: DAC Member Countries' Education
ODA by Sub-sectors, 2004 and 2008 252

Table 9-2: Global Trends of Education Policies
and Vocationalism 256

Figure 9-2: Trend of Enrolment in Primary and
Secondary Education in Ghana (1971–2016) 259

Table 9-3: The Proportion of Secondary-level Pupils in Vocational and Technical Education by Region and by Category of Country 268

List of pictures

W.E.B. Du Bois (1868-1963) 79

Booker T. Washington (1856-1915) 81

Thomas Jesse Jones (1873-1950) 99

J.H. Oldham (1874-1969) 104

James Aggrey (1875–1927) 107

Map of the Gold Coast Colony (1896) 152

On the day of Achimota Inauguration (1927) 189

Achimota School's Emblem 217

Acknowledgments

This book is based on my Ph.D. dissertation submitted to Indiana University, USA, in 2003. It has been a long while since then. At that time, of course, I dreamed of publishing it as a book. Some people also suggested that I do so. However, I left the field of history soon after I received the degree and shifted to studies on educational development in contemporary Africa and on donors' aid policies on education in developing countries. I maintained the passion for history and always thought of resuming it someday. However, 'someday' seemed to be in the distant future.

In November 2016, in Kampala, Uganda, I attended a conference on African potential, organised by a group of scholars of humanities and social sciences from Japan and various African countries. My presentation was about civics textbooks for secondary schools in Ethiopia. Deep down inside, this topic is linked to my interest in the historical and cultural roots of contemporary educational discourse which drove me to conduct a historical analysis of colonial education for my dissertation. But such link would not have been understood by anybody, given the distant outlook of the topic I presented.

That was where I met Prof. Francis B. Nyamnjoh from the University of Cape Town, South Africa. I do not remember how it happened, but he requested me to send the soft copy of my dissertation to him, and I did so while we were there. His reaction was prompt. On the same day, he suggested that I publish it as a part of the series he edits.

Unless somebody encouraged me, I was not motivated to revisit my dissertation and publish it. Therefore, I accepted Prof. Nyamnjoh's offer zealously, taking it as the opportunity to reward myself for my effort fifteen years before. However, the process of revision was much more difficult and time consuming than I had assumed. For several months, my progress was like that of a snail, in spare moments from routine tasks and other research. Still, I was excited to feel that various papers and books I had written on the contemporary themes in the last fifteen years were along the continuum of what I wanted to discuss in this historical piece. The more I was convinced of its analytical importance to make sense of my scholarly career, I could not compromise my desire to organise my argument.

When I was writing my dissertation, I did not fully digest why my internal self was pushed to pursue this theme of the British discourse on colonial education during the inter-war period and its adaptation in Achimota School.

Before joining the Ph.D. programme, I was working as an education expert to provide consultancy services for international cooperation projects funded by aid providing agencies. As Chapter Nine of this book outlines, in the late 1990s, the global aid community committed itself to achieve universal primary education around the world. Those countries which had a low enrolment rate for primary education received a large amount of aid. Back then, education experts like me were busy visiting such countries for feasibility studies for school construction, designing programmes for training teachers or developing curriculums. The tasks often brought me to sub-Saharan African countries, where school-based education tended to be far from universal.

After working this way for several years, I started to feel that urging everybody to enrol in school should not necessarily be considered as a sign of ensuring human rights to education. I had thought of potential diversity of the processes of education in traditional societies before the introduction of Western style schools. I became curious to know the logic and justification behind the massive movement for universal primary education. I wanted to know the real meaning of education in the contexts of the African societies I visited. That is why I decided to return to university to pursue a Ph.D.

As a person who was a technical specialist in educational development, my primary objective was not necessarily to conduct a historical study. Rather, I wanted to know how school education was introduced to Africa with what kind of intention, as a basis to make sense of today's educational practices. Still, I remember the fascination on a hot afternoon of the year 2000, when I found Governor Guggisberg's statement on education in Balme Library of the University of Ghana by chance. That was when I decided on my dissertation topic.

I started to learn historiography from scratch, not having studied history during my undergraduate and master's periods. I would like to express my deep gratitude to the professors who cultivated me as historian cum comparative educationist. Special appreciation goes to my former advisors Professor Emeritus Edward McClellan and Professor Robert Arnove, and Professors John Hanson and Margaret Sutton.

With my background as a specialist of contemporary educational development, as soon as I acquired the degree, the path was prepared for me to return to contemporary research. It was difficult to develop an academic career in either way, as African historiographer or as contemporary comparative educationist. But I chose the latter. That I thought was more true to my original cause.

For fifteen years since then, I have studied educational policies and practices in Africa from various perspectives. In that process, although I did not make any overt connection, I often felt that my past effort of digging into the origin of school education in Africa helped me to examine the contemporary discussions more deeply and critically than otherwise.

Also, I have published two edited books on global discourses on educational development and the policy adaptation in a few African countries (Yamada 2010 and 2016). The analytical perspective employed in these two books was similar to this book on colonial education. The accumulation of such works convinced me that what I want to do is consistently encompass different time periods and spaces. Namely, I want to untangle how issues like national development, citizenship and human capital formation were discussed in relation to education, and what kind of mechanisms there were to shape policies on these issues.

Once again, I would like to express my heartfelt appreciation to Prof. Francis Nyamnjoh for giving me this opportunity of publication. I hope this delay in finalising the manuscript will not fade his support. Also, I would like to thank Profs Motoji Matsuda, Itaru Ohta, Eisei Kurimoto and other senior Africanists in Japan, who are the leaders of the Africa Potential research project and linked me with Francis.

There were also people who had kind words to say on a small number of historical papers I have published, despite that I had abandoned that theme a long time before. Their words of encouragement made me retain my desire to revisit this historical study one day. Particularly, I would like to extend my gratitude to Prof. Peter Kallaway of the University of Cape Town, South Africa, who found my name in the programme of the 2010 World Congress on Comparative Education Societies and came to my session. He invited me to the colonial education workshop held in Cape Town in 2013 too. The encouragement from a figure whose work I had cited many times became a source of energy for me.

My graduate school mates, Profs Kara Brown and Doyle Stevick of the University of South Carolina invited me to make a talk on my dissertation in their university during my stay in the USA as a Fulbright scholar in 2013. While I studied the impact of black industrial education in the American South on Africa, I had not thought seriously how this education model and black activism for enfranchisement was transmitted to the contemporary southern youths. It was an important opportunity for me to think about this topic from a different angle, to talk in front of young students and faculty members, both black and white, in a place close to the original site of American black industrial education. Some of the questions I received then stayed with me to think more deeply about and helped me in revising the manuscript.

In Japan, Prof. Katsuhiko Kitagawa of Kansai University did not forget my study of Achimota and colonial education, and gave me opportunities of presentations from time to time.

I am not so much exposed to the academic standard of African historiography to judge the quality of this book as a historical study. However, if my perspective as comparative educationist, who has analysed contemporary educational practices and policies, has added any value to it, the long detour in my scholarly career might have had some value. I would like to thank all scholars, friends and my family who supported and inspired me along this path.

The cover photo of this book captures the members of a boarding house in Achimota School in the Gold Coast in 1929, two years after its establishment. I chose this photo to represent the image of educational practices in an African colony, reflecting the global discourse on colonial education. African students wore jackets with the Achimota School emblem of black and white piano keys, which were intended to symbolize inter-racial harmony. While they dressed like British bourgeois boys and sat with their British house masters and mistress, they were taught not to lose their African identity and to appreciate the 'dignity of labour'. This book seeks to untangle how such conflicting messages were combined and presented as if consistent.

November, 2017
Shoko Yamada

Part I

Framework of the study

Chapter 1

Introduction

'What does it mean to be an African leader?' 'What are the attributes of the character of leaders and how could those be developed through education?' These were the questions occupying the minds of people involved in the discourse on education in British Africa. The issue of educating Africans began to gain attention from the beginning of the 20th century, both in the metropole and in the colonies. Against this background, in 1910, colonial education was discussed at the World Missionary Conference at Edinburgh, the first major effort to integrate the various Protestant missions' views on education. Education fever reached its height in the interwar period, during which the Phelps-Stokes Fund, an American philanthropic organisation, sent two commissions to investigate African education (1920 and 1923), the British Colonial Office established the Advisory Committee on Native Education in British Tropical Africa (ACNEBTA) (1923) and the ACNEBTA issued its memorandum on education in Africa – the guiding principles for colonial education policies (1925).

The Gold Coast Colony in British West Africa, which largely overlaps with the area known as Ghana today, was a remarkable case that illustrated a widely shared enthusiasm about colonial education; it was discussed and studied extensively by many people, from members of the ACNEBTA in London to missionaries, colonial officials, American philanthropists, African intellectuals and traditional chiefs on the ground. The culmination of this process was the establishment of Achimota School in 1927 as the model school for training 'African leaders'. Achimota was viewed in London and in the international arena as a dream project, utilising the best wisdom the British could gather for African education. The idea of establishing a school for leadership training arose at the intersection of educational demands in both Britain and the colony, from Europeans and Africans, missionaries and government officials, African intellectuals and the public. These interest groups brought different views and expectations about education to the process of developing the policies on British colonial education and the model school to showcase them.

This book will focus on the discourse on education for Africans from around 1910 until the 1930s. Although the pace of exchange was not as fast as today, the advancement of communication and transport technology enabled those people involved in this process to lend and borrow ideas from other continents without much time lag. Such transfer of ideas caused convergences of policy options in different contexts, albeit with a great deal of reinterpretations. There were some popular terms which were sprinkled into texts written by the colonial officials, missionaries, European and American educationists or ideologues in Africa and diaspora. Words like 'adaptation' or 'character training' gave the sense of contemporariness and legitimacy, hinting that the policy or the practice in hand was based on the successful model elsewhere. The coincidences of motivations and mutual enforcements of concepts and policies happened even beyond the immediate domains of colonial education, interacting with global economic, political and social concerns, linking the local and the global through the chains of discourse on multiple facets.

1-1 Framework of analysis: actors, structure, norms and context

In this book, the analysis will be presented around two foci of decision making: one is the *Memorandum on Education Policy in British Tropical Africa*, the educational policy guideline issued by the British Colonial Office in 1923; another is the Achimota School established on the Gold Coast Colony in 1927. Readers may consider that they cannot be paralleled, because the former is a document and the latter is a school. However, they are common in the sense that there were long processes for them to be made public with series of meetings, public debates, informal exchanges of ideas and media reports. In this sense, the *Memorandum* and Achimota School are the windows through which observers can capture the intentions of actors, norms they relied on in promoting their positions and the politics of decision making. While the *Memorandum* allows us to examine the interactions at the global level, Achimota serves to know the application at the local level. Meanwhile, both in the metropole and the colony, the *Memorandum* and Achimota School were frequently referred to together in the official documents, letters of key actors, reports and minutes of various meetings. Therefore, with these two foci, global and local discourses can be analysed as a seamless, mutually enforcing process, instead of separate ones. Because of the great attention given to them and some key terms frequently used in the discourse on them, I could examine the meanings attached to these terms, the intentions and backgrounds of using such definitions. The different characteristics of actors resulted in the diverse ways of using popular terms, their modes of interaction and the outcomes of such interactions.

In addition to the geographic layers from the global to the local, this book also attempts to capture the inter-related constructs of the discourse, namely, structure, actors, norms and context. As I have noted above, discourses are not objective or value-free explanations of the world. Rather, they are processes of appropriating certain worldviews through the collective attempts of describing and understanding them. The knowledge accumulated or took shape through such processes are affected by the complex power relations in which different actors and institutions work to establish a dominant interpretation of what they consider to be the 'reality' (Said 1995; Spivak 1987). There were perceived needs of educating African leaders and of defining the attributes of such personalities. Such shared concerns drove actors – both institutional and individual – to promote their interpretations of the reality and the prescriptions to mend problems. As I present in this book, the continuous acts of selling ideas were so dynamic that one can clearly see how they constructed the core norms of colonial education, which then served as the basis of further discussion and application to practices in the colonies (cf. Foucault, et al 1988:17–18; Foucault 1972: 79–90).

At the same time, actors do not act on their complete free will. There were certain rules of the game which were shared in this discursive field of discourse on colonial governance and education. In presenting their worldviews, references to certain key terms such as 'character training', 'adaptation' or linking to the framework of colonialism and management of 'inter-race relationship' were expected. Those voices which do not follow such cognitive structure, because of ignorance or lack of exposure to the context of the discourse, were systematically excluded. Such tacit but practical knowledge of the rules shaped the *habitus* – system of practice – among participants which regulated their behaviour (Bourdieu 2000, 148–183). The *habitus* took shape through the accumulated exchanges of ideas and cross-references between them. In the sense that the participation requires *habitus,* those Africans who could take part in the discourse were limited to intellectual elites, most likely having been educated in Europe.

In this book, the consistent backbone of the analysis is the interactions among actors and their power relations. Still, the interactions did not happen in a vacuum and it is important to understand the conditions by which the discourses were characterised and delimited. One such condition is the structures, regarding which I would like to highlight both tacit and explicit ones. While the knowledge of unsaid rules of games was the former type of structure, the latter was also clearly elaborated during the inter-war period. The Colonial Office and various ad-hoc councils and research missions including the ACNEBTA served as the formal tone-setters of discourse. The regulations and guidelines which these institutions of formal structure announced became the normative foundations on which anybody who tried to influence the policy making and practices of colonial education had to ground their arguments.

Another pillar of my analysis will be norms and ideas. The process of negotiating the policies and practical measures to train African leaders had a highly political nature based on the diverse socio-political interests of the people who were involved in it, both in the metropole and in the colonies. At the same time, the discourse about African education cannot be fully understood without dealing with the larger picture of educational theories and practices in Euro-American societies of the time, which inspired ideas about African education.

The common characteristics of educational thought in the early 20th century were experientialism and an emphasis on morality and practicality. One source of inspiration came from American progressive philosophy of education, which is largely known by the name of John Dewey. The American model of black industrial education was another source of philosophical stimulant for thinkers on African education, especially after it was promoted by the commission dispatched by an American philanthropic institution named the Phelps-Stokes Fund. Furthermore, in the following chapters, I am also going to suggest the traits of British moralism prevalent since the era of Queen Victoria, embedded in both elite (public school) education and mass education.

In addition to those prevalent educational thoughts, one should also consider the influence of theories on colonial rule, which were quickly taking shape in this period, such as indirect rule and trusteeship (Bassett 1994; Cooper 2005). Meanwhile, in the effort of systematising the rule of colonial subjects based on scientific research evidence, there were increasing numbers of academic studies by anthropologists, biologists and epidemiologists (Hammond 1928; Hetherington 1978; Kallaway 2012). A large part of such studies were commissioned by metropole governments, religious bodies and philanthropic societies. In the political discourses on colonial education in Africa, actors picked elements from these theories and ideas to back up their arguments. Since they packaged pieces of ideas in a rather opportunistic manner without close examination, the references may not always do justice to the original thinkers. Sometimes, mutually contradictory ideas were combined as if being a seamless justification for some policy proposals. Regardless of the tendency of sloppy and shallow treatment in the political process, one should not overlook the important role these philosophies and theories had played to support the structure and interactions of actors. As Parsons states, to harmonise the goals of the society with patterns of practices, there is a demand for norms and values to match them up, which is typically fulfilled by the religious system (1968). In the discourse on African colonial education, academic theories and models of perceived successful practices served this function.

In terms of actors, in this book I will analyse the behaviour of both groups and individuals. At each level of discourse, there were linked but different groups of actors. For the development of the *Memorandum* in the metropole, the people involved were the staff of

British Colonial Office and headquarters of Christian missions, American philanthropists and academics. In the policy making in the Gold Coast colony, educated nationalists, African people with traditional authority, European missionaries and colonial officials took part. Further, when the preparation of educational contents for Achimota School started, pedagogical concerns of European teachers, which were linked with their imagination of African racial capacity and needs, played a role. Some of these groups had formal institutions and others were people who got together when their interests converged. For example, educated nationalists and African chiefs had overlapping members and raised voices together, particularly when they argued for the maintenance of 'African' tradition and dignity against outsiders. However, a large part of educated nationalists were the emerging elite who did not come from families with traditional backgrounds. Therefore, internally, their concerns would not always coincide but would even collide. Observing these actors in the discourse as groups is to examine the status roles they collectively embody in the structure of designing and implementing colonial education. The status role is the function attached to some social status or position, and performed by actors to reach their desired goals while fulfilling the demand to operate the structure smoothly (Grabb 1990: 101). For example, officials in the Colonial Office would make statements in line with the British government's overall colonial policies and interact with other actors in a manner which would be expected of public servants. Missionaries had their own collective identity and roles to embody. The fact that the discussions in the metropole and colonies circled around similar topics and logical framework suggests that the status roles embodied by these groups of actors were reproduced even when they occurred in different geographical locations and levels of administrative structure.

    While such collective behaviour of groups was a significant determinant for the direction of discourse, there were certain patterns among them, predictable according to the interplay between the constituting elements of their identities and the contexts of negotiation with other actors. What was more unpredictable and, sometimes, crucially influential was the subjective agency of individual members of such collective actors. While they represented their positions as collective actors effectively, behind the scenes of key conferences, adoption of regulations or promotion of educational models, there were influences exercised by small numbers of individuals with subjective commitment and personal acquaintance with one another. This book untangles the effects of such individual agencies, based on the detailed reading of archival documents including their personal letters. These people acted based on what they believed to be important. Such beliefs were based on their experience as educators, administrators, researchers, nationalists or missionaries. At the same time, each person's personality characterised his behaviour. There were the visionary, the realist, the strategist and the balancer. The experience, personality and context of discourse led them to interact in certain ways, on behalf of the groups they represented, but based on their interpretation of the status role and values of the decision to be made (Bruner 1990; Mills 1940).

In sum, this book is going to treat the global process of constructing the framework of colonial education for British Africa conditioned by the motivations and power relations among actors – both collective and individual – norms, politics and structure. The discourse happened not only at the global level in the metropole but also in various colonies. Perceived successes of educational practices in various colonies were shared and transplanted to different places with substantial reinterpretation of ideas. Not only sharing experiences among practitioners in colonies and protectorates horizontally, some ideas were brought up from the ground to feed the high-level discussion for developing the normative umbrella of the common colonial education guidelines. It was the multi-layered and multi-faceted process of globalising educational ideas and models. While it was a grand dynamics transcending continents, the book is also going to present a microscopic analysis of motivations and acts of subjective agencies that influenced the tone and direction of discourse both in the metropole and in the Gold Coast Colony.

1-2 Attention to education in the colonial and post-colonial Africa

Education has been an issue of hot debate throughout the modern history of Africa. During the colonial period, especially from the beginning of the 20th century, European powers extended their territorial rules and introduced administrative structures. Together with projects to develop the production bases of primary commodities and the economic infrastructure such as roads, railways and deep-water harbours, education was given significant weight as a means to train the colonial subjects not only in terms of basic literacy, numeracy and vocational skills, but also of morality and values of being ruled. Across the African continent, there arose resistance to such colonial education, both from the elite and the masses, condemning the European-imposed second class education of Africans and the teaching of submission, depriving Africans of rights to educate their own people.

Many historians analysed resistance movements to colonial rule from political and economic perspectives. However, it should not be overlooked that education has always been among the major issues for which African leaders fought either by writing, talking or physical confrontation. For example, many newspaper editors and authors in West Africa, who strived for self-rule and promoted the revaluation of the African tradition, wrote extensively about education and were deeply involved in teaching at or managing schools (Edward Wilmot Blyden, J.E. Casely Hayford or John Mensah Sarbah to name a few). Another familiar example would be the resistance of the Kikuyu in today's Kenya, which eventually led to the Mau Mau revolt, started in 1952. This is generally explained as a political and economic conflict over the ownership of land which the Kikuyu claimed to be their ancestral land. At the same time, education was a very closely linked issue. With disgust for the missionaries who tried to control the African mind by means of education and undermine the African culture, the Kikuyu established many schools independently from the colonial government and missionaries. Such schools were called *harambee* schools – *harambee* means 'self-help' in Swahili, a major language in East Africa. Regardless of the pressure of being closed down by the colonial government, they were estimated to be 200–400 in number at the end of World War II (Keller 1983: 57). As these cases represent, for Africa nationalist leaders and ideologues in the colonial and post-colonial periods, education seemed to be a symbol of incorporeal dominance and the seizure of control over administration and contents of education ('Africanisation') was considered to be indispensable for 'decolonising the mind' of Africans (Ngũgĩ 1986).

Africanisation of education has mostly been the issue of identity and self-consciousness, which affects the minds of people inwardly. Meanwhile, in Africa, the external or functional values of education were also recognised, particularly when they thought of schooling at the personal level. Colonial education created the track for schooled people to access power, status and resources. Europeans expected contradictory roles for education to develop Africans, on the one hand, who can read and write in a European language and adopt a Western attitude to a proper extent and, on the other hand, who do not lose the African mind and are not uprooted.

The term 'education' itself is a much broader concept than schooling. According to *Collins English Dictionary*, it means 'the act or process of acquiring knowledge' (Forsyth 2014). Although it is common to assume that such 'act' happens at institutionalised sites, namely schools, educationists consider informal processes of knowledge acquisition such as home learning or apprenticeship to be as important forms of education as schooling. It is also not only for children and adolescents but for all human beings throughout their lives. While there are spots of African communities which had their own scripts before colonisation[1], a large part of Africa had a tradition of transmitting knowledge and educating people through oral and visual means such as folk stories, proverbs and symbols (Adeyemi & Adeyinka 2003; Boateng 1983; Komba 1998, Lowden 2000; Mullins et al, 2003). Because of the expansion of the school education system during the colonial period and the thirst of Africans for the access to it, such traditional forms of education, which were situated in the social contexts and human relationships, have been pushed aside as if there was no proper education before colonisation. In this drive for elevating the status of school-based education with modularised, curriculum-based teaching, not only Europeans but also the African elite and the public colluded. As I demonstrate in this book, Europeans tried to 'adapt' curriculums which incorporate what they consider the positive aspects of African tradition while eliminating evil ones. The African elite resisted schooling with lower standards under the name of adaptation. Regardless of the severe contrast of interests, the debates over the rights to education were made always on the ground of schooling, which were shared by both the coloniser and the colonised.

For decades after independence, discussions have recurred about using African languages as the medium of education, teaching African values and traditions and introducing traditional events to school programmes (Semali 1999: 309-314; Tedla 1995). For example, some political leaders of newly independent African states, such as Nyerere of Tanzania and Sékou Touré of Guinea, had gone as far as initiating complete reforms of the education system based on the traditional value of self-help and service to the community. Except for these extreme cases, however, when it came to practical decision on the curriculum and the school system, most of the governments across different countries and time periods, have tended to increase academic content and extend instruction time in a European language rather than to allocate more time for learning African culture or to Africanise education fundamentally (Brock-Utne & Hopson 2005; Brock-Utne 2000). This fact indicates that, despite anti-colonial ideology or nostalgia for the good old days, for the present worldly benefit of individuals, they aspired to a higher and better school certificate following the Western framework rather than to promote African pride. The phenomenon which Dore named 'Diploma Disease' is prevalent in Africa as much as in other parts of the world (1976).

Further, in Africa, it is closely linked with antagonism towards and admiration of Western culture, which are both sides of a coin. The paradox between the realist demands and ideology will never cease in Africa unless it fully overcomes the post-colonial mentality and integrates itself into the global standard, or alternatively, detaches itself from the Western value framework and establishes a completely different mechanism of education based on African epistemology.

Issues related to education are, therefore, political, economic, social and psychological in their nature and have constituted the fundamental basis of controversy inherent in the African nation-states and citizenship. Based on the case of Indonesia, Anderson argues that the anti-colonial nationalism was moulded by the native 'bilingual intelligentsias' who were educated in the Western manner and were exposed to their worldview, particularly 'the models of nationalism, nation-ness, and nation-stated produced elsewhere in the course of the nineteenth century' (1991: 113). The same applies to Africa. Most of the primary figures in African anti-colonial nationalism used common terms with their colonial masters in their resistance movements and had lived in Europe or North America.

In the course of their intellectual resistance, they united with political activists in the Americas, such as Marcus Gurvey and W.E.B. Du Bois, and held a series of Pan-African Congress meetings. The Pan-African Congress lasted from 1919 to 1945 and was absorbed into the Pan-African Federation in 1946. In this process, African delegates played key roles, which included first national leaders of independent African states such as Jomo Kenyatta of Kenya, Kwame Nkrumah of Ghana and Hastings Banda of Malawi. The nationalist consciousness and resistance to colonialism could not exist without sharing the epistemology shaped by European political and intellectual history. In this sense, anti-colonial nationalism was a 'derivative discourse' which depended on the models and language originated from the colonial power (Ania 2005: 158; see also Memmi 1965; Fanon 1967). The primary channel for those political leaders and ideologues to contact European culture and their epistemology was school. After education in the colonies, many of them went to the metropole on scholarships, awarded for their academic excellence, to pursue university degrees. Academic excellence could not be independent of exposure and internalisation of European culture, albeit unconscious they might have been.

The discourse this book is going to untangle is what happened in the hybrid space of ideological negotiation between the coloniser and the colonised intelligentsia, among the educators, administrators, politicians and missionaries, and between the Americans and the British. They had diverse, often conflicting, interests, but shared the common rule of the game. 'Education for Africans' was the topic which symbolically represented the psychological and cultural roots of the colonial confrontation. Also, debates over education which persisted in post-colonial Africa cannot be fully understood without knowing this historical origin. The period which this book will highlight is when the formal education systems were established in respective African colonies and protectorates, with regulations on accreditation, subsidies for school operators and standardisation of contents to be taught. Before then, schools run by missionaries were independent of colonial administration and were not part of the network of the colonial social services.

Nowadays, according to the Millennium development Goals (MDGs) and following Sustainable Development Goals (SDGs) agreed at the United Nations summits in 2000 and 2015 respectively, education is a human right and basic – primary and lower secondary – education is expected to be compulsory and free, under the responsibility of the government. Such arguments can happen only when based on the shared assumption that there are national education systems and that school education follows the common framework universally. Also, despite this shared assumption of universality, contents to be taught in schools are influenced by the social contexts and interpretations, which are far from value-free. I hope the analysis presented in this book will provide an opportunity for contemporary scholars and practitioners of education to revisit the difficult and controversial nature of this issue at its stage of systematisation, despite the unanimous interests of various stakeholders. That, I wish, will enrich the discussion on 'adapting' global agendas such as SDGs to local contexts in more nuanced manners.

1-3 Data used for the analysis

I collected data in two ways: documentary search and interviews. Archival research was the main part of my research and the greater part of the analysis presented in this book relies on it. Interviews with graduates of Achimota and other secondary schools in the Gold Coast Colony serve to supplement documentary analysis, in which we seldom hear the voices of students who actually experienced the education discussed by politicians and educationists high above their heads.

When it was established, Achimota was a comprehensive educational institution covering from kindergarten to teacher training college. However, I have focused my analysis on the secondary branch of Achimota for the following reasons. First, the original plan was to make it a secondary institution, as a stepping stone to establish a university. Therefore it is more logical to trace the development of this plan rather than to divert attention to the fringe added at the last moment. Also, branches other than secondary education had been either moved away or terminated during and after the Second World War, because of the financial difficulties and the change in the political climate.[2] In addition, because of its character change from the late 1930s onward, I limit my analysis of Achimota until the 1930s, when the philosophies of its founders were clearly reflected in their practice. Achimota as an educational institution which covered the upper to the lower streams of education was short-lived, only about 20 years. For the large part of its life, Achimota was a secondary institution. Achimota in its early days was often referred to as the 'College'. However, because of my focus on the secondary part of it, I call it the 'School' to clarify that it does not include the teacher training college and other branches.

1-3-1 Documentary research

The following archives were visited to collect primary records about education in colonial Africa: in the US: the Rockefeller Archive Center, Phelps-Stokes Fund Library, New York Public Library and Hampton University Archives; in the UK: the Public Record Office, School of Oriental and African Studies' Library at the University of London and Rhodes House Library at Oxford University; and in Ghana: the national archives in Accra, Central regional archives of Cape Coast, the Institute of African Studies at the University of Ghana and several school libraries including Achimota, Mfantsipim and Adisadel.

The Rockefeller Archive Center (RAC) has a collection on philanthropic institutions for black education, including the transfer of its model to Africa. The records I looked at are reports, minutes and correspondence of the International Education Board and General Education Board. While the RAC has a series of personal files of executive members of Rockefeller organisations, few of them had to do with educational transfer to Africa. The individual file of Jackson Davis, the director of the General Education Board during the period concerned, is among these few relevant ones. There was a file specifically on the Phelps-Stokes Fund, which maintains correspondence regarding financial assistance to the Fund's domestic and international activities of black education. A small file named 'Africa Education' is a scattered but useful source to grasp the involvement of American philanthropic organisations such as the Rockefeller organisations and the Carnegie Corperation to African education, especially in Southern and Eastern Africa and in Liberia.

The Phelps-Stokes Fund entrusted most of its archival materials to the New York Public Libraries, especially the Schomburg Center Library. The materials kept at Schomburg Center mostly treat the domestic activities of the Phelps-Stokes Fund and American black education generally. At the Phelps-Stokes Fund library, I had access to minutes of board meetings from its inception in 1910 to the 1960s. The minutes I read there were the most useful piece of data for my analysis of American intentions of transferring black industrial education to Africa, and for an understanding of the development of the Phelps-Stokes' involvement in particular. It was in July 2001 when I visited the library in lower Manhattan, very close to the financial district. After September 11, the Fund's New York office closed for months as it was within the restricted area; I hope the tragedy did not damage any of these important archival materials for future researchers.

Hampton University was one of the two institutions, with Tuskegee in Alabama, whose educational philosophy and curriculum were promoted to Africa. It keeps records in very good shape, but unfortunately for my purpose, they are exclusively about Hampton's domestic works. I could find only a few records on individual students from Africa.

In the UK, the purpose of visiting archives was to learn about the policies and discussions among the British government and mission societies. The Public Record Office is the largest governmental archive in the world and maintains the biggest collection of the British Colonial Office's political documents on education. The Colonial Office was divided into roughly two kinds of sections: technical sections and geographic sections. The technical section which concerned my research was the Advisory Committee on Native Education in Tropical Africa (later the Advisory Committee on Education in the Colonies). The collection on the Advisory Committee (CO 1045) maintains bound minutes of the Committee's meetings and correspondence between the Committee and executive officials (governors, colonial secretaries and directors of education) in respective colonies. Geographically specific records which are relevant were: CO 96 Gold Coast Correspondence; CO 98 Gold Coast Sessional Papers and Reports; CO 554 West Africa Correspondence; CO 847 General Africa Correspondence; and CO 323 General Correspondence.

Protestant missions sought to influence the official educational policy of the Colonial Office by taking part in the work of the Advisory Committee. Acting as a long-term and influential mission representative on the Committee was J.H. Oldham, Secretary of the International Missionary Council. In order to understand the views on the educational policy of Oldham and missionary societies behind him, the combined records of the International Missionary Council and its associate body, the Conference of Missionary Societies in Great Britain and Northern Ireland (CBMS-IMC), have been used. CBMS-IMC archives were entrusted to the School of Oriental and African Studies (SOAS), University of London. Another useful collection at SOAS was that of the Wesley Methodist Mission Society (WMMS). I looked through the Gold Coast District synod minutes and West Africa correspondence. Correspondence and reports about schools operated by the Wesleyan mission and about the Gold Coast Board of Education, which was attended by a representative of the Wesleyan mission, were useful sources to understand the local missionaries' attitude toward African education and toward other Europeans and Africans.

As for private records, the Oxford Rhodes House Library maintains numerous valuable sources. For instance, it contains the private records of Lord Lugard (Governor General of Nigeria 1914–19 and also a member of the Colonial Office Advisory Committee on Native Education), of J.H. Oldham and of A.G. Fraser (the first principal of Achimota School). A large part of the Oldham collection had been transferred to SOAS with the CBMS-IMC collection. A gem for educational historians is the collection of manuscripts by educational administrators and teachers who worked in British Africa in the late colonial period. In the 1980s, Oxford University initiated the Project on the Development of Education in Pre-independent Africa, which interviewed and collected manuscripts of those individuals involved in education. Among files useful for my research were those of Lionel Bruce Greaves, Wesleyan educational missionary; J.R. Marshall, Achimota staff member and later Deputy Director of Education, the Gold Coast; W.E.F. Ward, Achimota staff member and later Deputy Education Advisor of the Colonial Office, London; and Samuel Hanson Amissah, the first Ghanaian principal of Wesley College, Kumasi, the Gold Coast.

In Ghana, I visited the National Archives in Accra and the Central Regional Archives of Cape Coast. I visited the Cape Coast archives because secondary education in the early 20th century was centred in two coastal cities: Accra and Cape Coast. But in fact, a substantial part of the records are preserved in the UK, not in Ghana. There were some useful local official records I found in these public archives, though. I also visited the library of the Institute of African Studies, University of Ghana. There, I read through newspapers published on the Gold Coast between 1910 and 1940, which include *Gold Coast Times, Gold Coast Nation, Gold Coast Spectator, Gold Coast Leader, Gold Coast Independence* and *Vox Populi*. At some secondary schools, I asked to see the old student register books. All of the schools visited – Achimota, Mfantsipim and Adisadel – had handwritten register books which kept individual students records, such as age of entry, parents' address and previous schools attended. Even though it took much energy and time to copy this data into a computer database, since the style of record keeping is not the same in schools or even at different periods within the same school, the reference to these student data is limited in this book.

In addition to archival records and reports, this book has made great use of academic journals dealing with African matters and education. The most important journals were the Advisory Committee's publication *Oversea Education*, the International Missionary Council's *International Review of Missions*, the International Institute for African Languages and Cultures' *Africa, the Journal of the Royal Society of Africa* and Hampton Institute's *Southern Workman*. Articles in journals published in the colonial period are part of the primary source material and are listed at the end of the book as such.

1-3-2 Interviews

I interviewed members of the older generation who graduated from Achimota and Mfantsipim secondary schools in the colonial period. Interviews were conducted between January and August 2002. The total number of interviewees were 23 (see Appendix for details), 13 Achimota alumni and 10 Mfantsipim alumni. The conversations were informal and in-depth, taking between 30 minutes and two hours. They were tape-recorded as far as possible and were transcribed except for the few cases where interviewees asked me not to.

The purpose of the interviews was primarily to discern the perceptions of people about the secondary education they received. The interviews contributed students' vivid memories to this book, which were not available from any written materials. The reason I interviewed graduates of two schools was to contrast the educational experiences of Achimota with those of another, well-accepted but very different secondary school. Mfantsipim was jointly operated by the Methodist mission society and African nationalist leaders. Its discipline was to promote Methodist morality while also taking pride in high academic performance. Achimota was a government school whose philosophy was more to adapt education to an African background than to increase students' academic performance. As it turned out, it is difficult to tell if the philosophical difference made any significant difference in students' experience at the two schools. None of them had experience of both schools to be able to compare. Also, their memories were more of boyhood/girlhood at school than that at a particular school with a specific educational philosophy.

After long years since their school days, their memories must have been reinterpreted according to their later experiences and perceptions. Still, by examining the ways they represent their memories in relation to their background and personalities, the study of life stories serves the researcher to reconstruct the impact of education in these schools from students' perspectives (Casey 1995).

Going to secondary school in the late colonial period was itself the privilege of the few. Therefore, in addition to the old age of potential interviewees, the original pool of people who would meet the criteria of this research was small. As for the selection of interviewees, I relied on alumni networks and personal connections. I asked the school principals to give me contacts of old alumni, and I visited alumni associations. Whenever I interviewed someone, I asked him/her to introduce me to schoolmates. The limitation of this approach was that I could only locate people who still keep contact with their schoolmates. The reason for their keeping contact was one or a few of the following: they were very healthy and active for their age, they lived in urban centres, they were not retired yet, or their children went to the same school and they keep contact with the alumni organisation or the school. It was difficult to even identify who were in the generation schooled in the late colonial period. As a result, the oldest among my interviewees were at the schools in the early 1930s, younger ones as late as in the 1950s. I cannot, therefore, use the parts of interviews that are closely related to the context of a specific time, such as boarding life while school buildings were occupied by the army. On the other hand, I found that there are commonalities in the school life across different time periods, such as relationships with teachers, students' self-discipline under the prefect system, sports and the tacit messages students received from the schools. I only used parts of interview data which showed such consistent nature, so as not to bring in perspectives which seem to be specific to students of later generations to the analysis of Achimota in its early days.

1-4 Structure of the book

This book has three parts. Part I provides the framework of the book, composed of this introductory chapter and Chapter Two which overviews scholarly works in the relevant fields. Literature reviewed in Chapter Two will fall into the following fields: history of education and politics in colonial Africa; theories on global exchanges of ideas and transfer of educational models; and equilibrium between general and vocational education. Based on the overview in Part I, Part II will provide the analysis of discourse at the global level, focusing on context, structure, actors and norms. Part III will go to the national and institutional level in the Gold Coast Colony and Achimota School, while the dimensions of analysis continue to be context, structure, actors and norms.

Chapter Three describes the context in which the issues on African education were discussed in the metropole. Firstly, I will discuss the political economy of the period between the first and second wars in Europe and its implication for colonies, particularly in Africa. Then, I will discuss how education is systemically embedded in colonialism.

Chapter Four introduces main actors involved in the discourse and the roles played by them. Mission societies played a critical role in the formation of colonial education policy in British Africa. They not only achieved coordination among themselves to develop a consensus view about African education beyond denominational differences, but together with the Colonial Office they devised the basic framework of educational administration that placed the Director of Education of each colony under the supervision and guidance of the Advisory Committee on Native Education in Tropical Africa. The mission societies played another important role in that they incorporated the other major group of actors: American philanthropists. American philanthropists actively promoted the application to Africa of a vocational education model developed for the black population in the American South. The chapter also picks up some key individuals who connected groups and scripted the discourse: J.H. Oldham, Tomas Jesse Jones, Gordon Guggisberg, and James Aggrey among others.

Turning from the politics of discourse, Chapter Five will focus on the normative aspect of the colonial discussion on education. It traces back the original educational philosophies and ideas which fertilised the ideology of the 'education for Africans' piecing together ideas from different sources. Especially, the chapter reviews three educational models/ideas which seemed to have directly influenced the philosophical discussion about African education. These were: American progressive educational philosophies; an agricultural and industrial education model for the American black population; and British moralism rooted in Victorian era in education.[3] They were all quite different in their perceived goals and promoted pedagogies, but they all converge in their stress on 'character training' and practical education 'adapted' to the students' background. This commonality among different educational models/ideas reconciled the mixture of ideas and represented the coexistence of seemingly conflicting ideas in a school's or a colony's educational principles.

Chapter Six opens Part III which focuses on the discourse at the national and institutional level. The chapter reviews the history of school-based education along the coast of the Gulf of Guinea from the 16th century. Then, it will present the political economic context of the Gold Coast Colony in the inter-war period. The Gold Coast was one of the most lucrative colonies among British territories because of natural resources, particularly gold and cacao. The colonial government invested greatly in constructing economic infrastructure such as deep-water harbours and railways. The chapter highlights the era of Governor Guggisberg, which was the most dynamic in the late colonial period. Guggisberg is also known for his commitment to expanding education and initiated the establishment of Achimota School.

Chapter Seven describes the main actors involved in the educational discourse in the Gold Coast Colony, particularly in relation to Achimota education, and analyses their interactions and intentions for participating in them. A strong pressure group was the emerging nationalists. Among their demands on the colonial government, establishment of a degree-granting university in West Africa was one of the most earnest, for they perceived it as a means to political representation and higher appointment of Africans in the colonial structure. Traditional chiefs, who were often the political opponents of nationalists, also saw the benefit of more and better education for Africans. In addition to the appeal of these politically active Africans, the desire of the African public for more schools was constantly pressuring the government to expand access to education. European missionaries were still another group of people who influenced the educational discourse. As major operators of schools in Africa at the time of systematisation of colonial rule, missionaries faced the necessity of cooperating with the government to maintain their dominance in the field of education. Groups of people who participated in the political debates on the Gold Coast were not so aggressive as to try to overthrow the colonial regime itself, as was seen in East and Southern Africa; rather, what they tried to achieve was relative advantage in the power conflict within the framework of the colonial rule. And education was the key issue in this struggle for relative advantage in the colonial structure.

Chapter Eight provides a detailed analysis of the philosophical debates about African education, which were inspired by Euro-American educational ideas, and Achimota as the experimental school. Two key terms of the discourse, 'character training' and 'adaptation,' will be used as the grid to locate diverse views on the type of personalities schools were to develop, on the balance between Europeanisation and maintenance of African tradition and customs, and on the educational methods utilised to achieve the perceived goals of education. Achimota School, as the model school of 'adaptation', assumed the role of codifying what elements of 'African tradition' should be taught at school and to which African elements Achimota's education should be 'adapted'. The European staff of Achimota made extensive and sincere efforts to define and reduce the 'African tradition' into teaching materials and school activities, which covered the areas of history, music and performing arts, languages, dress and manners. In the last section of Chapter Eight, I will present my analysis of interviews with people who went to Achimota School between its year of establishment (1927) and the early 1950s, who internalised the philosophical messages of the School's founders.

Chapter Nine of Part IV is to situate the historical case of Achimota and British colonial education in the longitudinal discussion about vocational and general secondary education in Ghana and the world. I overview secondary education policies in Ghana since independence to today in relation to changing trends of education development programmes in the global discourse. There have been rises and falls of vocational education. The education policy right after independence followed suit of that of the colonial period and prioritised secondary and higher education for developing skilled professionals and leaders. During this period, secondary vocational education had received the highest proportion of the budget in the history of independent Ghana, which continued to decrease throughout the 1970s and 80s. The chapter discusses the revivals of vocationalism in the late 1980s and recent 10 years, and points out the roots of ideas in global discourse and local socio-economic and historical contexts. In this chapter, the comparison is made not only between Ghanaian education policies and changing global normative trends, but also between policies and practices. The analysis reveals that, regardless of the clear shifts of ideas at the policy level, patterns of enrolment and public responses have been pretty consistent. The perception that academic secondary education will lead to white collar jobs and vocational education is the imposition of inferior education is deeply rooted in the minds of the Ghanaian public. This strong shared conception has effected the watering down of various policy intentions, without fundamental discussions about contents and intentions.

Lastly, the book concludes by drawing out the implications of this educational study for policy analysis and for African historiography. This work will attempt to untangle how different interests were negotiated in the process of policy formation, instead of accepting the statements in the announced policies on their face values. The book also suggests that the theoretical framework of educational transfer, which dichotomises 'the borrower' and 'the lender' of educational policies, is limited in its ability to capture the dynamics of global discourse. My analysis will demonstrate that the London-made policies were not strictly adapted to the Gold Coast but were selectively used according to the Gold Coast's political, economic and social context. This analysis will also reveal that the Africans were not mute receivers of policies brought from outside, but they exercised strong influence on policy formation. Still another theoretical contribution of this book is that it tries to capture the discourse as a multi-dimensional process consisting of contexts, structure, actors and norms. Although the British officials and missionaries agreed to ask for American advice at the political level, this fact did not necessarily mean that the American educational models were faithfully followed in Africa. Educational norms and ideas circulated largely independent of political process and influenced practices on the ground not only through London but directly from America, continental Europe or other colonies in Africa and other continents. Further, my study contributes to African historiography by bringing the perspective of an educationist to the studies on colonialism. While colonial education has been studied by historians, most of them saw school as one of the sites of cultural encounters, but not based on educational ideas and pedagogy. So far, little attention has been given to the study of 'character training' and 'adaptation' as educational ideas. This book will contribute to African historiography through the lens of educationist, while also seeing it from political and cultural aspects.

Notes

[1] Scribner and Cole conducted a study of psychological and cognitive effects of literacy in multiple scripts among Vai people who had their unique traditional script, while learning English at school and Arabic for Islamic religion (1981).

Among people in the Horn of Africa, there is Ge'ez script which is said to have its origin in 9th–8th century BC, adopted by the Ethiopian Orthodox Church and lasts until today in Ethiopia and Eritrea. The spread of Islam from the 7th century AD brought Arabic script to Africa, although the population who are literate in Arabic beyond chanting from the Quran is limited outside of the Islamic countries along the Mediterranean. Except for them, most of the scripts used in Africa are Latin. There may have been small groups who had their own scripts in the past but there is no concrete record on them and, even if they existed, such scripts have disappeared.

[2] The lack of housing for students caused by army requisition resulted in the closing down of the kindergarten and lower school altogether. Teacher training and engineering classes were transferred to the University College of Gold Coast, which was established in 1949 (Agbodeka 1977: 144–55).

[3] The period which this book covers was under the rule of King George V. Therefore, the word 'Victorian' refers not directly to her regime but the values and moralities which took shape in her era and had lasting influences in various forms across the British Empire.

Chapter 2

Literature review

2-1 History of colonial education and education in Africa

2-1-1 Chronology of education in British West Africa

The earliest works to have reviewed the development of education in the British West Africa appeared in the very last years of colonial rule. Colin Wise and F.H. Hillard, both of whom had experience in teaching and educational administration in West Africa, published histories of education in British West Africa in 1956 and 1957, respectively (Hillard 1957; Wise 1956). The contributions of these early works were that they largely provided a chronology of British West African education. Some of these chronologies started from the 16th century when the first European schools were introduced for the mixed-blood children between European traders and African women at forts along the Western coastal line called 'Castles'. Others started from the mid-19th century, and focused on the process of systematising mission-led education under British colonial rule. While most of the historical synthesis in the early post-independence period was by the hands of Europeans, works by Africans offered different and often conflicting views on the British colonial heritage on education. *Nigerian Education,* edited by Ikejiani (1964), represents the anti-British sentiment which was shared among African intellectuals in the post-colonial era.

As for the Gold Coast Colony, there have also been several scholars who attempted to summarise its history of education. In 1959, McWilliam and Kwamena-Poh published the first overview of education in the territory that had, two years previously, gained independence from the Great Britain and was now known as Ghana (1975, first published in 1959). Several attempts to write the educational history of Ghana followed in the 1960s and early 70s. David Williams centred his analysis on the educational policy of Governor Guggisberg, which stressed the moral uplift by means of education (1964). Williams's essay was valuable as the first work which paid any attention to the 'character training' aspect of education in the Guggisberg era, but there should be some reservation about accepting his conclusion which stated that 'character training' was an educational failure, arguing that it dwarfed the value of examinations and ended up lowering the average examination results. In fact, examinations were not designed to measure the impact of 'character training'. Also, the judgment about the moralistic influence of school could vary according to viewpoints, which cannot be determined in a uniform way. The issue of moral education on the Gold Coast received a passing reference in a history by Anim too (1966). Charles Martin (1976) was still another one who presented a history of Ghanaian education from the period of the Castle Schools to the report of the educational review committee released in 1966. So far, the most comprehensive history on Ghanaian education is that by Phillip Foster (1965).[1] Starting from the Castle Schools run by Portuguese, Dutch and Danish traders and missionaries, he provided fine details about the process of educational expansion, the relevant ideologies and local discourse, all of which were sprinkled with figures and numbers. In the latter part of the book, he specifically tracked the development of secondary education and its influence on national development, as well as the social impact it had from the late colonial period to the time immediately after independence. Graham's history of Gold Coast education was a thematic one that loosely followed chronology (1971). There were mainly three themes he focused on: (1) girls' education and teacher training; (2) vocational (agricultural and industrial) education; and (3) higher education. After Graham, academic enthusiasm shifted away from the general history to the more specific issues of education in colonial Ghana. Although many scholars included a part or a chapter of their work that focused on Ghanaian educational history, their work was mostly background for their main argument, and they rarely provided critical analysis beyond simple description.[2]

2-1-2 Reflection on the British policies and planning on colonial education

There were many memoirs and reviews by the figures who exercised influence either in the metropole or in the colonies regarding education. Margaret Read, a pioneer educational anthropologist, published *Education and Social Change in Tropical Areas* in 1955, based on her long years of fieldwork. W.E.F. Ward, who was a colonial educator in Ceylon and later in Achimota also published his experience and views on colonial education (1959). Another example of this sort was the work by Meyhew, who had worked as educational administrator in India, the editor of the journal *Overseas Education* and as a joint-secretary of the Advisory Committee on Education in Colonies (ACEC) (1939).

The early scholars tended to accept the British colonial education policies not only as statements but also as realities, assuming that there was no difference either between statements and intentions or between policies and implementation. Thus, Ipaye (1969) attempted to compare British and French educational philosophies in West Africa based on the idea, which was then widely accepted, that British education was 'adaptive' and French was 'assimilative'. This type of dichotomy resulted from acceptance of written statements without seeing the diversity in the implementation of these policies.[3] In fact, neither British nor French policies were that strict nor did they have a clear long-term strategy. In other words, colonial enterprises were collections of makeshifts meant to meet emerging realities.[4]

In terms of policy making in the metropole, there was limited access to the major Colonial Office documents for certain periods. Therefore, the works by earlier historians mostly relied on published materials and some personal records, which restricted a more rigorous critical analysis. Still, under such limitation, one of the earliest reviews of policy statements of the ACEC was conducted by Lewis in 1954.

Starting from the 1960s, scholars' attention was enlarged from simple chronologies to more critical analysis taking into account other perspectives than that of the colonial officials in the metropole and in Africa. *Church, State, and Education in Africa*, a volume edited by David Scanlon, reviewed interactions between missions and states in former British colonies (Scanlon 1966). In 1964, Godfrey Brown reviewed British colonial educational policy throughout the process from its formation in Britain to its implementation in the field, in relation to the intentions of mission societies, the development of the trusteeship theory and African reaction (Brown 1964). This article was an attempt to provide a general understanding of the policy process in British African education, including the different levels and actors of decision making. Clatworthy was commissioned by the US Department of Health, Education and Welfare to extract lessons from the 'British experience of cross-cultural educational planning' for evidence-based planning of human resource development (1969). In addition to the records of Colonial Office, missionary bodies and individuals who were involved in the process, he interviewed J.H. Oldham, Secretary of the International Missionary Council and one of the figures which this book is going to focus on. Since then, there have been sporadic but continuous studies on the colonial education policy-making process in the UK (Lewis 1971; Whitehead 1981 and 1989; Ball 1983; and Gray 1990). Sivonen (1995) extensively examined British mission societies' perspective on the formation of British policy on colonial education. Kallaway focused on the influence of academics (2012). Meanwhile, Whitehead had analysed this policy-making process by focusing on specific issues: for example, the role played by the journal *Overseas Education*, established by the Colonial Office, for the objective of sharing practical experiences of education in British colonies around the world (2003); or the discourse on the vernacular education, the education using local languages as the medium of instruction (1995).

The studies on British colonial education policies and planning, particularly when the colonialism was at its terminal stage or in the early post-colonial era, had the nature of policy studies to find implications of earlier practices in public administration. It was particularly so because the establishment of United Nations Educational, Scientific and Cultural Organization (UNESCO) in 1945 was under the auspices of the British Colonial Office and key actors of the Advisory Committee on Colonial Education had been transferred to occupy decision-making positions in this new international organisation mandated to set the tone of discussion on educational issues globally. Therefore, at least in the field of education, colonial discourse had not been broken by the independence of former colonies but continued without fundamental changes. Therefore, one can find the roots of theories on human capital development and manpower planning, which became dominant prescriptions for post-colonial international development, in British colonial education discourse. That is why many practitioners and researchers who were commissioned by the governmental and inter-governmental agencies looked into the history of the ACEC and British policies on colonial education for lessons to learn. It is a stark contrast to the post-colonial discourse and the sentiment which occupied the minds of intellectuals in newly independent Africa, Asia and Latin America. It also has a different academic dynamics from that among scholars fascinated by the American involvement in British colonial education, who tended to have a Marxist orientation.

2-1-3 Studies on the American influence on colonial education

European mission societies and American philanthropic organisations actively participated in the formation of the British educational policy. Particularly, many scholars' eyes were attracted by the involvement of the Phelps-Stokes Fund, a New York-based philanthropic foundation that specialised in education in British colonial policy formation. Among some academics, it was nearly accepted as given that the educational 'adaptation' policy was a transplant of American black industrial education to Africa via London. The issue of American influence on colonial education in Africa was brought into the limelight in the 1970s. Berman (1971) was rather harsh in criticising the Phelps-Stokes Fund and its staff for imposing, without asking for African opinions, an inferior form of education which stimulated much criticism from American black intellectuals. Then there is King's detailed analysis of American black industrial education and its transfer to Africa, which is a classic of its sort (1971). Both Berman and King studied and grasped the international discourse on African education from American perspectives well. However, as they put heavy weight in their analysis of American influence, they inclined to make light of British motivations to invite American as well as African responses to the educational models brought from outside. Both Berman and King focused geographically on Eastern and Southern Africa, where racial conflict was more severe and Europeans were keener on applying the American model. In these sub-regions, discussion about the American model of Black industrial education was more frequent and African voices were less represented in educational policy making than in British West Africa. Therefore, it is understandable that documentary analysis of educational discourse tended towards reaching the conclusion that the American influence was massive.

Also, the role played by the Phelps-Stokes Fund was enlarged in the imagination of Marxist scholars, who saw it as an example of imposing racial and class-segregated education. The long-lived distaste among Africans for vocational education was endorsed by such educational historians, who equated 'adapted' education with a form of vocational education which had been developed in America for an 'inferior' race (D'Souza 1975; Marah 1987; Peterson 1971). South Africa has a strong school of educational historians whose analysis is highly critical of colonial rule, which, they argue, imposed segregated education which served the political intention of Europeans to suppress Africans (for example, Kallaway 1996 and 1984; Krige 1997; Molteno 1984; Proctor 2000). Since a large number of the studies on African colonial education have been by the scholars in this school, one could form an assumption that the situations analysed by them are applicable not only to Southern Africa but to other parts of Africa. In fact, the situation in West Africa was very different, because there were fewer Europeans, and the African elite exercised a strong power on policy making there.

After the academic enthusiasm in the 1970s on studying American involvement in African education, this field was nearly abandoned except for studies on specific educational institutions that were said to have followed American models (Berman 1972; Jacobs 1995; Livingston 1975). In 1983, Bude appraised the outcomes of educational adaptation in various parts of Africa, starting from the belief that the 'adaptation' concept was originally promoted by the Phelps-Stokes Commissions. He concluded that most of the attempts at adaptation failed because Europeans introduced the concept without 'tak[ing] into account African needs structures'. As he put it, 'European-American paternalism, which ultimately regarded Africans as immature people having no understanding of the "well-meant" plans of their "protectors", was doomed to failure' (p. 349). To determine if an adaptation policy had successfully taken root or not, many scholars assumed that the adaptation policy had substance. However, as for education in colonial Africa, the adaptation was not practised as stated in the policy. On the one hand, the effort of 'adaptation' to local environment had been made by missionaries long before the colonial discourse in the 1920s. On the other hand, as it became the later colonial period, it became common for schools to claim their commitment to the 'adaptation' policy for the interest of legitimisation, whatever the reality was. In sum, Bude's attempt to determine the American influence was based on a shaky assumption that there was a fixed policy of 'adaptation' following the American model and that it was implemented as stated.

In 1995, *The Teachers College Club* by Fleische shifted the attention from philanthropic organisations to an American educational institution, namely, the Teachers College of Columbia University (see also, Hunt 1984). While the Teachers College accepted students from various parts of the world, white South Africans were the largest groups from Africa in the first half of the 20th century. By closely examining the backgrounds, dissertations and careers of a few South African alumni of Teachers College, Fleische considered the influence that the educational ideas these people were exposed to in the Teachers College had on the development of educational policy in South Africa. As Fleische concluded, one of the reasons that South Africa was active in adopting American black industrial education was that, for some influential educationists there, such kind of education was familiar and made a positive impression, from the time when these people were at the Teachers College.

Still another work which examined the American influence on African education was that by Steiner-Khamsi and Quist in 2000. They applied the theory of educational borrowing and lending to this historical case. From this theoretical perspective, Steiner-Khamsi and Quist assumed that what was called 'adapted education' in British

Africa was another name for an American black industrial education model which was developed and implemented in Hampton and Tuskegee Institutes in the American South. Unlike their assumption, as I am going to demonstrate in this book, American input was only one of various educational ideas British Colonial Office relied on to develop its education policy in Africa. Owing to this assumption, they called Achimota School of the Gold Coast, which aimed at developing African leadership by means of 'adapted education', one of the 'Tuskegee clones in Africa' together with Booker T. Washington Institute in Liberia, the vocational institution established by American philanthropists (Steiner-Khamsi and Quist 2000: 288).

The series of works on American involvement in the discourse on African education shared the belief that there was a massive and substantial influence by Americans. Also, despite the abundant studies on American influence, there are few studies on the British and African reactions to it. There have been many studies on the formation of British colonial education policy as well, but the trends of research on this same phenomenon seen from the different sides of the Atlantic have not been communicated well.

2-1-4 Local politics of education in Africa

Different from scholars who focus on policy making and its determinants at the global level, there have been many analyses of the colonial and post-colonial discourse and practices on the ground in Africa. Articles and books published in Europe and America during the colonial period were mostly written by educational missionaries and colonial administrators involved in education.[5] One of the challenges of the historiography of African education has been the lack of written records as the source of analysis. Because of the tradition of oral transmission of knowledge, indigenous documents are almost non-existent, which naturally led to the reliance of historians on the records of Europeans and small groups of African intellectuals. Therefore, it has been a critical concern of African historiographers that recorded history does not reflect a large part of African voices and that there is no clear answer to the question how historians can recover the perspective of silent African commoners. In this way, African historiography has developed in close relation with the effort of reconstructing the perspectives to counter the hegemony of European powers (Cooper 1994; Engels & Marks 1994; Feierman 1993; Trouillot 1995).

Since independence, despite the lack of records, many scholars attempted to investigate African reaction to Western schooling. This focus on the African perspective reflected the academic atmosphere of the wider African studies which were critical of, often aggressive toward, colonialism. *African Reactions to Missionary Education*, a volume edited by Berman (1975), was among the earliest works which focused exclusively on mission education as seen from the eyes of the African public, against the socio-political background of the time. As for the Gold Coast, Mobley spent considerable space in his *The Ghanaian's Image of the Missionary* on African reaction to mission education (1970). Yates claimed, based on her analysis of the case of Congo, that there were three stages of African reactions to the western-type schools: indifference, curiosity and finally widespread acceptance (1971). As school-based education penetrated their lives, Africans came to realise the economic advantage of schooling in getting access to salaried employment, the social status of being an 'educated man', and exposure to Western culture, which motivated Africans to accept schools. Povey's study of autobiographic novels by African writers supported this point about the economic and non-educational motivations of Africans for attending schools (1966).

Against scholars who saw African reaction to colonialism primarily as 'resistance' or 'conformity' to hegemony, there arose a movement among African historians which claimed that the interaction was more complex and that Africans found ways to regain the control of power outside of hegemonic discourse (Cooper 1994: 12–3; Engels & Marks 1994: 8–15). The strong demand for education often led Africans to seize control of schools themselves. This movement for gaining control of education was more widespread in Eastern and Southern Africa than in other parts of Africa, and such a movement naturally attracted the attention of historians who were critical of colonial hegemony. Ranger (1965), based on an analysis of independent school movements in Kenya, stated that there were three ways by which Africans attempted to control education: (1) by controlling mission education within the church; (2) by inviting the government to establish schools independent of mission control; and (3) by establishing independent schools of their own, free from both the missions and government control. Anderson (1970) provided still another categorisation of African responses to formal education based on his study in Kenya: resistance, acceptance, selection and adaptation. The issue of control is critical for understanding African involvement in educational discourse. Thus, although the works which focused exclusively on independent school movements decreased after the 1970s, many scholars devoted some space in their writings to the issue of the African attempt to control schools.[6] More recently, Summers provided detailed examinations of African reactions to education at grass-root level. Her *Demanding Schools* (1997) investigates the complex power relations and motivations among Africans in the case of a school established at Umchingwe, Southern Rhodesia. Another of Summers's works, *Mission Boys, Civilized Men, and Marriage* (1999), focuses on the 'fetish' appeal of education and Christianity, which were not the substance but external elements of them – such as European ways of clothing and living or European materials including books – and its effect of changing the African lifestyle in Southern Rhodesia.

The encounter with European culture at school, church and other sites transformed local societies in various ways. However, the influence was not only from European to African culture, but vice versa. Moreover, Africans did not swallow whole European lifestyles and ways of thinking; they were selective. As Comaroff and Comaroff (1997) state, it was a 'dialectical encounter' in which changes took place on both sides, although such changes were different in manner and degree. Thus, in her book on the changing meanings of sacred sites and rituals in the life of the Anlo people in Eastern Ghana, Greene (2001) analysed this selective, mutual influence. Sacred sites, to which geographical and spiritual meanings were attached, changed their location in the minds of Anlo people as they encountered European culture, which separated the material from the spiritual. At the same time, European missionaries and colonialists adapted some elements of the Anlo culture in their practices so as to make themselves more acceptable to the population.

Also, the Anlo did not adapt every aspect of European culture but only selected things which could strengthen their existing beliefs.

Among historians of African culture, the idea of 'modernity/modernities' has been a central concern. Europeans in the colonial period assumed the role of the 'moderniser'. However, 'modernisation' as a cultural encounter had plural meanings and implications according to one's perspectives and to localities. As a school was one of the most powerful sites of European cultural transmission – sometimes referred to as indoctrination – historians who focused on colonial education rarely saw that the process was dialectical. Meanwhile, Levinson and Holland state that however strong the school's power is to make students conform to the dominant social values and culture, schools are not only sites of cultural transmission but also sites of producing a new culture in the interaction among students and between teachers and students (1996: 9). This aspect of schooling – cultural production – has been largely neglected among historians who studied education in colonial Africa. To this gap of analysis, this book will also aim to make a contribution with the close analysis of education in Achimota School.

From the late 19th century on, a few of the African elite who were educated in European-operated schools and were politically active began to participate in the debates on education, which, until then, was virtually dominated by Europeans. Whereas ordinary Africans demanded education in the 3R's for the economic and cultural benefits such studies brought to their children and, by extension, to their family as a whole, African ideologists advocated not only mass education but also leadership education. Their insistence on secondary and higher education often clashed with the European hesitation to expand the higher orders of education beyond the needs of those concerned with European trade and state administration. Ashby's grand epic of discourse on higher education was the first to illuminate the long-lasting controversy between Africans and Europeans on this matter (1966). Later, Emudong (1997) examined the interaction between the nationalists and colonial officials in the 1940s' Gold Coast, and Okunor (1991) investigated the educational ideologies of nationalist leaders in West Africa. For African ideologists of the colonial period, the campaign for the establishment of a higher educational institution had a symbolic meaning beyond the access to knowledge. These ideologists thought that to have a university was a necessary condition for the political advancement of Africans. Given that view, many historians referred to the struggles for a university in the context of nationalist movements. Among the scholars who have focused on nationalism on the Gold Coast and in West Africa, Kimble (1963), Kay (1972), Holmes (1972), Edsman (1979) and Boahen (1987) have provided some analysis of the relationship between nationalism and the debate on higher education. Another work by Boahen (1996), a history of Mfantsipim Secondary School in colonial Ghana, demonstrated the process by means of which African intellectuals' pressure for literary secondary education influenced the direction of the School.

To what extent the European curriculum should be 'adapted' to the African context was another source of conflict between Africans and Europeans. The African public, which was mostly pressuring the authorities for education in English writing and reading, resisted any form of education which was not literary education, that is, which was not exactly the same as British children received. Therefore, scholars who had studied the African reaction to education rarely missed the opportunity to mention the conflicting views on cultural relevance and on non-literary, vocational education between Europeans and Africans. One volume edited by Brown (1976) attempted to reveal the kind of education which existed before the aggression of the Europeans, and how European and 'indigenous' values interacted through the process of adapting European education to African contexts. Contrary to Brown's contention that there was a dichotomising of 'indigenous' and European education, Ranger (1983) claimed that what was called 'indigenous' or African tradition were, in fact, colonial inventions. Fluid customs and the rules of African institutions were fixed by Europeans as 'tradition' and education was 'adapted' to this invented tradition.

As for vocational education, Ocaya-Lakidi and Mazrui wrote specifically about African reaction to it in Uganda. According to them, African students 'merely tolerated' vocational subjects because they were 'a means to be able to remain in school and so be able to learn English' (1976: 355). Summers (1997) made a similar argument.

Yates's article (1976) provided complex opinions on vocational education expressed among missionaries in Zaire, some of which were not necessarily positive about vocational education. She also revealed that from the point of view of missionaries who needed African catechists who could read and write English, literary education was sometimes more of a direct skill preparation of Africans. Kallaway (1996) focused on a European scholar, Fred Clarke, who worked in South Africa and was sceptical about a vocational education which trained Africans in a set of skills pre-selected by Europeans. Clarke's view, influenced by the American progressive educational philosophy of the early 20th century, was that students should learn to cope with a changing environment, not a fixed set of skills. The contribution of Kallaway's article is that it demonstrated that there was a European theorist who was against the dominant trend toward vocationalisation. Pointing this out is important, since British colonial administrations obliterated a large part of criticism of vocational education in the public records. Thus historians who base their analyses exclusively on governmental archives tend to neglect atypical European opinions about vocational education. Victor Murray was another British educational theorist, a contemporary of Clarke, who was publicly against vocational education in Africa who proposed his theory on native education in Africa in 1929. So far, however, no serious study has been done on Murray's educational philosophy, which would reveal the contested nature of educational 'adaptation'. Agbodeka, (2002) who studied vocational education in the Gold Coast Colony, claims that vocational education was promoted on the Gold Coast from the mid-19th century on. He considered why it never took root, and concluded that it was contrary to the persistent aspiration of Africans to attain literary knowledge and thus access to salaried employment.

2-1-5 Educational practice and experience of schooling

In the late 1970s, Kelly pioneered a field in the history of education which had been mostly neglected until then: the schooling process and African students' reactions to it (see Mak 1997). Whatever was discussed outside of school, the actual transmission of knowledge, skills and values to students occurred inside school. Kelly attempted to reveal not only the type of knowledge taught but also the tacit messages transmitted by teachers in various aspects of school life (the hidden curricula). Based on an analysis of history and other textbooks used in French West African schools, she concluded that the schools prepared students for an adult world which did not exist. Africans were educated to be unlike 'blacks' – their uneducated peers – but at the same time, it was also imprinted that they could not belong to the world of the French coloniser (1983 and 1986). Along a similar line as Kelly, Colonna (1997) analysed the influence of the evaluation of students by teachers in an Algerian school on students' attitude. By examining the types of students who were called 'good' or 'bad', Colonna demonstrated that the school sent a message to students that obedience and harmony in groups were of higher value than individual excellence.

There have been some attempts to contrast educational experiences at schools operated by different missions. Carmody (1991) studied the Jesuit educational philosophies and the role played by schools in the conversion of Africans to Roman-Catholic-Jesuitism in Zambia. Meanwhile, the Presbyterian missions are said to prefer segregating students from African societies by having them live in boarding schools and to discipline them strictly. It is widely accepted that the Presbyterian missions were among those who placed great stress on manual work and skills training much earlier than those who embraced the colonial policy of adaptation. In contrast, Methodist education was primarily literary (for example, Wyllie 1976). Boateng summarised the Presbyterian education in Ghana partly based on his own experience of school life, as that of 'harsh discipline and strong religious indoctrination' (1975: 76). Miescher (1997) studied how the educational experience at Presbyterian boarding schools contributed to the construction of masculinity in colonial Ghana. According to him, missionaries made a distinct effort to remake African men and women through exposure to 'cultured' western manhood at school.

In the same vein as masculinity for male students, schools contributed to the construction of African female character too. Gaitskell wrote about formation of femininity in a 'subordinate race' in various educational settings both inside and outside school. Her

Upward All and Play the Game (1984) focused on girls' socialisation through Girl Guide activities. She also examined the girls' vocational curriculum in South Africa, which was distinct from that of boys (Gaitskell 2002). Needlework as a vocational subject for girls was given a symbolic importance as a signifier of femininity. Girls received not only such skills training 'appropriate' for girls but also were taught to help transform African families according to the Victorian Christian notion of good households, although there was no ground for such a notion in African homes. A similar argument about training in morals and skills for girls in French Africa was made by Barthel (1985).

A relatively new field of study related to the schooling process that emerged in the late 1980s was one that examined the link between British public School morality and 'character training' in African schools. A large number of colonial educators, either government or mission, were graduates of public school and believed in the virtue of the moral education they received there. Public schools taught students specific values in all aspects of school life; these values were selflessness, discipline, loyalty, helpfulness to others and a sense of honour. Mangan has written much on this topic (1982; 1986; 1987). According to him, the trust in team sports and the boarding arrangement to develop a specific type of character was transferred to African schools. Thus, there was a dissemination of a moral ideology which was conducted with the ethnocentric attitude that Africans could be brought morally to the height of British upper class children in public schools, if they received 'character training' through the same educational tools (for instance, team sports). Rich (1991) demonstrates how this public school morality was spread by its graduates in their work as colonial administrators, at clubs and at schools in various parts of British Empire. Ranger (1983) also devoted some space to this issue in *The Invention of Tradition in Colonial Africa*. He argued that public school graduates went to Africa as administrators and ran their districts like public school prefects, inventing their own little traditions to define and justify their roles. As such, in practice, public school tradition was modified by administrators and teachers according to their needs on site. The Boy Scout movement, which was actively promoted in British Africa in the 1920s and 1930s, was a derivative of the public school morality. Originally, it was started by a retired military man, Baden Powell, so as to provide character training of a public-school type for working-class children who were not fortunate enough to go to the public schools. Rosenthal (1986) described how the movement expanded to 'less-fortunate' children throughout the Empire and how it contributed to the development of a sense of obedience among colonial subjects.

Lastly, I would like to introduce some memoires and chronicles by former teachers and students of Achimota and other schools in West Africa. These works, even though written much later than the period with which we are concerned (1920s–30s), serve as primary sources rather than analytical literature. Achimota teachers, who were among the first group that arrived on the Gold Coast and who were directly exposed to the founders' educational philosophies, later wrote about these early years of the School based on their memories. The works by Kingsley Williams (1962) and W.E.F. Ward (1965) are in this category. Ward also wrote a biography of the first principal of Achimota School, A.G. Fraser. This biography contributes to our knowledge of the psychology of an educator-cum-theorist of the time who left numerous public and private statements. The two histories of Achimota School that were published in the 1970s were both by alumni and attempted to locate the School in the context of nation building (Agbodeka 1977; Setse 1974). Thus, the contribution of this unique educational institution to independence and national development caught the interest of graduates and educational historians. However, the limitation of works by Achimota sympathisers is that they do not question its educational philosophy but rather blindly accept it and take pride in the 'innovative' and noble intentions of the founders. To critically review a school's educational practice, one should include the framework of its education philosophy in one's analysis. Only in this way can one assess how and to what extent the school experience had an impact on students' character formation. Boahen's work on Mfantsipim School on the Gold Coast (1996) is somewhat different, although he was also an alumnus of the school. He described the curriculum and school activities, but a large part of the book was on the political discourse of the Europeans and Africans who were involved in the establishment and development of the school. Mfantsipim was the first secondary school on the Gold Coast in whose development African nationalists were deeply involved. The book vividly describes the interactions among African leaders, Methodist missionaries and the colonial officials. Hubbard (2000) published a history of Katsina College in Nigeria. The difference between Hubbard and earlier writers of African school history was that he attempted to examine the effect of internationally popular educational ideas on the college and its curriculum.

As I mentioned earlier, school was not only a site of receiving European cultural influence but more significantly of cultural production. The values transmitted at school were uniquely created in the daily interactions between African students and European teachers. However, there are still limited studies on this process of cultural production and socialisation in colonial schools in Africa. Early 20th century colonial education was characterised by its emphasis on the role of education in the moral upliftment of Africans. What did it actually mean and how was it practised in school? We need more studies not only about the philosophical debates at the high policy-making levels in the metropole and in the colonies but also the practices and experiences of teachers and students.

2-2 Perspectives on global discourse and transfer of educational models

2-2-1 Theories on borrowing and adaptation of educational ideas

The development of the field of comparative and international education is closely related to the demands of the 'borrowing' and 'lending' of education policies between countries. One of the major aims of comparative studies of different educational systems and policies has been to seek out and analyse good practices in other countries and to relate these other countries' attempted solutions to their educational problems to the situation at home (Noah 1984: 155; Phillips 1989: 267). Noah and Eckstein reported that from the beginning of the 19th century, educationists travelled to foreign countries, mostly in Europe and North America, in search of ideas to be borrowed (1969: 31–2). In the beginning, the approaches to the study of foreign systems were largely unsystematic, and scholars had naïvely assumed that there was 'the one best policy and practice for all contexts' (Arnove 1999: 7). According to Noah and Eckstein (1969: 32), Horace Mann, an American educator who is known as the 'Father of the Common School', visited several European countries and reported 'on whatever happened to catch his eye' and thought 'institutions, even whole systems, could be reproduced at will on foreign soil'. In 1816–17, Marc-Antoine Jullien, the 'modern father of comparative education' (Phillips 1993: 14), developed a questionnaire to systematically identify good educational practices with the expressed intention of transferring those practices to other systems. Many comparative educationists regard Jullien's questionnaire as the starting point of the tradition of 'examination of, and borrowing from, foreign models of provision in education' (ibid). However, Jullien still believed that by systematic examination, one could extract a perfect educational model applicable to all countries regardless of the particularities of each context. The departure from this universalistic attitude of comparative studies and borrowing/lending occurred with the study on foreign education provision by the Office of Special Inquiries and Reports of the English Board of Education at the turn of the 20th century. Michael Sadler, the director of the Office, stated:

> In studying foreign systems of education we should not forget that the things outside the schools matter even more than the things inside the schools, and govern and interpret the things inside. We cannot wander at pleasure among the educational systems of the world, like a child strolling through a garden, and pick off a flower from one bush and some leaves from another, and then expect that if we stick what we have gathered into the soil at home, we shall have a living plant. A national system of education is a living thing, the outcome of forgotten struggles and 'of battles long ago.' It has in it some of the secret workings of national life. (Sadler 1900, cited in Phillips 1993: 15)

After Sadler's pronouncement, arose basic agreement among comparative educationists that education systems are the products of and are influenced by the political, historical and socio-cultural contexts in which they are developed, and therefore cannot be transferred to other settings without adaptation (see for example, Arnove 1999; Finegold, et al 1993; Halpin & Troyna 1995; Phillips 1989; Robertson & Waltman 1993). It was not a coincidence that the concept of educational adaptation in British Africa arose at the same time. As people came to accept the diversity of contexts in which seemingly similar education policies were embedded, comparative educationists became more cautious about the transplant of education policies than earlier scholars had been. They argued that well-conducted cross-cultural studies could provide general features of successful education policies and so help policy makers to identify the potential of transfers (Arnove 1999: 15–16; Noah 1984: 159). At the same time, they pointed out the difficulties of transplanting educational policies into soils in which they were not grown. Thus, Noah expressed his impression that more than half of the international borrowing/lending of educational ideas and practices has failed. Despite these expressed concerns, the enthusiasm of policy makers for finding solutions to their problems elsewhere had not disappeared.

2-2-2 Motivations for transferring educational ideas

Many comparative educationists have pointed out that the transferred policies are not always those that achieved the targeted goals in the original countries, regardless of the advantages claimed by the importers. Policy makers tend to give more weight to other considerations than the effectiveness of the policies to be borrowed/lent. Referring to the convergence of British and American vocational education policies, Finegold et al (1993: 6) argue that what matters in decision making are 'not only ... common problems, but also a similar interpretation of the state's proper role in solving these problems, ... the historical linkages between the two nations' languages, cultures, and state structures ...'. .

According to Ginsburg, et al (1991), there are two approaches to the analysis of the motivations for introducing a new educational policy: the equilibrium approach and the conflict approach. The equilibrium approach believes that educational reform begins when there is an agreed need for change. In contrast, scholars of the conflict approach believe that the reform involves some power relationship: coercion, resistance or a lack of any other means than reform. As far as one can imagine, it would be quite unlikely that all the policy makers involved reach agreement on one specific educational policy, as the equilibrium approach suggests. It is more natural to think that there is some kind of power relationship, either confrontational or negotiated between people who intend to introduce different policies.

The externalisation theory is one of the major attempts to explain this power relationship. According to Steiner-Khamsi and Quist (2000: 276-277), 'When policy makers fail to receive sufficient political support ... for carrying through a contested [educational] reform, ... references to "examples abroad" or to "lessons" learned from abroad are used as effective means to externalize and justify the needs of action'. For scholars who take this analytical standpoint, the transferred policies' symbolic roles in the political discourse are more significant than the particular characteristics of the policies. Thus, supporters of a borrowed policy advertise its superiority, and opponents try to make it appear to have uncertain or negative consequences. Policies imported as such may be met with resistance, adjustment or compromise among the citizens affected (Dolowitz & Marsh 1996). Still, the reason for educational borrowing, according to the externalisation theorists, is not necessarily its substantial values but legitimisation of the policy that is already favoured (Robertson & Waltman 1993: 29; Halpin & Troyna 1995: 307–308; Phillips & Ochs 2003: 454).

Other scholars emphasise the international influence beyond the specific needs and contexts of the countries involved in the educational transfer. According to them, political and economic trends and power relations in the global community drag a country's education policy in the direction of external determination with only a limited range of choices given to its own people. To explain the massive simultaneous transplant of a same model to multiple sites, classic theories of borrowing and lending seem not to fit. Also, in this type of multilateral transfer, the relationships between the 'lender' and the 'borrower' tend not to be equal, where the lender grasps the hegemony. Referring to the transfer of American and European models of education to their colonies in the 19th century, Yates (1984: 533–6) argued that such a form of transfer was 'selective lending'.[7] She claimed that comparative educationists tended to see the 19th century as 'a period of borrowing' from among European and American countries themselves, but they neglected the fact that there were efforts of transferring their education models to the colonies in a form which they perceived as appropriate for them (p. 533).

2-2-3 Global mechanism for developing a common policy framework

In explaining the diffusion of some policy ideas to multiple societies simultaneously, some have pointed to a shared assumption that a certain type of school culture is a universal condition for running a nation effectively. 'World culturalists', as they are called, assume the existence of a shared 'world culture' that makes a particular schooling model appeal to multiple countries (Boli, et al 1985; Benavot et al 1991; Meyer & Ramirez 2000; Baker & LeTendre 2005). Baker and LeTendre (2005) demonstrated such voluntary adoption is likely to happen among countries with little difference in economic and diplomatic power. However, when one analyses the diffusion of educational models and ideas from industrialised countries to developing ones, or from the metropole to the colonies, such assumption of power equality is less likely to apply.

'World-system theorists' sharply point this out (Arnove 1980; Samoff 1999). The world-system theory, as developed by Immanuel Wallerstein, extends the Marxist notion of the exploitative dynamics of class relations to the whole world (1974). According to Wallerstein, just as the bourgeois capitalists exploit the working class, so the economically advanced 'core' countries exploit less developed 'periphery' countries and strengthen the core–periphery relationship through political influence. Several scholars applied the world-system framework to their examination of the relationship between international organisations and aid-providing countries, on the one hand, and developing countries, on the other (Brock-Utne 2000; Jones 1992; Mazrui 1997).

Many scholars have pointed out the limitation of reducing countries and regions into two categories: core and periphery. Two kinds of criticism arose, primarily among scholars of colonialism. One criticism was that such distinctions as core–periphery are produced by hegemonic discourse. The dominant powers, to justify their cultural and political superiority, needed to construct 'others' in contrast to themselves (Said 1995). These scholars call for the rethinking of relationships from the viewpoint of 'others' or the people of the Third World. As they argue, actual relationships among different parties cannot be explained simply by the 'synchronic panoptical vision' (Bhabha 1994: 86) of the 'metropole-colony axis' (Stoler & Cooper 1997: 28; see also Escobar 1995; Gupta 1998).

Given such criticism, while world-system theorists focus on the vertical relationship between the core and the periphery, 'multilateralists' pay attention to the processes by which organisations (predominantly aid-providing agencies) with different motives and characteristics interact with each other and formulate the shared norms and agenda of international educational development (Chabbott 1998, 2003; Jones 1999; Mundy 1999, 2007). According to Ruggie (1992: 565–7), multilateralism refers to an international governance of multiple countries working in concert on a given issue, which involves not only formal institutions but also norms and practices.

2-2-4 Limitations of conventional analytical framework

World culture theory, world-system theory and multilateralism have been employed and have effectively explained, from different perspectives, the global discourse and practices of international educational development during colonial and post-colonial eras. However, these theories are all based on the assumption of one model or a couple of dominant models that influence the whole world either voluntarily, through coercion or through multilateral efforts to promote the common good. They do not assume a multipolar power structure, which may influence actors from different directions at different levels, causing intermingling of diverse sources of influence. In reality it is often difficult to tell who the borrower and the lender of a policy idea are because of the constant cross-feeding of ideas. The resultant hybrid ideas, which often occur unconsciously, are adapted by the respective participants to their own societies and sometimes brought back to the global discourse after a fundamental metamorphosis. In this sense, the analysis of the global mechanism of international educational development, which is one of the core interests of comparative educationists, would require a new step to theorise the changing landscape through a multipolar structure among actors who constantly cross-feed and hybridise ideas.

Another limitation is the divorce between the academic examination on the process and decision of educational transfer and that on implementation and its outcomes. There are certainly many cases where transferred educational models have failed in new sites. While there have been many reports from the field to international donor organisations which claimed the 'success' of transferred educational reforms, academic writings have been much more critical of the outcomes of such educational transfer. As for the colonial era, Bude (1983) argued that the educational reforms which took place in British Africa based on the adaptation policy of the colonial administration failed almost without exception. He attributes the failure of adaptation to a lack of understanding of and interest in African needs on the part of Europeans. Similar case studies are abundant for the post-colonial period. One such study, by Ferguson (1990), is on a rural development project in Lesotho funded by the World Bank. According to him, the project failed to achieve its goals because of the Bank's institutionalised neglect of the specificities of the local context and because of its tendency of fixing countries with diverse conditions by means of a stereotype of 'Lower Developing Countries'.[8] Others argue that the failure of the imported model is caused by the lack of continuity in aid organisations' policies and, by extension, the funding, as well as the power struggle between aid organisations and various sections of a government (for example, Agelasto 1996; Lillis & Lowe 1987; Mayer, et al 1993; Nagel & Conrad, Jr 1989).

The analytical framework for educational transfer tends to limit researchers' attention to the decision making that takes place at the point of transfer. However, the studies of colonial and contemporary practices of educational transfer demonstrate that international and local discourse are not separated but are linked with each other and with practices, so that the continual re-interpretation of jargon in this discourse makes the implementation of a prescribed educational model very different from the intentions of the original.[9]

2-3 Perennial debate over vocational versus literary education

As a basis for my investigation of colonial discourse on education in Africa, it will be useful to give an overview of the different opinions about the objectives and forms of vocational education. In the late colonial period, one of the differences in educational views between the African elite and the British was the degree to which the contents of education should be vocationally oriented. Achimota School was established as a model school by the British colonial authority to train African leaders. In this sense, its education was supposed to be different from schools run by missionaries or by the local initiatives of Africans. On the one hand, there is a shared objective to provide the highest level of education equipped with good teachers, curriculum and facilities. On the other hand, the British were cautious not to uproot these educated leaders from African society and be excessively Europeanised. Facing the strong demand for political and administrative autonomy from native intellectuals in Asia and in Southern and Eastern Africa, British educators and administrators shaped a rough consensus that the model school for leadership education should not be biased toward literary education but be balanced with vocational and moral education. Vocational education, in this context, was considered as a middle ground between no schooling and excessive exposure to the European elite culture and value system. It was imagined as formal school-based education, somehow insulated from the society surrounding it, but with a set limit on the access to knowledge. The scepticism of such European intention behind vocational orientation in education created a strong negative image of vocational education throughout the post-colonial period in Africa, even though the memory of the colonial past had faded and the decisions on educational policies have been made by the Africans themselves. Also, it is ironic that West Africa has had highly developed and widespread practices of apprenticeship, an informal mode of educating disciples by masters through hands-on experience of work (Hart 1970; Anokye et al 2014; Sonnenberg 2012). Learning vocational skills might have been possible without school, but there have been constant efforts, from the colonial period to the present, to integrate vocational training as a part of the school system.

In this section, I will review theoretical debates on vocational education not restricted to the colonial period, but in a broader framework. As much as the concept of 'adaptation' was inseparable from vocational education in the colonial period, after independence too, the relevance to learners' environment has been the issue which has almost always driven the policy makers towards vocational education. The global trends have periodically swung between vocational and literary education, with which the national education policies of African states have also shifted their focus. Whenever vocational education was highlighted, in its background, there was criticism of literary education that the knowledge taught in school is not relevant to the world of work and life for the graduates. Also, vocational education has often been advocated as if it is the magic bullet to cure various social, economic and political issues. Since many issues were said to be solved by means of vocational education, it is necessary for the purpose of this book to examine the expressed views on it so as to critically untangle the intentions of different stakeholders involved in the discourse.

The bodies of literature reviewed in this section are about vocational education at the secondary level, unless otherwise stated, because vocationalisation is often considered as an issue after the general basic education, when the learners are tracked into university-bound academic courses and vocational ones. There has also been discussion about including vocational contents in basic education, particularly in relation to subjects such as social studies or life science, so that those who terminate schooling at the basic level can also transit smoothly to the world of work and life. In either case, a fundamental concern of the promoters of vocational education is to ensure smooth transition from school to the societal role of the person by improving the relevance of education, while the actual definition of 'relevance' would vary depending on perspectives.

2-3-1 Justifications for vocational education

Economic justification for vocational education

The justification which is most likely to be mentioned is the economic one, based on the assumption that training in the types of skills which match the demand of the labour market will increase the productivity of individual workers and, as a result, contribute to national economic development. Starting from the late colonial period, it was considered that the vocational curricula of secondary schools ought to be designed according to estimated demands for skilled manpower. Technological modernisation from the 20th century onward prepared the ground for argument that efficient industrial development should be supported by the supply of manpower equipped with skills to meet the specific needs of the industries. Such economic justification as emerged in the colonial period was succeeded by international organisations established right after the World War II, which advocated vocational education programmes in secondary education (e.g. ILO 1946; ILO 1950; UNESCO 1961). A telling example was UNESCO, the United Nations agency specialising in education, science, and culture. It was established in London in 1945 and the large part of its initial high-level staff members were British education specialists who had promoted the importance of 'manpower forecasting' and vocational education.

The human capital theory, developed in the early 1960s, views education as an investment for increased economic return. Unlike earlier economic theories, which treated education as a service consumed by individuals, early human capital theorists considered human beings as important capital, who together with physical and financial capital, contribute to the production process. Along this line, the importance of interventions to improve the human capital element, such as education or health care, are highlighted in order to enhance the productivity of workers (Becker 1964; Schultz 1971). The issue then was to specify the level at which investment in education is cost efficient. Initially, the investment in vocational programmes at secondary school was considered to be cost efficient. Accordingly, the inflow of financial and technical assistance from overseas to this sub-sector of education took a large share. In 1963, the World Bank launched a large-scale loan programme for vocational education in developing countries. Eating up the share of the general secondary education, the World Bank's loan for vocational secondary education, between 1964 and 1969, occupied the second highest proportion (20 per cent) of the total loan for the education sector (World Bank 1995; Jones 1992: 125). Accordingly, the proportion of secondary school students in vocational education had risen to 15–20 per cent during the period 1950–1960 in Africa, although it decreased to less than 10 per cent in the 1970s (Benavot 1983).

Contrary to the assumption of vocational education advocates, however, empirical data do not often demonstrate higher rates of return on investment in vocational secondary education than in academic secondary education. Rather, it is more common that net returns for vocational education are lower than those for academic education. When the capacity of vocational schools to produce a workforce exceeds that of the labour market to absorb them as workers, overproduction of vocational graduates leads to wages lower than the costs of education or unemployment. Such instances have been reported for the following African countries: Benin, Mozambique, Niger and Somalia (Ziderman 1997: 357). Based on evidence from Tanzania (East Africa) and Colombia (Latin America), Psacharopoulos argued that 'the expense of schools [which introduced practical subjects] was considerably more than that of the conventional academic schools. ... [However,] graduates from [vocationalised] secondary schools do not find employment more quickly than graduates from conventional schools and ... do not demonstrate higher initial earnings than those from traditional academic schools' (Psacharopoulos 1988: 275). Other studies find that there is no significant difference between the earnings of vocational and academic graduates. Ziderman cites studies on Cote d'Ivoire (West Africa), Indonesia (South East Asia) and Peru (Latin America) which support the findings of Psacharopoulos (1997: 357). To make things even more complicated, there is often gender bias in the rates of return on different forms of education. Horowitz and Schenzler have demonstrated that in Suriname (Latin America) private and social rates of return on vocational secondary schooling are negative for females but positive for males (Horowitz & Schenzler 1999: 15–7).

Still, more recent studies report positive rates of return on vocational secondary education. A study in Turkey, where up to half of all high school students are enrolled in vocational and technical high schools, shows that male graduates of such schools not only have a higher probability of waged employment but also significantly higher wages and rates of return than general academic high school graduates (cited in Ziderman (1997: 359). Even Psacharopoulos, who has been a strong opponent of vocational secondary schooling, has become less dismissive of the effectiveness of vocational education lately. Analysing data from eleven countries in Latin America, he found that over half (six) of these countries 'show that the [social] rate of return for vocational secondary education is higher than that for secondary general education' (Psacharopoulos 1994: 7).[10] It was also reported in this study that, in seven out of the eleven countries, the private returns on secondary education do not significantly differ between general and vocational education.

Political and ideological motivations for vocational education

Although there is little empirical evidence either to confirm or reject the hypothesis in favour of vocational secondary education, governments of developing countries have not lost their enthusiasm for providing this type of education. This fact suggests that there are motives other than just that of increased productivity involved. Such governments often have political reasons for advocating this type of education. One of most frequent justifications for vocational education is the reduction of youth unemployment. J. Lauglo (cited in Bacchus 1988: 35) found in Kenya that 'the efforts at [vocationalisation] had not been so much an attempt to meet certain projected manpower needs as an essentially political response to a situation in which the school-leavers from the regular academic programs of the schools were increasingly having difficulties in finding jobs'. Macroeconomic performance of a country does not directly correlate with the employment growth. In fact, in Africa, after the long stagnation until the mid-1990s, economic growth rate had been high, averaging above 5 per cent, with some growth centres such as Cote d'Ivoire and Ethiopia exceeding 7 per cent growth rate. On the other hand, the employment prospect had not seen much change during the same period (around 8 per cent regional average) with a significantly higher unemployment rate for the youth between 15 and 24 years old (around 14 per cent) (World Bank 2017). In such a situation, governments often see the vocational education as a useful policy measure to prevent these unemployed school leavers from becoming a threat to social stability.

Second, some governments state that vocationalisation will give students a wider variety of subjects to choose from than is available in strictly academic education, and will thus increase the equity in educational opportunities. Benavot points out that this emphasis on equity reflects a global ideological tendency toward egalitarianism that has been going on since the 1950s (1983: 73). There has also been an attempt to increase the number of vocationally oriented rural schools, which have been promoted in many areas as a way to increase the opportunities for the rural population to be schooled, while avoiding an overly academic curriculum that is considered irrelevant to rural life. The advocates of this scheme argue that it will enhance the equity of *access* to education. However, this is a slippery justification. Lauglo and Lillis argue that distinct tracks in both academic and vocational programmes may lead to an inequality of *future prospects* for students (1988: 13). According to their argument, the inclusion of vocational subjects in a general secondary curriculum (the 'vocationalisation' of general secondary education) can be justified by egalitarianism, but not by the creation of a separate-track vocational education. This issue of separate-track and vocationalised secondary education will be explored more deeply in the following sections.

Third, one justification for vocational education that has recurred since the colonial period is that vocational education can change youths' aspirations from white-collar jobs to manual employment. In some cases, this argument is justified as a means to improve the earnings of the poor and other disadvantaged groups by reorienting them to locally available jobs (Ziderman 1997: 361). In other cases, it is argued that the reorientation of students to manual work and agriculture, which are dominant occupations in rural areas, will halt urban migration, while such attempt 'did little to stem the tide of urban migration (Tanzania, Kenya, Rwanda, Ghana, Benin, Uganda and Botswana all tried this out.)' (Honig 1993: 4; see also, Sifuna 1992: 6). There are also instances when governments have had the intention of using vocational education in schools to keep students out of higher education ('cooling out') (Gill & Fruitman 2000). There are a limited number of seats in higher education, and the government often deliberately limits the intake of students to higher education, because (1) the government cannot afford the cost of higher education if it expands too much; and (2) there are not as many white-collar jobs as there are university graduates.

Last and a less frequent justification for vocational education is the idea of populism. Some countries, especially socialist countries, promote vocational education as a way for the masses to go back to 'real life', and this tendency is coupled with the sentiment of anti-intellectualism. Lauglo and Lillis (1988: 7) thus say of populism that '[it] typically celebrates the importance of work as a source of moral fiber, self-reliance and civic virtue. Productive physical work is, from this perspective, educational in that it develops valued personal qualities. Populism may be skeptical of formal schooling on the grounds that it unduly distances the young from their cultural origins, or because school removes a person from the hurly-burly of "real-life" situations in which true character is formed'. This link between morality and vocationalism was also a widely accepted justification for promoting vocational skills training in colonial Africa, which is one of the key issues in this book.

The governments which plan and implement vocational schooling with the non-economic objectives tend to pay less attention to the nature and dynamics of industry and the nature of jobs available there. On the other hand, political, social and ideological goals of vocational education will not be achieved unless parents and students internalise the messages of the providers of education that vocational education is as good as general education. However, because of the historical root of vocational education in Africa, both the general public and government officials do not believe in the equality of two tracks of education in a real sense. Therefore, the value system surrounding this form of education has not fundamentally changed, which makes it difficult to achieve the goals explained above. For parents and students to find positive prospects after education in vocational programmes, the availability of employment is important. Primarily, this is the matter of economic condition of the society. At the same time, unless the general perceptions about the vocational education and the capacity of their graduates change, the chances of employment for the vocational graduates will continue to be hindered.

2-3-2 Criticism of tracking and the vocationalisation of the general secondary curriculum

After the enthusiasm to invest in vocational education in the 1950s and 60s, which I mentioned earlier, there was a period of downfall of vocational education. It was largely because of the disapproval of vocational programmes as a separate track from general secondary education. It was criticised to have systematically disadvantaged the vocational students in pursuing higher education and white-collar jobs (Verner 1999). Not only the employment of the graduates, but also the recruitment of students to different tracks are often biased by class and gender and help to reproduce social inequalities (Bhola 1995: 27–8). As regards class, Psacharopoulos reports that the outcome of his research in Tanzania shows that the average difference in family income and the number of years of a father's education between students of academic secondary schools and students of agricultural schools are 7,400 shillings and 1.5 years respectively (1988: 262). As for gender, Kerre reports that in Kenya women's enrolment in technical education is below 40 per cent (1999: 206–7). Therefore, at least in some countries, social and gender bias between vocational and academic tracks of secondary education was demonstrated to exist.

Also, some critics argue that students' aspirations for jobs have nothing to do with the content of the education they receive. In his influential paper 'The Vocational School Fallacy', Foster states that what schools teach does not matter as much as the job structure and expected opportunities it brings in the wider society (1966). According to him, in independent Ghana in the mid-1960s, the primary employer in the formal economic sector was the government, which preferred to employ graduates of academic secondary schools over those of vocational schools. As a result, academic schools are more 'vocational' than their counterparts in terms of preparation for the world of work. Not only in Ghana in the 1960s, but also in many other places, schools' role of providing credentials for students for certain types of job is perceived by students and parents as more important than the actual curriculum. In Africa, given the low social acceptance of vocational school certificates, the chance of the vocational curriculum actually making an impact on the labour market becomes smaller.

Having realised the problems of separate-track vocational education at the secondary level, in the late 1970s, international organisations and African governments began to shift their emphasis from separate-track vocational education to diversifying the general secondary curriculum through the introduction of vocational subjects. As all students have equal access to general subjects, and not exclusively vocational subjects, this form of education is seen as being less biased than the separate-track secondary education for different classes, sexes or races. It is also said that a diversified curriculum will increase the rates of return on investment in vocational education. Because it provides a range of subjects from which students can choose, according to their aspirations and the labour demand, vocationalised secondary education is thought to be more adaptive to changing needs. McMahon et al stress that the question is not between vocational and general education. For them, the two types of education are not substitutive but complementary. The more important task is to figure out the 'optimum degree of vocationalization of the curriculum'; the balance between practical skills and theories (1992: 181).

As was the case with separate-track vocational education, vocationalised secondary education quickly became a global trend. International and regional conferences hosted by various international organisations began advocating a vocationalised secondary education, whereas they had previously advocated a separate-track vocational education. For example, Colin Power, the Deputy Director-General for Education for UNESCO, stated at the Second International Congress on Technical and Vocational Education held in 1999 in Seoul, South Korea:

> UNESCO's activities ... should aim at *including vocational subjects in general education curricula* to facilitate the young generation to obtain generic technological knowledge and key pre-vocational skills – making Technical and Vocational Education and Training (TVET) for all an integral part of national educational policy. (UNESCO Regional Office for Education in Africa (BREDA) 1995: 29; emphasis is added)

However, there are several issues which vocationalised secondary education cannot solve and where it remains uncertain whether it has positive effects or not. First, vocationalisation is as expensive as separate-track vocational education. The facilities, equipment and materials necessary to teach vocational subjects add up to several times more than those needed to teach general subjects. The change in the way of providing vocational instruction has not made any difference to costs. Second, it is doubtful if vocationalised secondary education is more socially just than separate-track vocational education.

The efforts in the 1990s to mitigate the tracking effect by vocationalising general education and generalising vocational education did not persist for too long. After all, from the public, there had been constant demand for more academic education and the distinction between vocational and general secondary schools persisted in most of the countries which introduced vocationalisation in the 1990s. Implicit tracking of students according to their backgrounds was reported from many countries. As students' and parents' perceptions have not changed much, the socio-economic backgrounds of students will probably continue to affect students' choice of subjects. What is necessary for the sake of achieving equity is a holistic approach, taking into account not only the education system itself, but also the wider social, economic and political environment.

There is still another question. Can formal education, however vocationalised it is, be flexible enough to meet the changing and diverse labour demands? Some scholars are sceptical about this (for example, Foster 1966: 154–6; McGrath & King 1999: 216). In 2012 in sub-Saharan Africa, the informal economy is estimated to have yielded as much as 63.6 per cent of the Gross National Products (Kolli 2016: 5), while this sector has mostly not been captured in the government records and neglected in the large-scale manpower forecast. As a result, formal vocational education, whether separate track or combined with general education, where the curriculum is designed based on the large-scale forecast of manpower needs, is likely *not* to meet the skills needs in the largest part of the economy. Even though vocationalised secondary education provides a wide range of practical subjects from which students can choose, flexibility at the school level is limited, compared to the flaws in the large-scale assessment of labour demands. In addition, the needs for skills training in the informal sector are diverse. By their nature, enterprises in the informal sector are small- or micro-scale, and the work is influenced by the local socio-economic environment. Locality and diversity are the major characteristics of the informal sector and its labour demands. In such a context, recently, utilisation of non-formal channels of education gradually caught the attention of policy makers and scholars as a possible solution to the mismatch between vocational education and the labour market. Accordingly, it became a fashionable policy measure after the mid-2000s to establish the skills development mechanism which seamlessly coordinates formal and non-formal training and education.

2-3-3 Implication of vocationalism in Africa

The literature cited in this section indicates that orientation toward vocational subjects and programmes often emerges from the concerns of social unrest, lack of employment, slow economic development and maintenance of class- or gender-based segregation. In most of the cases, these concerns are inseparably tangled and vocational education is promoted as if it is a magic bullet to solve all these complicated issues. At the same time, it is often difficult to specify the causal relationship between increased budget or teachers for vocational subjects and schools and the solution of the perceived problems.

Analysing the differential patterns of student enrolment in technical and vocational education across the world, Atchoarena and Caillods (1999:71) argue that there is a positive correlation between the level of an economy's development and the relative importance attached to technical education. However, a positive correlation does not necessarily imply a causal relationship. For example, sub-Saharan Africa has been the most aid-dependent region in the world by any measure. In this sense, educational provision in sub-Saharan African countries is vulnerable to the policy changes of international organisations. Therefore, it is reasonable to attribute the declining proportion of vocational students in sub-Saharan Africa as much to the reduction of external financial assistance as to the industrial structure of the country. As I will discuss in more detail in Chapter Nine, the decline of vocational secondary education was indeed a global phenomenon between the 1950s and early 70s, although the decline in Africa was the sharpest compared to other regions. At the same time, though, international organisations' policy shifts are not the only reason for the decline in emphasis placed on vocational education at the secondary level. For Africa's departure from vocational secondary education, Benavot offers two reasons: (1) education in Africa entailed basic instruction in literacy and numeracy rather than specialised skills training, in spite of recurring calls to the contrary (see also Foster 1966); (2) the industrial sector, which would require formal skills training, was still immature. Rather, the formal economic sectors which were expanding during this period were those in public service, which required academic qualifications rather than vocational skills (Benavot 1983:69).

Although three decades have passed since Benavot published his article, the basic industrial structure and relationship between education and employment has not changed much. In the case of Ghana, according to the national census of 2010, 93 per cent of the labour force was employed in the private sector, 86.1 per cent of which was informal. Thus, the formal private sector employment was only 7 per cent (Government of Ghana, 2010). A dual economy, consisting of a large 'traditional' sector and a small 'modern' sector of salaried employment, is still a common feature of many sub-Saharan African countries. In assessing the impact of formal vocational training on productivity in the traditional sector, Little (1984: 96) points out that the contribution of specific skills training to agricultural production is fairly small, although a general increase in schooling may contribute to technology innovation. In sum, unless it is fundamentally overhauled to match the industrial structure in most sub-Saharan African countries, simple adaptation of vocational education models brought from elsewhere would not contribute much to overcome labour market challenges in a true sense.

Such analysis of the status of vocational secondary education confirms that the true aim of vocationalism could be more to serve socio-moralistic goals rather than to address the demands of the labour market. Such moralistic justification of vocationalism has not been heard much in the international discourse but has been consistently used in the Gold Coast during the 1920s–30s, the period which this book focuses on, and after the independence of Ghana. Global ideologies and the socio-economic environment of the world have influenced the domestic process of policy making very much, but in contrast to the international fluctuation of policy on vocational and secondary education, the Ghanaian discourse has a certain continuity.

Notes

[1] The impact of secondary and higher education on social mobility stimulated the interest of several educationalists in the 1960s and 70s. Scholars who presented statistical analysis of students' background, such as parental education, parental occupation, place of birth and ethnicity were:

Bibby and Margaret Peil (1974); Philip J. Foster (1963); G.E. Hurd and T.J. Johnson (1967); Margaret Peil (1965); and Weis (1979).

[2] For example, see the chapter on 'The Development of Education', in Antwi (1992). See also the chapter on 'The Colonial Educational Heritage', in E.A. Boateng (1996).

[3] Although they fail to fall into simple stereotypes, it is still common for contemporary historians of colonial education to compare the policies and practices of colonial powers (for example, White 1996; Madeira 2005).

[4] Mackenzie (1993) states that cooperation between the colonial administration and missions in the field, which was often explained as a characteristic of British colonialism, was 'pragmatic collusion' to cope with the pressures from various sources rather than any conspiracy to control education for Africans.

[5] See the list of archival sources at the end of this paper.

[6] For example, Stephen Ball (1983: 256–8) examined the cases in Kenya and Nigeria in which Africans 'resisted' the curriculum as 'applied' to the African background and attempted to control schools.

[7] Along the same line as Yates, Persianis made a case for 'selective lending' by the British to colonial Cyprus (1996).

[8] Ferguson, however, states that the project had an unintended impact on the extension of the government's power, given investment in large scale infrastructure.

[9] Anderson-Levitt and Alimasi (2001: 40, 51) analyse the multi-level and multi-dimensional process of educational appropriation in Guinea. According to her, 'the Guineans were either redefining a donor-introduced word to suit their own values or borrowing an international "buzzword" to label a prior Guinean concern. ... Once Guinean educators put certain Western notions ... into practice, they created a new, "creolized" version of it'.

[10] There have been suggestions that the conventional rate of return analysis does not correctly measure the effectiveness of schooling. According to critics, 'weak-willed acceptance by employers of the status of certificates from vocational [schools]' results in lower wages for graduates of vocational schools than their productivity would justify (Honny 1999: 199). They thus argue that, because of this wage bias, the rate of return analysis based on the earnings of graduates is not accurate.

Part II

Global discourse on colonial education in Africa and its constructs

As the 20th century approached, colonial rule was systematised and so was educational administration. Unlike earlier periods, education was no more a free land for missionaries but was considered to be a part of public service. Even though missions remained the major operators of schools, they became heavily dependent on grants from the government. As the conception of educational administration was transforming in Africa, there grew demands on the part of missions and the Colonial Office in London to develop a policy framework which would justify the enlarged commitment of colonial governments to education and cooperation between missions and the governments.

In Part II, based on the theoretical framework set in Part I, I am going to shift the focus to a core part of the analysis: global discourse centred on the Colonial Office in London, while involving diverse stakeholders in North America, Europe and the British territories in Asia and Africa. I will first set the background by overviewing the economic and political context of the United Kingdom and the world from 1900 to the start of the World War II (Chapter Three). Particularly, the focus will be given to the inter-war period between 1919 and 1939. In this period, despite the fragility of the basis and gradual decline of its economic and political supremacy, the UK was still maintaining its position as the prime global power. The economy of the colonies, particularly those exporters of agricultural and mineral resources, including the Gold Coast, was in a quite good shape. Technological advancement continued from the 19th century fostered the trust in scientific analysis and planning based on it. The recognition of the necessity of planned colonial rule, tacitly linked with the uncertainty of political and economic situations in Europe, was the important background to understand why the issue of colonial education caught the interest of various groups of people and why it was discussed in the manner that I demonstrate in this book.

In 1910, colonial education was discussed at the World Missionary Conference at Edinburgh, the first major effort to integrate the various Protestant missions' views on education. Education fever reached its height in the interwar period. In 1920 and 1923, the Phelps-Stokes Fund, based in New York, sent commissions to investigate educational conditions in West, South and Equatorial Africa, mostly in those colonial territories ruled by the British. In the same year as the second Phelps-Stokes Commission, the British Colonial Office established the Advisory Commission on Native Education in British Tropical Africa.

American philanthropists had their motivations and background for selling their educational model for Southern blacks to Africa. At the same time, there were logics of the British officials, missionaries and educators, and the realities they faced. Such different but overlapping realities among actors pushed them to take part in moulding the policy framework for colonial education in Africa. They needed a shared framework which would create a space for mutually beneficial relationships. In this sense, the 1925 *Memorandum* was the joint product of these different interest groups across the Atlantic. The words and phrases used in the *Memorandum* resemble not only those in the Phelps-Stokes reports, but also in the various reports by the missionary societies in the UK. They were mutually inspired and cross-referred ideas from others' reports and conference minutes.

Chapter Four will focus on the political aspect of the discourse in which British colonial education policy was formulated through the negotiation of different interests. While I will roughly follow the chronology of events, the main part of my analysis will follow an actor-oriented approach. The reason for such analysis is that I consider it is the negotiation of interests and the agency of the individuals involved in the process, which determine the nature of historic events. Based on this consideration, a greater attention will be paid to the psychology and ideology of individuals involved than has traditionally been done. I will first discuss the characteristics of some collective actors and their motives for lobbying for African education, which will then be followed by the examination of the personal traits that were common to major individuals who led the discourse.

While it is important to know the motivations of actors and the processes of their interactions, as I have argued in Chapter One, one cannot fully understand the discourse without knowing the normative framework they refer to. There are theories on education, governance, colonial rule, and social and religious norms which inspired ideas about African education. To untangle the link among politics, structure and norms, Chapter Five will examine theories and norms which were available in this historical period for actors of discourse to borrow essences to legitimise their conceptions of African education in the contemporary theoretical map.

The common characteristics of educational thought in the early 20th century were the emphasis on learning through experience and moral education which were often phrased as 'character development'. Within this broad spectrum, there was the American progressive philosophy of education, which has often been associated with the name of John Dewey. The American model of black industrial education, which was promoted by the Phelps-Stokes Fund and other American philanthropic organisations, also highlighted the importance of experience and morality. Furthermore, the traits of British Victorian moralism, which again placed significant weight on the class- and gender-based moral training, could be found in both elite (public school) education and mass education.

While Part II will focus on the global discourse and the factors which conditioned it, I fully recognise that what was discussed there did not always impact on the practices or implemented as originally intended. It is true that there was a fashion to refer to certain educational ideas in the context of colonial education in Africa. Still, whether they were implemented is a completely separate issue to be examined. Such will be the topic of Chapter III, which will focus on the discourse in the colonies and the actual process of developing and implementing the educational programmes of Achimota School.

Chapter 3

Context which conditioned the discourse

3-1 Political economy of the inter-war period in Europe

From the beginning of the 20th century, British economic superiority was fading gradually. While the industry structure in the United Kingdom had remained unchanged, the United States emerged as the industrial power, supported by the development of new technologies based on steel and electricity, and a dynamic workforce. One of the contributing factors which sustained the comparative supremacy of the United Kingdom was its position as the financial centre, which was not only connected to Europe but had a worldwide network, and the resources it could collect from the widely extended overseas territories (Briggs 1968: 37–8). However, by the end of the First World War the instability of such position of the UK surfaced. The large part of the credits it provided to European countries turned out to be irrecoverable at least in the short run. Instead, the demand for capital to reconstruct the war-damaged facilities, particularly in continental Europe, was absorbed by the United States, the emerging global creditor (Martel 2005: 78).

Despite these unfavourable factors and the gradual shift of power away from the pre-war big three, namely, the UK, France and Germany, up to 1925, most European countries were recovering from the war, with generally high rates of economic growth. The rush for infrastructure reconstruction in the war-devastated France and Germany, and to a lesser extent the UK, raised the demand for commodities and services of firms in the countries whose properties had been destroyed. Capital which had been stocked during the war was released into the market in the form of investment, which created the positive cycle of supply and demand for a while (Aldcroft 2013: 35–40).

During this economic boom, colonies were increasingly incorporated into the metropolitan economy, mainly as the suppliers of raw materials for home industries which produced consumer goods for European and overseas markets. The Gold Coast was one of the British African colonies which were viewed as the pivotal suppliers of agricultural and mineral resources. The major export products of the Gold Coast were cacao and gold. In the case of cacao, its international market price had risen sharply after the First World War (Figure 3-1), driven by the appetite of European consumers for luxury grocery items. Small scale cacao farmers of the Gold Coast responded to this opportunity of access to and gain from the global market.

Figure 3-1: Cocoa Export Price, 1900-1940

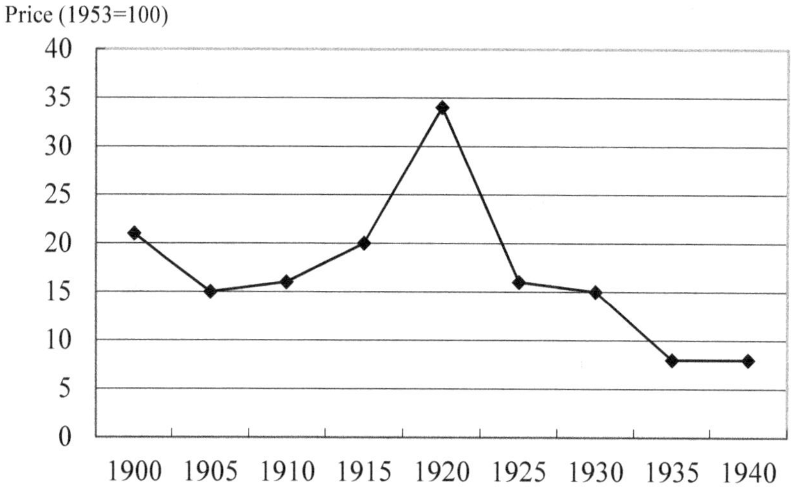

Price (1953=100)

Source: Kay (1972): 338-9

Accordingly, the cacao export from this West African colony soared (Figure 3-2). Even after the decline of international prices, export continued to grow. Interestingly, such positive economic prospects in some colonies, like the Gold Coast, which exported raw materials, were not so much caused by the economic planning of the metropole but by the calculation of the benefit by the individual *homo economicus* in Africa.

Regardless of such a favourable situation in the colonies, the foundation of the metropole's economy remained shaky. Accordingly, colonies were gradually expected to be financially self-reliant. Therefore, from the 1920s, the colonial authorities stepped in to control and tax small-scale local producers, which yielded ample revenue in the colonies and was reinvested in 'modernising' projects. Typically, such projects were directed at the economic infrastructure to expand economic capacity and to social welfare such as schools and hospitals (Martel 2005: 88; I Brown 1989: 76–80).

Figure 3-2: Trend of Cocoa Export, 1900-1940

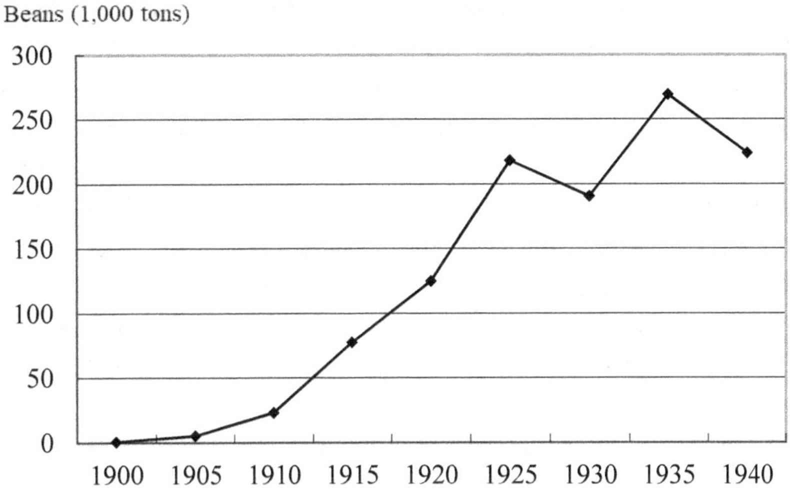

Beans (1,000 tons)

[Line chart showing cocoa bean exports from 1900 to 1940, with values starting near 0 in 1900-1910, rising through ~25 in 1915, ~75 in 1920, ~125 in 1925, ~220 in 1930, dipping to ~195, peaking near 270 in 1935, and declining to ~225 in 1940.]

Source: Kay (1972): 338-9

The violent boom of the economy in Europe was followed by a sudden downfall. The shortage of supply caused by war damage raised commodity prices which gave the economy a positive outlook temporarily. However, as the supply caught up with the demand, the financial market cooled down. After the Great Depression, between 1929 and 1932, the value of international trade shrank by more than 65 per cent (Briggs 1968: 60–1). Such a downturn of the economy, coupled with the often unfriendly diplomatic relationships among European powers caused economic protectionism. Unlike earlier periods when there was little barrier to cross-border transfer of goods and capital, after the Great Depression, the governments of economic powers raised tariffs to protect their domestic economies while formulating the exclusive economic bloc among diplomatic allies. Because of such intervention of the government in the economic practices, the intra-trade within Europe decreased while the partners of trade became more diverse and globalised (Aldcroft 2013: 44–58; Briggs 1968: 80). Meanwhile, the price of cocoa fell calamitously by 40 per cent in the recession years 1937–38 (Briggs 1968: 76). This suggests that the economies of colonies which achieved rapid growth owing to raw material exports were also severely damaged.

Because its economy was closely linked to that of the metropole, the Gold Coast Colony experienced a sharp rise and fall in revenue. It is a very significant background for understanding the characteristics of the model school established in this colony: Achimota. The plan for Achimota emerged in the late 1910s and the school was inaugurated in 1927, before the Great Depression. In sum, the process of actualising the idea of model school for African leaders was backed by the abundant resources and visionary leadership of Governor Guggisberg, together with the principles of colonial rules which were gradually taking shape based on the notions of scientific planning, welfare-state and paternalism toward colonial subjects.

3-2 Interventionist government and scientific planning

The First World War was the all-out war, which required governments to mobilise whole populations in a totalitarian manner, and they started to intervene in economic activities by controlling the supply of commodities or mandating private enterprises for contributions to the state objectives. Such interventionism persisted throughout the fragile post-war period. Keynes, a British economist, made a major paradigm shift in the economy theory from *laissez-faire* to planned macro-economics, in the face of the recession in the 1930s. He proposed that the government regulate the economic mechanism by devaluing currencies and increasing public investment in social infrastructure (Briggs 1968: 45–50). There were a few implications of such interventionism: one is that it required a plan, which is based on the systematic analysis of the market demands, resource supplies and a trade mechanism. Instead of assuming that free economic interaction would bring about an optimal resource distribution guided by an invisible hand, Keynesian economy promoted the analysis of the current state as the basis of a plan to achieve the set goals. Such policy framework would then be translated to actual implementation measures. In relation to this move toward regulation and planning of the economy, there arose the expectation of scientific research, which would feed the administrators and policy makers the data and ideas for making informed decisions. This high esteem for research was also closely linked with trust in technology and scientific findings which enabled the rapid modernisation of European social lives and industries. Therefore, the interventionism, policy planning and regulation, trust in science, and sense of mission to 'modernise' the world were knitted closely and constituted the shared orientation among European government officials during the inter-war period. Further, such common basis of public administration was indicated to enlarge the space of the responsibility of the government and the society, compared to the earlier *laissez-faire* approach, for filling the gap between desirable conditions for individuals and the realities. The disparities of living conditions and income between the classes had increased with the economic recession. Partly for the political concern to divert the domestic dissatisfaction, the European governments stepped into social welfare, so that the basic requirements for life would be fulfilled for the majority of citizens.

Such shift of norms to guide public administration incurred a parallel change in the principles of colonial administration. In 1929, the Colonial Welfare Act was adopted which stipulated 'up to a £1 million a year in Treasury grants and loans to aid the development of colonial agriculture and industry with the express purpose of promoting trade with or industry in the United Kingdom' (cited in Kallaway 2012: 412). Not only in agriculture, but also for basic economic infrastructure, the colonial governments invested greatly. Such investments were, while presented as welfare programmes for colonial subjects, also important means to justify their continued rule over the overseas dependencies, regardless of the hardship at home and resistance in the colonies. These normative changes which guided public administration were as important background as the economy of the metropole. It is no coincidence that, in the Gold Coast, the first general hospital in Kohle Bu and a deep-water harbour in Takoradi were constructed during the governorship of Guggisberg (1919–27), same as Achimota School. Further, the scientific approach of public planning was also adopted by the Colonial Office's Advisory Committee on Native Education in Tropical Africa, who commissioned various scholarly research programmes (for example, Murray 1929; Hailey 1938). The frequent reference to the reports of the Phelps-Stokes Commissions by the members of the Committee has to be considered along this line of 'scientific' planning. While the Commissions were dispatched by an American philanthropic organisation, their comments served the objective of the British colonists to authorise the plan with the scientific evidence provided by the external experts.

3-3 Education in the systemic web of colonialism

Although the British government gradually formalised its administrative commitment in its colonies and protectorates in Africa, according to Stanley, the British never willingly extended their colonial rule. The British government's stance was to step into colonial issues only when there were obstacles to fulfilling the commercial interests and missionary zeal of British citizens. Therefore, extension of British formal control was 'less a reflection of strength ... [than] an acknowledgement of failure or weakness' in the diplomatic or military setting of favourable conditions (Stanley 1990: 45). The principle of indirect rule was, in a sense, to run the colonies with fewer personnel and less funding. It was a system of colonial administration introduced by Frederic Lugard in Northern Nigeria in the 1900s, whereby British officials ruled 'indirectly' through the existing administrative institution: chieftaincy. *Dual Mandate in British Tropical Africa*, the book Lugard wrote about the colonial administration based on his experience as High Commissioner of Northern Nigeria (1900–06) and Governor General of all Nigeria (1914–19), became the blueprint of British colonial administration and was referred to extensively by colonial administrators in Africa. By utilising the traditional system, Lugard proposed to avoid friction caused by introducing a European administrative system, and to enforce laws and collect taxes with minimum investment.

Not only with traditional chiefs, but coordination with European missionaries also was considered an effective means of low-cost colonial administration (Lugard 1922: 193). It was much more cost effective for the British government to support missions in providing social services, including education, than to duplicate the governmental ones from scratch. Also for the mission societies, such partnership was desirable. In their overseas posts, until this time, they had always suffered from the lack of financial support from the home offices; home offices naturally had a limit to the portion of funds they raised in the UK that they were able to direct to Africa. In addition to the financial constraint, missionaries in the field were vulnerable to political and military pressure either from African traditional chiefs or from colonists. Association with the colonial government was, therefore, beneficial for missionaries financially as well as politically. It was a pragmatic and symbiotic relationship (Berman 1975: 16–7; Mackenzie 1993). Moreover, the cooperation between the government and Christian bodies in education was already common at home: England, Scotland and Ireland. The grant-in-aid scheme for non-governmental schools, which was widely employed in British colonies, was originally developed for education of the working-class children at home in the mid-19th century (Rubinstein 1969). It was a British tradition to have representatives of religious bodies on the school boards, and these people's opinions carried weight.

Partly to convince the British constituency of the importance of colonial rule, colonies were made financially independent basically, except for some subsidies through the Colonial Office, London. This financial policy brought about some dilemmas: (1) there became a gap between rich and poor colonies, depending upon factors such as mineral reserves, capacities for crop production, location, etc.; (2) To achieve financial stability, colonial governments gradually enhanced their commitment to the development of industrial bases, which caused conflicts with traditional societies and the need for further investment to control (Stanley 1990: 47–9). The more resources and energy invested in colonial rule, the more the British government needed to justify its involvement. In this context of formal and enlarged involvement of the British government brought ideological discussions on 'education for Africans' to the forefront. The argument for Europeans' civilising mission, which had been used by missionaries, was now taken up by the British government itself. The British colonists came to assume the paternalistic 'white man's burden' to guide and uplift the primitive races in Africa. In 1915, a letter from the Wesleyan Methodist Head Office, London, to an African minister in the Gold Coast region said that their role was to help Africans in a way which 'the elder brother or the father can afford to the younger brother or the son' so that Africans could reach 'the stage of adolescence and young manhood'.[1]

Until Africans would reach the level at which they could take leadership positions in every aspect of national life, whether in the mission or government organisations, the Europeans were to stay in the colonies to guide them. In this sense, colonial rule was said to be a 'trusteeship' until colonial subjects would be ready to 'self-govern' (Hetherington 1978: 46–93). Education was considered an important part of social services, which would enhance the capacity of Africans as citizens of the colonies and the British Empire. In the collective statement adopted at a meeting of British missionary societies in 1923, a paragraph said:

> In the long run the welfare of a colony depends on the advancement and education of the people as a whole. This wider view of the purpose of education seems also to be required by the obligations of trusteeship. It is of vital importance to the future of Africa that those responsible for the administration of the Continent should not yield to the pressure of immediate needs and follow the path of least resistance. It is in the ultimate interests both of the native inhabitants and of the Western Powers themselves that educational policy should be definitely directed towards promoting the welfare and advancement of the whole population.[2]

Now education was considered an indispensable part of social welfare in the colonies, whereby both the European and the African would benefit. The fact that the quote comes from missionary records and not from the colonial documents indicates that mission societies, at least in the metropole, shared with the government the ideology of the 'trusteeship' as central to the development of educational programmes. In the field of education, rather than being embarrassed by the governmental commitment, mission societies made active efforts to participate in policy making and establish a reciprocal relationship. Because of the pragmatic reason of cost-effectiveness, the government also appreciated the cooperation with mission societies. Along this line, the Colonial Office looked to Christian organisations for input on colonial education policies.

When the Advisory Committee on Native Education in Tropical Africa was established in 1923 in the Colonial Office, London, J.H. Oldham, secretary of the Conference of Missionary Societies of Great Britain and Ireland (later International Missionary Council), was appointed as a member. Meanwhile, the cooperative set-up of mission societies and the government in London was duplicated in colonies, too. Representatives of mission societies were appointed as regular members of the Education Boards, following the guidelines of the *Memorandum of Education in Tropical Africa* issued by the ACNETA. For example, in the Gold Coast Colony, representatives of the Wesleyan Methodist Mission, Scottish Presbyterian Mission,[3] English Church Mission and Roman Catholic Mission were the regular members of the Education Board, which met annually throughout the 1920s, and 30s. Other regular members of the Board of Education were: Governor, Director of Education, Principal of Achimota School (after its establishment in 1927) and some Africans. Occasionally, sub-committees were formed, which met more intensively than the general committee.

As I will discuss in Part III, the mission–government relationships were not as friendly in the colonies as they were in London, because they faced real issues instead of just negotiating in the conference room. In the case of the Gold Coast, when the 1925 Ordinance increased the governmental control of the content and quality of education, missionaries resisted for the sake of preserving the space for religious education and protecting their names as providers of the literary education that Africans wanted. However, local quarrels did not cause flaws in the grand design of the cooperative project of colonial education.

3-4 Pan-Africanism and inspirations for nationalism in Africa

As further discussed in Chapter Seven, African ideologues pushed the colonial governments to provide more opportunities of literary education for Africans. They condemned vocational education as the imposition of education with lower standards and claimed literary and equal quality of education to Europeans. While they demanded education at all levels, including primary and secondary, the symbolic ground of competing debates against colonists was higher education. Such argument of African intellectuals on education cannot be fully understood without seeing the parallel black activism in the Americas. As much as the British colonists looked for the model of handling the inter-race relationship in the south US, African intellectuals admired the American black ideologues and their struggle for emancipation. A quick review of the newspapers published by the African intellectuals in West Africa during this period will reveal, from the frequent reference, their strong interest in the inter-race relations in America and black leadership.

One of the figures who influenced the mind of African nationalist leaders was W.E.B. Du Bois, a prominent African American sociologist and a vocal promoter of civil rights and liberal education for blacks. Born in Massachusetts, unlike his cohort American blacks who grew up in the South, Du Bois's environment would have been a little less restrictive for him to persist with his academic aspiration. He entered Harvard University and received a scholarship to study at the University of Berlin. He was the first African American who earned a doctorate and acquired a faculty position at Atlanta University.

W.E.B. Du Bois (1868-1963)

During his stay in Berlin in the 1890s, he wrote a thesis on small-scale farming in the American South, which played some role in introducing the American 'Negro Question' to German academics. Later, Max Weber, one of Du Bois's advisors in Berlin, wrote *Capitalism and the Ethics of Protestantism* after his visit to the Tuskegee Institute, which was widely known for its industrial (vocational) education model for the freed blacks, in Alabama and conceptualised differential states of development according to the characteristics of races. The link between the discourse on the inter-race relationship in the American South and German sociology, and by extension, the American sociologists trained in Germany is an interesting issue to examine as is the contribution of academic research in legitimatising the racial hierarchy of the Tuskegee model of black industrial education (Zimmerman 2012). Although it is not the purpose of this book to follow this line further, it would be important to point out that, despite Du Bois's lifelong insistence on civil rights and equal opportunities for the blacks, his statements often inspired the international observers to the opposite effect. Weber was more attracted by Tuskegee education than liberal education for the blacks, while it was likely that Du Bois had planted the interest in the educational issues in the American south in the mind of Weber.

In Chapter Four, I am going to demonstrate the impact of the Tuskegee model of education on the discourse on British colonial education in Africa. Booker T. Washington, the founder of this Institute was another American black, whose name rose frequently to the mouths of actors involved in this discourse. Trained at the Hampton Institute, one of the two model black institutes frequently referred to internationally (the other being Tuskegee), he was the primary black promoter of agricultural and industrial education. His theory was simple: Find the way to be happy in a given position, rather than expecting too much and being frustrated. His 'Cast Down your Bucket' story was often cited in the white media as indicative of his ability as a race mediator. The story goes as follows: A ship was lost at sea for many days. Each time other ships passed nearby, the passengers asked for water, but the answer was always 'Cast down your bucket where you are'. Finally, dying of thirst, the passengers cast down their bucket. What they pulled up was fresh, sparkling water from the mouth of the Amazon River. The lesson of the story was that, if they paid attention, there were many things blacks could do to better their situations without demanding things which are not in their hands now (*The Southern Workman* 1922: 209–10). This parable was introduced in a speech which was labelled by W.E.B. Du Bois, a black ideologist who argued for higher education and enfranchisement for blacks, as the 'Atlanta Compromise'.

Du Bois stood at the opposite end of Booker T. Washington in his view about the training of black educators and leaders. Du Bois argued for the education of the 'talented tenth', a small group of black intelligentsia, whereas Washington thought it was more feasible to train leaders who acquired practical skills and to show the masses how to lift themselves up in the existing social structure. Du Bois strongly believed that black leadership should be fostered through liberal education, and he starkly opposed to introducing to the black schools a form of education different from that taught in white schools, namely industrial education (Anderson 1988: 104–8).

Booker T. Washington (1856-1915)

Records show that African intellectuals had access to ideas of proactive black leaders on the American continents, such as the pan-Africanism of Marcus Garvey, a West Indian activist, and the black intellectualism of ideologists like Du Bois. Apparently, they were influenced by such movements. Still, as I will discuss later, African intellectuals were less critical of Tuskegee than of the European model of vocational education, and tended to accept its value. Considering that there was an unnegotiable discrepancy between Du Bois and Washington regarding views on education, it is ironic that the symbolism of ideas originated from America could even blur such fundamental differences when transferred across the Atlantic.

Putting aside such confusion, still the influence of American black activism on African nationalism was significant. Also, the black literature movement to write the life of African Americans from their own perspectives had also made an impact on African writers. Not only in Anglophone but also in Francophone countries, such transocean solidarity took shape. For example, anti-colonial literary works by Caribbean writers of African diaspora led to a movement called Negritude and involved Africans such as Léopold Sédar Senghor, the first President of Senegal, and Léon Damas of French Guiana.

Turning back to Du Bois, in 1909, he co-founded the National Association for the Advancement of Colored People (NAACP) and also became the editor of *Crisis*, the journal of NAACP. Based on these capacities, he set forth arguments in writing and spoke on the promotion of the rights and dignity of the blacks. Aside from such dynamic activities in the US, he also brought together political leaders from the continents of North and South America and Africa. Although there were precedents of such cross-continental meetings of African descendent leaders, the Pan-African Congress, which first met under the leadership of Du Bois in 1919, can be considered the first one which systematically gathered leading figures and tried to collectively work for racial emancipation and unification. The Congress was held a few times until 1945 and was taken over by the Pan-African Federation, whose formation was now led by African nationalists such as Kwame Nkrumah who became the first prime minister of Ghana, Julius Nyerere, the first president of Tanzania, and Jomo Kenyatta, the first president of Kenya. These African leaders, who brought about independence to the colonised homeland, were initially the recipients of ideas and zest from Du Bois and other leaders from the Americas but gradually gained control of their own emancipation discourse and practised it in their respective contexts.

It is beyond the scope of this book to closely follow the development of Pan-Africanism and thereafter. I will limit myself to report that Du Bois spent his later years in Ghana, invited by his sworn friend, Nkrumah. He passed away in 1963 at the age of ninety-five. It was the day after his death that, in the US, Martin Luther King made the famous speech to demand desegregation, which started with the statement 'I have a dream ...'.

3-5 Overlapping spaces of global influence

In this chapter, I have overviewed the political and economic context which conditioned the global process of building the consensus view about the principles and desirable approaches of practices of African colonial education. While the issue of concern is education, as I have demonstrated, the values behind the educational models and policies which became the mainstream cannot be fully understood without situating them in a broader framework. Without the particular atmosphere of the inter-war period, backed by the economic and political conditions of Europe and its overseas territories, the nature of discourse on colonial education might have been very different. Also, the general trend of scientific planning and shift to welfare state, which emerged as responses to the instability of the politico-economic conditions of Europe after the First World War, were the significant background for the reason why the Colonial Office stepped in to develop the policy framework and structure for the educational administration in the colonies.

Since there were not many practices of curriculum-based school education in Africa before colonialism, analysis of discourse on it tends to fall into the hierarchical contrast in which the models and ideas perceived by the actors from the colonising Europe have influenced colonised Africa. However, there were significant external reference points in the Americas and continental Europe, which had affected, either substantially or symbolically, both the Europeans and Africans. Africans were not passive recipients of American influence via Europe, but they imported ideas through their own channels. I have touched on Pan-Africanism and debates over the position of African Americans in North America in this chapter, despite that they may not be the factors which directly influenced the making of colonial education policies or the erection of a model school in an African colony. The scepticism among African nationalists of vocational education has to be examined not simply as the matter of resistance to European domination but the extension of political solidarity with diaspora leaders in America and admiration for their activism for black emancipation. While education was not the issue which Pan-Africanists have acted on collectively at the both ends of the Atlantic, in both sites, the debate over vocational versus liberal education was heated and fundamentally related to the sense of dignity.

Colonial officials, missionaries and American philanthropists created their own global discursive space to mould the common products of colonial education. That space was also institutionalised by the advisory committee in the Colonial Office in London and the Board of Education in the colonies. Meanwhile, African intellectuals did not only participate in the colonial discourse – either as resistors or collaborators – but also created their own channels of alignment with their American counterparts. Only because the latter discursive space was not directed at education much, the discussion about it will be limited in the following chapters. However, its latent influence on the education discourse was too significant to be overlooked altogether.

Notes

[1] Goudie to Hammond, 6 August 1915, WMMS West Africa, Correspondence, Box 769/1395.

[2] Africa Education Group, International Missionary Council, 'Christian Education in Africa' 1923–4 (year of record uncertain), CBMS-IMC Box 218.

[3] The Scottish Mission took over the educational and other work of the Basel and Bremen missionaries after they were deported in 1919 for being nationals of an enemy country (Germany) in WWI.

Chapter 4

Genesis of British colonial education policies

This chapter focuses on the political aspect of the discourse in which American educational ideas were promoted and British colonial education policy was formulated through the negotiation of different interests. First, I will untangle the political process following the events that happened in this course and the interpretation of their meanings from the perspectives of different actors. Then, I will present the personal traits that were common to the key individuals in the discourse: a British mission spokesperson, an American philanthropist and an African educator who advocated American black industrial education. The common attributes of these key figures were, according to the hegemonic perception of white Anglo-American society, tactfulness in mediating different interests and 'cooperativeness' in working for the tacit common goal. Those who were uncompromising and did not align their views to the hegemonic values were disparaged. The 'good' representatives of the white interest groups from the US and UK negotiated and moulded a set of educational ideas for Africans, while 'good' representatives of Africans gave consent to them. Together, these people contributed to the joint project of developing a comprehensive education policy for British Africa, excluding uncooperative agitators from the whole process.

Until the early 1920s, governments in the British colonies had not developed comprehensive educational policies, although there were some random regulations on grant-in-aid for mission schools. Education was almost entirely dominated by missionaries. As the number of people educated in mission schools grew, a group of African intellectuals emerged to challenge colonial rule, demanding the right of representation and self-determination. In such a political climate there arose criticism among government officials, business people and travellers about the 'bookish' nature of missionary education and the danger of 'denationalising' Africans. Then, literary education was disparaged for feeding the aspirations of Africans to achieve the same status as Europeans and inculcating in them contempt for African culture. According to Thomas Jesse Jones, Educational Director of the Phelps-Stokes Fund:

> A popular pastime of travellers to and from Africa [was] the exchange of jokes and ridicule concerning the 'mission boys' who [were] said to represent the futility and harm of educating natives away from 'their place' in the colonial scheme arranged by Western civilization for the Africans. (Jones 1925: 249)

Europeans working in Africa thus came to see the importance of establishing clear frameworks and standards for educational practice in Africa, and before the Phelps-Stokes Commission in 1920, there had already been considerable effort toward this end (Oldham 1934). Missionaries – the major providers of education – had been building up scattered but numerous types of schools in Africa. Also, by this time, colonial rule had extended from key centres to wider areas in a more systematic way. To justify colonial rule, the political ideology of 'trusteeship' was developed, arguing that Europeans stayed in the colonies to guide the colonial subjects until they would be ready to 'self-govern' (Hetherington 1978: 46–93). Social services, including education, were strengthened, partly to help demonstrate that colonial rule served the welfare of its subjects, as opposed to European rivalry for resources and wealth.

At home in Britain, mission societies organised the World Missionary Conference in Edinburgh in 1910, at which a special commission was formulated to investigate various educational issues in the mission fields. Being criticised for its 'bookish-ness', mission education was seen to require revision. At the same time, education was acknowledged as an important tool for mission evangelisation. Mission societies therefore endeavoured to redevelop aspects of mission education and adapt to the changing socio-political environment, while protecting space for religious education. Both in the field and in the metropole, mission societies collaborated closely with the governments, which provided financial and administrative support for educational operations carried out by mission societies. In return, mission societies provided input for governmental policy making based on their field experience. In sum, even though there was no unified effort involving all parties concerned, the time was ripe for the British mission societies and the Colonial Office to develop education policy and administrative systems for African territories, without the need for formal consultation with a third party. Even so, they did look to America for advice and for a model for education in Africa.

The Phelps-Stokes Fund, which had become a major funder and ideological promoter of black industrial education in America, and its educational director, Thomas Jesse Jones, responded to the call and played a role as advisor. The Commission's report, published in 1922, consisted of two parts: general policy recommendations along thematic lines, and reports and recommendations for each colony visited. The thematic recommendations can be summarised into three areas: adaptation of the form and content of education to the socio-economic and cultural background of students; cooperation of the colonial government with missions, Africans and the commercial sector at various levels; and development of an administrative system and organisation.

While it would seem puzzling for those who try to make sense of the process only by following the events and discussions in the UK, *The Memorandum on Education Policy in Tropical Africa* articulated by the British Colonial Office in 1925 repeated the emphasis of the Phelps-Stokes report on adaptation, cooperation among stakeholders and the establishment of an administrative system. J.H. Oldham, Secretary of the International Missionary Council, and Thomas Jesse Jones were two major figures responsible for this convergence of argument. Records suggest that they had close communication in the process of writing these documents.[1] Jones stayed in London and consulted with British officials and mission representatives while writing the Commission's report. Oldham, who contributed to mission policy documents and the Memorandum for the Colonial Office, was responsible for connecting the Phelps-Stokes Fund with the Colonial Office. Moreover, such interchanges of educational ideas could not happen without support from the British authorities, especially in the metropole, for American input – although it was not necessarily motivated by purely educational concerns.

In sum, my aim in this chapter is to demonstrate how collective interests of actors were negotiated through formal and informal channels and determined the contents of the *Memorandum*. While the issues of discussion were education, the concerns which drove them to take part in the formation of the general framework of colonial education were not so much educational but more pragmatic. Also, key decisions were often made by a small group of people. The discourse analysis with micro-focus on individual and collective actors will reveal a different picture from the history of formal events and publicised documents, which has tended to suggest a grand alliance between mission societies and the Colonial Office in the metropole, with a widespread cascading impact on the education policies in British colonies.

4-1 Convergence of interests

4-1-1 Formulating the Alliance of Mission Societies

In the colonies, the groping for an educational policy framework began around the beginning of the 20th century and involved both the colonial administrators and mission societies. Nigeria was one of the progressive centres of governmental initiative in education. Lord Lugard, the architect of the principle of indirect rule, was keen on educational administration too. During his governorship in Nigeria (1914–19), Hanns Vischer, who later became the first secretary of the Advisory Committee on Native Education in Tropical Africa, was there as Director of the Northern Nigerian Education Department. Based on the proposal of Vischer, Governor Lugard drew up a memorandum on education in Nigeria in 1915, which influenced educational policy making in other parts of British Africa (Hubbard 2000: 35–40; Sivonen 1995: 48–9). The need for an Empire-wide framework of education policy and central coordinating body was perceived, therefore, partially as an endorsement of the changes that were already happening in the field. Meanwhile, as the British government increased its commitment to education in colonies, mission societies in London felt a pressing need for coordination amongst themselves and to clarify their stance in the field of education. As Oldham stated:

> If Christian missions [were] to achieve their distinctive purpose, and at the same time to co-operate, as they [had to] do, with government in education, they [had to] know clearly what they [wanted]. If they [had] not a clear policy of their own, they [would] have to accept one dictated by government or to withdraw from the educational field altogether. (Oldham and Gibson 1931: 16)

Mission representatives thought if they did not present a clear policy agreed by all Protestant mission societies, their principal position in education would be threatened by the government which had enhanced its commitment.

It was in 1910, on the occasion of the World Missionary Conference at Edinburgh, that Protestant missions made the first major effort to integrate their education policy. At this conference, a special commission was formulated to investigate various educational issues in the mission fields. At this point, African affairs did not yet catch much attention from the missions. It was important, however, that at this conference the continuation of collaboration of Protestant missions in the field of education was agreed upon. In the decade following the Edinburgh Conference, Oldham and other major mission actors extended the network and collected information, and their ideas ripened about the missions' role and mission–government cooperation in education. The Continuing Committee on Christian Education set up in Edinburgh sent a commission to West Africa in 1914, which was chaired by A.G. Fraser, later Principal of Achimota School, to examine the educational questions from the perspective of missions.[2] The stage was gradually ready for missions and the government to develop mutually agreed education policy in Africa.

4-1-2 Inviting the American experts

In 1920, the Phelps-Stokes Fund, based in New York, sent a commission to investigate educational conditions in West, South and Equatorial Africa. Every party working in Africa, whether the missionaries or the colonial officials, felt the urgency of setting the framework and standard of educational practice in Africa. Missionaries had been accumulating scattered but useful and numerous experiences operating different types of schools in Africa. Colonial administrators had begun developing administrative and theoretical models of colonial education in some of the British Tropical African colonies. At home in Britain, mission societies had established the International Missionary Council, headed by J.H. Oldham, to reach consensus amongst themselves on the role and meaning of mission education in the field. The British could have developed an Empire-wide education policy and a mechanism to standardise educational practices in different parts of their overseas territories without any formal consultation with a third party. Even so, they looked to America for advice and a model for education in Africa. The Phelps-Stokes Fund, which had become a major funder and ideological promoter of black industrial education, and Thomas Jesse Jones, the Fund's educational director, took the call for the role of advisor.

It was the Baptist Foreign Missionary Society which officially requested, through the North American Missionary Conference, that the Phelps-Stokes Fund would send an educational commission to Africa.[3] Several other missionary societies in the US expressed interest in the Phelps-Stokes' Commission and promised their cooperation.[4] Although the direct request came from within the US, the British were no less keen to make an educational survey in Africa. In fact, without a request or at least permission from the British government and mission societies, it was impossible to investigate schools and to meet relevant people in British Africa. From records, we know that J.H. Oldham and the International Missionary Council, the consortium of British Missions headed by Oldham, were the driving force behind the visit of the Phelps-Stokes Commission to West, South and Equatorial Africa. Oldham assured the Commission that the British missionary societies and government officials in the field 'would undoubtedly be in every respect cooperative'.[5] He also recruited a sole British member to the Commission, Rev. Wilkie, chairman of the Scottish Mission at the Gold Coast. His letter to Wilkie urging him to join the Commission was suggestive. The letter said that Thomas Jesse Jones was considered 'a leading authority on everything relating to the Negro', and for Wilkie to join the

Commission was not only important for 'the future of education' in British Africa, but also for himself.

> In my letter of March 15th I wrote about a commission which the American boards are sending to West Africa. It is a very strong commission and Professor Monroe of Columbia University said in my hearing that its chairman, Dr. Thomas Jesse Jones, was the best man in America who could have been chosen for Chairman and that anything he reported would carry the greatest weight in the best educational circles in America. Dr. Jones is a leading authority on everything relating to the Negro in America and has written the best report in existence on Negro education.
> ... In the course of discussion ... your name [was suggested] as the British member. I said ... that I know of no one better... On thinking matters over ... I came to the conclusion that, not only are you the man best qualified for the job, but in view of the developments to which we look forward in the Gold Coast, service on this commission might be of great value both to you and to the future of education in the Gold Coast.[6]

At this stage, the British Colonial Office did not give any official recognition to the Phelps-Stokes Commission, which was different from the second Commission to East Africa in 1923. Despite this lack of official recognition, however, the Phelps-Stokes Commission was still considered to be 'quasi-official', thus it was received by the governor and high colonial officials in each colony it visited, guided to not only mission-run schools but also government schools, government agricultural extension centres, training centres, etc. (Jones 1924).[7] The Commission's report, published in 1922, consisted of two parts: general policy recommendations along thematic lines, and reports and recommendations for each country visited. The thematic recommendations could be summarised into three areas: adaptation; cooperation with missions, Africans and the commercial sector at various levels; and organisation and administration. In the area of adaptation, Jones made recommendations under the headings of: health; use of environment; preparation for home life; recreation; vernacular instruction;

character training; and religious life. Recommendations on adaptation followed the educational ideas of Thomas Jesse Jones, the chairman of the Commission. Echoing the idea of American black industrial education, he recommended to 'adapt' various aspects of school life to the social backgrounds of students aiming at fulfilling 'four essentials': (1) sanitation and health; (2) agriculture and simple industry; (3) the decencies and safeties of the home; and (4) healthful recreation. Jones's recommendations on adaptation are consistently directed toward these 'four essentials'. In the latter half of the report, he presented recommendations for each of the six colonies he visited, which were the Gold Coast, Nigeria, British South Africa, Angola, Belgian Congo and Liberia. While the description of social and educational situations was different from colony to colony, the recommendations were nearly identical. They converged on religious education, mission–government cooperation and adaptation.

The report received enthusiastic praise and high regard both from missionaries and colonial officials. For example, Sir Gordon Guggisberg, Governor of the Gold Coast (1919–27), said:

> I must state my conviction that one of the most important events that occurred in the history of the progress of the African peoples is the publication of the [Phelps-Stokes] Report.[8]

As I will discuss later, it is dubious how much Guggisberg agreed with the Commission's educational ideology or its analysis of African conditions. Even so, British colonial officials and missionaries still expressed great appreciation for the Commission's work. Putting aside the persuasiveness of the report's ideological content, other political and circumstantial factors also made people speak favourably about American educational ideas. Whatever the cause, it was undeniable that the Commission to West, South and Equatorial Africa initiated a new period of administration and policy making for education in British Tropical Africa.

4-1-3 Jointly moulding the global policy framework

In 1923, J.H. Oldham approached the Colonial Office with a memorandum which proposed basic principles of educational policy in Africa prepared by the Education Committee of the Conference of Missionary Societies in Great Britain and Ireland.[9] This Education Committee had been meeting regularly since the World Missionary Conference in Edinburgh in 1910. Four of the six sections of the memorandum were devoted to stressing the role of missions in education and the importance of mission–government cooperation in educational provision in Africa. To promote such cooperation, the memorandum proposed the establishment of Advisory Boards in Britain and each colony. The two papers, the Phelps-Stokes' report and the Conference of Missionary Societies' memorandum, echoed the importance of religious education and government–mission cooperation.

It is not clear how much actual input was made jointly by the writers of the two papers. But there is much circumstantial evidence of collaboration. First, it was J.H. Oldham who made the Commission's visit to Africa possible. Second, Thomas Jesse Jones was in London while writing up his report. Moreover, mission societies' cooperation with the government started at this stage of drafting the memorandum. The Conference of Missionary Societies' memorandum was written not only by the Conference's own initiative, but following the request of the Colonial Office. It was drafted by Oldham according to the request of Ormsby-Gore, Under Secretary for the Colonies, 'to write on African Education' and was 'approved by the Education Committee of the Conference of Missionary Societies'. Oldham submitted the draft to Ormsby-Gore for review in the Colonial Office before finalising it.[10] The direct result of this was the Colonial Office's decision to hold a conference, 'the agenda for which [was] [Oldham's] letter and enclosed memorandum'. The conference was attended by some Governors of African colonies and Thomas Jesse Jones.[11]

The trans-Atlantic collusion enhanced the pace of policy making. Within the same year (1923), the Advisory Committee on Native Education in Tropical Africa was established along the same line as that which the Conference of Missionary Societies proposed in its memorandum, especially under the section of 'Advisory Boards' (pp. 3–4). According to the constitution of the ACNETA, its functions were (1) to accumulate and distribute information about educational experiences in British Africa and good practices from other parts of the world including the US; (2) to advise educational officials and missionaries for the improvement of their practices, 'most effective and harmonious co-operation' with missions, and for better 'adapt[ation]' to the needs of Africans; and (3) liaison with the other nations to cooperate in African education.[12]

The mission societies' representative, Oldham, was appointed as a regular member of the Committee. Through the ACNETA, the Colonial Office made available for colonial officials the lessons of 'native education' from various parts of the world and within British Tropical Africa, and they introduced a platform for information sharing and provided a standard of educational administration and ideology with which the colonial governments were to comply (McWilliam & Kwamena-Poh 1975: 57). The Advisory Committee revised its constitution and extended its geographic coverage from tropical Africa to all the 'Colonies, Protectorates and Mandated Territories' in 1927. However, the basic functions of the Committee remained the same. It released reports and memorandums on various educational issues, among which were educational staff (1925), grants-in-aid (1933), higher education (1935) and vocational agricultural education (1937). It had also published the quarterly journal *Overseas Education* from 1929 to share and disseminate information about educational practices.

While the Advisory Committee was establishing the mechanisms of Empire-wide educational administration and policy making, the other actors in this colonial educational drama were active on their own terms. The Phelps-Stokes Fund sent the second Commission to East Africa in 1923. This time, it was officially endorsed by the British Colonial Office and it was virtually the first job of Hanns Vischer, Secretary of the ACNETA, to join the Commission as the official member representing the British government. In fact, Vischer was sent to the American South to acquaint himself with the 'Negro education' as a foundation of his responsibility as Secretary of the Committee on African education. The following remarks of W.G.A.

Ormsby-Gore, Under Secretary for the Colonies, shows how highly regarded Thomas Jesse Jones and the Phelps-Stokes Commissions were in British official circles for their expertise in black education. Proposing the toast at a government-hosted dinner for Thomas Jesse Jones in 1925, he said:

> We have got to evolve new standards, new forms of education which are suited to the highest needs of a people situated in [Africa]. ... It is ... of special value to Great Britain as a Colonial Power with tremendous responsibilities in Africa ... to [learn from] the work those who are facing and dealing with a not wholly similar but an analogous problem in the Southern States of America.[13]

The Under Secretary for the Colonies himself endorsed the value of black industrial education in the American South 'to evolve new standards' of education in British Africa.

In 1924, a wide-ranging mission conference at High Leigh was held to discuss the achievements of the Phelps-Stokes Commission in East Africa and the future educational policy of the missions in Africa in general. The report of the Phelps-Stokes Commission was presented by some of its members: Thomas Jesse Jones, Hanns Vischer, James Aggrey, C.T. Loram and Garfield Williams. Facilitated by Oldham and Lord Lugard, the conference agreed in the *Memorandum on Education Policy in British Tropical Africa* on the rough policy of African education to be followed. This document was issued by the Advisory Committee on Native Education in British Tropical Africa in 1925. The aims of education and its organisation were commonly defined in the High Leigh resolution and the Advisory Committee's *Memorandum* as follows:

1. Adaptation of educational objectives to the needs of the individuals and the community.
2. Differentiation of the education of the masses from that of the teachers and leaders.
3. Systematization of the inspections, supervision and guidance via regular inspector visits at all educational institutions.
4. Organization of the school system.

5. Cooperation of all interested parties: government, missions, white settlers and traders and Africans in the education of Africans.
6. Promotion of technical and vocational training where the dignity of manual work were [sic] taught.
7. Promotion of education for women and girls
   (Brown 1964: 370; Lewis 1971: 36; Sivonen 1995: 74).

The process of forming the central body, the Advisory Committee, and the development of its guidelines clearly demonstrates that British colonial education in Africa was a joint project of missions and the government from its very beginning.[14] In fact, the government welcomed the initiative of mission societies to draft the government policy and to bring in expertise from various sources, including the US.

In 1926, the International Missionary Council organised yet another conference on Christian missions in Africa at Le Zoute, Belgium. Among the issues discussed, education was one of the hottest, given the circumstances. This time, however, there was nothing fresh in the 'recommendations and resolutions'. These merely restated now familiar phrases: co-operation, adaptation and religious education.[15] The two largest groups of participants were those representing North American and British mission societies, followed by missionaries of other European nationalities and a few from South Africa. In the list of consultative members of the conference, one finds most of the familiar names in the discourse on African education: Thomas Jesse Jones; Anson Phelps Stokes, President of the Phelps-Stokes Fund; Jackson Davis, Director of the Rockefeller's General Education Board; J.H. Dillard, President of the Slater and Jeanes Funds of New York; C.T. Loram, Commissioner for Native Affairs of the Union of South Africa; and Hanns Vischer, Secretary of the Advisory Committee on Native Education in Tropical Africa. The Le Zoute Conference seems to have served for mission societies to reaffirm the policy on African education publicised by the government for the last time. It also made sure that American philanthropists maintained influence as external advisors.

Starting from the mid-1920s until the1940s, it became common practice for British colonial governments and mission societies working in Africa to send individuals to study American educational practices. In 1924, the Phelps-Stokes Fund established a scheme of travel grants for missionaries working in Africa to visit American educational institutions (annual budget was 5,000 dollar).[16] To this amount, the Rockefeller Board added 35,000 dollar for general African programmes of the Phelps-Stokes Fund, of which 10,000 dollar was earmarked for the visitors' programme.[17] Such a sum enabled more than two hundred and fifty white educators from across British Africa to visit American black educational institutions (King 1971: 179). After the two Phelps-Stokes Commissions, in 1942, another commission was sent from America to investigate African educational practices and conditions.[18] In the late 1920s, the Carnegie Corporation also provided a considerable sum to establish and operate in Kenya the Jeanes School, a training institution based on an American model of black visiting teachers to be sent out to rural schools (see Chapter Six). The Corporation also funded American educationists to visit and lecture in South Africa. Thus, massive efforts to transfer American educational experience were backed by philanthropic organisations in the northern United States. They were driven by a conviction of moral responsibility, as veterans of black education, and by financial power.[19]

4-2 Agencies of the key individuals: 'good' mediators of interests

Regardless of the grand design of colonial education, the number of people who were directly involved in the decision-making process was small. The same names appear repeatedly in the records of this process. Based on this observation, this section explores the personality, intentions and values of people at the core of the development of the *Memorandum* and trans-Atlantic transfer of the American black industrial education model: one American, one British and one African who received higher education in the US. In many cases they were the public speakers representing the perspectives of the British, American and African parties, respectively, and they were regarded as skilful mediators of different interests. By investigating their values and motivations, it emerges that the political goals shared among participants was to negotiate conflicting interests at different levels, from those of high officials in the metropole to those in each colony. Education was perceived as a means of such negotiation. It was a feature of the whole discourse that everybody reiterated the same themes: adaptation, development of useful citizens, practicality and better race relations. However, these are terms which can be interpreted in diverse ways. As I will demonstrate in Part III, the ambiguity of the key concepts created room for another layer of negotiation in the respective colonies. In the metropole, the consensus was made rather broadly, as if it was the normative wrapping paper that provided a uniform outlook by covering diverse realities. In this sense, the attributes of active participants in designing the policy framework were not necessarily their expertise in the field of education, but more the skills of balancing and mediating different interests.

4-2-1. Thomas Jesse Jones: salesperson of the American model

'The most active and vocal American in the discourse on African education was Thomas Jesse Jones. He had been the education director of the Phelps-Stokes Fund for more than a quarter of a century, as well as chairman of the two Phelps-Stokes' Commissions to Africa. Jones started his career as a researcher of black education in the South, first at the Hampton Institute and then with the Phelps-Stokes Fund. His theory of 'adaptive' black education was developed in the early days of his career. Throughout his life, Jones maintained the same line of argument, whether in speeches, during interviews or in writing.

Thomas Jesse Jones (1873-1950)

Certainly, it was not the freshness of his ideas that maintained Jones's reputation as agricultural and industrial education guru for so many years. As I have stated, it was the need of missionaries and colonial officials in Africa for an outside authority to assure their educational practices that enabled Jones' ascendancy. But this alone does not explain fully why Jones as an individual stayed in the position of authority without being replaced by other promoters of American black industrial education. Credit should be given to his presentation and mediation skills with respect to different interest groups as well. As his tactfulness in mediating conflicting interests was widely known, he was often asked to arbitrate conflicts. For example, when a conflict arose between the government and missionaries in Portuguese East Africa, Thomas Donohugh, Associate Secretary of the Committee on African Welfare of the Federal Council of Churches, wrote to the Phelps-Stokes Fund requesting Jones to negotiate between two the parties:

> Dr. Jones is by all odds the one best equipped to handle this very delicate situation most effectively. His personal knowledge of conditions in Angola and in Portuguese East Africa, from his repeated visits, his well-known tactfulness and courtesy in dealing with officials and other classes of individuals involved in the many sided phases of life in Africa, and his unusual ability to see all points of view sympathetically equip him to understand the delicate task better than anyone else whom we know.[20]

He had no more knowledge about Portuguese East Africa than about British Africa, which he had visited only a few times. However, it is important to note that he was accepted as an Africa expert with good negotiation skills.

At the same time, even though he was widely praised and his words prized proclamations, he was also frequently criticised. The flip side of the fact that his argument was clear and consistent was that he reduced diverse realities of different places to fit his 'four essentials' formula. There were people who were cautious about transporting the idea of 'essentials' for American blacks to Africa. Jones's critics thought Africa had its own mode of viewing things and its own essential needs, which were likely to be different from those of American blacks.[21] Other people thought that Jones came to Africa with foredrawn conclusions, developed before he even saw Africa. His acclaimed efficiency was the result of his starting to write his final recommendations for a colony on the second day of his arrival! For example, Jones wrote a long letter to Oldham on the fourth day of his stay on the Gold Coast, expressing his opinion that the major educational problem there was the lack of mass education 'in agriculture, simple manual arts, hygiene, and the simple but fundamental virtues of family life'.[22] He visited only one city

(Kumasi) before he determined that the prescription for this West African colony was his regular 'four essentials'. These foregone conclusions of his sometimes caused conflicts with local educators and interest groups. The Conference of Missionary Societies in Southern Rhodesia, for instance, determined that the Phelps-Stokes Commission's report *Education in Africa* mistreated educational work of missionary societies by using wrong statistical data as proof of substandard education at mission schools. In his letter to Oldham, Hardaker, the representative of the Conference claimed:

> The Statement [in *Education in Africa*] that most of the Mission Schools are third class schools which are 'for the most part ineffective and almost entirely lacking in supervision' is, in our opinion at variance with the true facts of the case, and constitutes a censure on the Mission, which is, we feel, quite undeserved. Dr. Jesse Jones, the compiler of the Report, admits that the 'education Commission was limited to the observation of only a small part of the work' (p. 217) and he did not, in fact, see a single 3rd class school in operation. We are therefore at a loss to know what justification there can possibly be, for a gratuitous statement, that is not backed up by Official Information, or actual observation; and we resent that our work should have been treated in so cavalier a fashion.

Jones often compared 'good' and 'bad' practices to make the 'good case' stand out more starkly. In the case of Southern Rhodesia, the mission schools were used to contrast the 'good' industrial education operated by a man named Keigwin. The letter of Hardaker followed:

> We further consider that the treatment given to the Keigwin Scheme, described as the 'most helpful influence' (in education) is disproportionate and biased, and overshadows entirely the work of the Missions. We resent this the more, in that the Report of the Commission is regarded as authoritative, and likely to be made use of in the further consideration of the problem of native Education in S. Rhodesia.[23]

As Hardaker duly worried, the Commission's and Jones's words carried weight in the circle concerned about education both in the metropole and colonies. More than a few people noticed that Jones was not ready to examine the reality with an open mind. What he would say was highly predictable, and how accurate his observations were did not matter as much as the fact that they were spoken by him. This attitude of fixing 'good' educational practice and its imposition on different contexts foreshadows the research done by international organisations in developing countries in the post-colonial era.

Jones was an arrogant man, who spoke and wrote as if his own opinion were self-evident truth that everyone agreed on. Hanns Vischer, who accompanied Jones in the second Commission to East Africa, criticised his egoistic pretension and domination of authorship harshly in his letters to Oldham. At the same time, even Vischer admitted that Jones was an excellent politician who could change his modes and attitudes according to the context and people he had to deal with.[24] The enthusiastic acceptance of Jones and the Phelps-Stokes Commission in Eastern and Southern Africa largely owed to his ability to speak about sensitive racial issues to different audiences, such as white settlers, missionaries, government officials and Africans, in ways that appealed to each of them. His comments were not always accepted favourably at first, but he had the skill to negotiate between different interests and make people accept his ideas in the end. This quality of a good negotiator kept Jones at the core of educational discourse.

4-2-2 J.H. Oldham: the spider of the missionary web

J.H. Oldham, Secretary of the International Missionary Council, was another good negotiator in this sense. He acted as the bridge between British officials and philanthropists, missionaries and educationists in America in the formulation of educational policies in British Africa. At the same time, he was the unofficial spokesman for many British and Irish Protestant mission societies before the Colonial Office, mediating between the interests of both. In the words of Adrian Hastings, Oldham was 'the spider at the heart of almost every non-Roman missionary web' (Stanley 1990: 146). In fact, his web extended beyond the missionary world. He also personally corresponded with governors and high colonial officials in the UK and in the field. American philanthropists often claimed that the establishment of the British Advisory Committee on Native Education in Tropical Africa was a direct result of the Phelps-Stokes Commission to Africa. Also the historians who have analysed the American involvement in British colonial education tend to assume that Americans brought about substantial and revolutionary changes to education in British Africa (Marah 1987; Steiner-Khamsi and Quist 2000). However, as my earlier presentation of the decision-making process has demonstrated, American philanthropists were able to influence British policy only through missionary channels, particularly through Oldham. In the beginning, Oldham was almost the only channel connecting the British and American groups involved in African education, although as time passed, frequent communication diversified contact points. Oldham's motivation to connect Americans with the Colonial Office and European mission societies was to enhance his credibility in his attempt to establish a mechanism for mission societies to participate in policy making. And his effort coincided with the motivation of the Colonial Office to invite external authority to legitimise its forthcoming education policy in Africa.

J.H. Oldham (1874-1969)

An indicative case of the mediating role he played was the one at the time of formulating the Advisory Committee on Native Education in Tropical Africa in the Colonial Office of 1923. Before the conference to inaugurate the Committee, for which high colonial officials were called from the field, he wrote to Jones, telling him to arrive in London before the actual conference for the sake of conferring with Governors in advance and making a greater impact on policy making:

> I had an interview to-day with Mr. Ormsby-Gore, the Under Secretary of State for the Colonies… He informs me that the three

Governors from West Africa are all arriving early in May and that they will certainly confer together quite early after their arrival in regard to educational policy.

... You will realize that it is in these preliminary discussions that policies actually take shape. Supposing at one or more round-table conferences the Governors of the three West African Colonies form certain ideas which are mutually agreed upon and which, in consultation with us, they believe to be acceptable to the missionary societies, those are the ideas that will go through and the discussions at the Imperial Education Conference will have no effect upon them.

... In view of my conversation to-day [with Ormsby-Gore] ... I see quite clearly that the crucial decisions are likely to be taken in May and if we want to have any influence on them we must have our ideas and our line of policy perfectly clear by the middle of that month. ... I most earnestly need your collaboration and the sooner you can reach this country the better. The key to everything important is to get in early.[25]

For Oldham, Jones was a powerful supporter, an established authority on black education, and someone necessary to have on his side if his scenario of government–mission cooperation in education was to succeed. His effort coincided with the motivation of the Colonial Office to invite an external authority to legitimise its forthcoming education policy in Africa.

Oldham was not so simple as to buy into Jones's education philosophy without reservation, however. While Oldham valued the idea of educational adaptation, he knew that it was not a peculiar conception of Jones but reflected popular educational thoughts of the time. Through his wide network, Oldham was acquainted with the latest educational philosophies discussed among scholars.[26] He also knew that the Hampton-Tuskegee model was far from an uncontested form of education in America. For Oldham, preachers from the Phelps-Stokes Commissions and even Thomas Jesse Jones were strategic tools, not the embodiment of fixed educational models to meet complex African needs. The British political ideology of trusteeship made it a part of their responsibility to help Africans become self-governing and produce their own leaders. The provision of advanced levels of education for prospective leaders was built in as a part of colonial rule's *raison d'être*, however hesitant the British government was in actualising it. Jones's philosophy, did not offer a strong enough educational ideology to justify secondary and higher education in Africa. Therefore, Oldham consciously balanced Jones's ideas with other educational thoughts such as those of Victor Murray who starkly opposed the vocationally oriented adaptation promoted by Jones. In 1931, Oldham sent Murray, a British educationist, who authored *The School in the Bush* (1929), to investigate educational issues in Nigeria (Sivonen 1995: 105). By bringing in Murray, Oldham probably attempted to avoid giving the impression, especially to aspirant Africans, that British colonial education was dominated by Jones's philosophy. He understood the political value of Jones's educational ideas in achieving missions' and British officials' goals in Africa but he also knew their limitations well.

Thomas Jesse Jones and J.H. Oldham had very different personalities. While Jones often appeared aggressive and stubborn, Oldham was a good listener and counsellor. But one commonality between them was their skill at negotiating different interests. In other words, their abilities were more in the political arena than in the philosophy or practice of education. This was so, even though Jones received a postgraduate degree from the Teachers College, Columbia University. To implement new educational policies, people had to mediate between often opposing interests. 'Coordination' was one of the popular terms employed: coordination between the government and mission societies, between races, between different levels of government, etc. At various levels, from policy making to implementation, coordination was given almost equal emphasis to the content of the education itself. Reference to specific educational ideas – including American black industrial education – was often an expedient to facilitate consensus building, rather than an expression of commitment to their educational values for African learners.

4-2-3 James Aggrey: a black mediator

James Aggrey (1875–1927)

James Aggrey, a celebrated speaker on black education, was born on the Gold Coast in West Africa. After studying at a Wesleyan Mission School, he was sent by A.M.E. Zion Mission to the US, and there he received his education at Livingstone College and at Teachers College, Columbia University (Author unknown 1927; Ofosu-Appiah, 1975; Smith, 1929). After thirty years in the US, he joined the Phelps-Stokes Commissions to Africa in 1920 and 1923 as the sole black member. He also joined the founding staff members of Achimota School on the Gold Coast as assistant vice principal and occupied this position until his death in 1927. As the editor of the *Southern Workman,* the journal of the Hampton Institute, observed, '[h]e was an eloquent speaker and made numerous addresses before native and European groups, endeavoring to foster better race relations' (Author unknown 1927, p. 393). In the speeches he made during his stay in Africa as a Commission member, he identified himself with great pride 'as a "Britisher", a product of the wise and generous policy of the British Empire'. He also acknowledged 'the indebtedness of Africa to the British people' and noted that the highest ambition of his race would be to profit from the 'lessons … taught by the Missionaries, Settlers, and Government Officials of Great Britain'.[27] His thankful, adaptive attitude was very much appreciated by whites in Africa. Rev. J.F.G. Orr, president of the YMCA in Kenya, praised Aggrey's presence as good for 'those who desired to understand the native mind and to have an opportunity of gaining first hand knowledge'.[28] Thomas Jesse Jones did not forget to promote Aggrey in his interview with Kenyan media:

> Dr. Aggrey is really of very great value in helping the black people to understand the whites and the whites to understand the blacks. ... It would be worthwhile for the white people to keep Dr. Aggrey permanently in Kenya to explain the white people to the natives![29]

Aggrey often used metaphors to express his views about race relationships. He compared the relationship of Africans and Europeans to the black and white keys of a piano. Unless blacks and whites worked harmoniously together, there would be no music. At the same time, he pointed out that they were separate, not mixing with each other.

Good Africans, from the perception of Europeans and white Americans, were those who were cooperative rather than confrontational. While the white's duty was to guide the black and be tolerant of differences, the black was expected to be thankful and adaptive. James Dillard, the first President of the Jeanes Fund, an American philanthropy which promoted black rural education, and a trustee of the Phelps-Stokes Fund, said, 'No problem can be solved except on the basis of the golden rule – co-operation and good will'.[30]

Aggrey echoed, 'The African never can rise to his own, unless there is co-operation between black and white'.[31] Within the circle of 'good' actors in the discourse – both Africans and whites – there was agreement that education was the way to create better race relations and avoid conflict, by developing the quality of 'good Africans' in the minds of students. Thomas Jesse Jones claimed, 'We are not interested in quarrels but in encouraging a type of education that in the long run, makes for sound relationships'.[32] At the same time, it was felt that any educational programme should be carefully designed so as not to develop people in a manner that did not fit the existing social structure. To this end, the Governor of Rhodesia noted that 'by the wise and careful direction of the channels and methods of imparting technical instruction, it may, and indeed it should, be possible to minimise the danger of economic rivalry between the two races'.[33]

It is difficult to tell if Aggrey was genuinely thankful to the whites or if such an attitude was merely adopted as a strategy for getting things done. Such speculation would also be difficult for another famous 'good' black mediator in the scene, Booker T. Washington. Critics like W.E.B. Du Bois, for example, criticised Washington's philosophy as the practical acceptance of 'the alleged inferiority of the Negro' (cited in Brown 1964: 369; see also, Peterson 1971: 149–51). But Alfred Young to the contrary argues that aggressive appeals such as political agitation or boycotts, which activists like Du Bois preferred, were not the only way to achieve the improvement of the social position of blacks. According to Young, Booker T. Washington's attitude, which looked like a compromise, was a strategic, alternative way of attaining this shared goal. Young argues that 'Washington took advantage of the imposed segregation of blacks in order to promote black hegemony through economic interdependence' (Young 1976: 232; see also, Dunn 1993; Gardner 1975).

In any case, hardly any criticism of Aggrey can be found in historical records. In many cases, Aggrey was looked upon as a successful African man who, after more than 30 years of absence, returned to Africa in an honourable position. It was ironic that while he was speaking for the Phelps-Stokes Commission, which advocated vocational and primary education in rural areas, African people tended to see Aggrey as an example of the benefits of higher education and foreign experience. It is not evident from the records to what extent he was clear about his own ideas on education for Africans. His reputation as an interpreter between races put him in a position as a 'representative' African educationist, trained in America. Indeed, there are abundant records which prove that he was a good mediator between Africans and Europeans. However, in spite of his official recognition as an 'educationist', one can only find scattered utterances from him on educational issues such as girls' education, leadership education and vocational education. He passed away unexpectedly in 1927, just when he had begun to write his own book on African education. In a way, he stepped off the stage before his reputation as an African educationist was ever really tested. He left very few bad impressions with either Africans or Europeans.

Although it is not easy to tell Aggrey's psychological status and reasons for being a 'good' black mediator, one can clearly see the whites' expectation of Africans from the way Aggrey communicated to white communities and the way he was praised. From the analysis of the two white actors, Jones and Oldham, and one African actor, Aggrey, it can also be seen that considerable political importance was attached to education by every party who participated in the discourse and that the 'coordination' of often conflicting interests was both the precondition and goal of education. Unless consensus was built on what and how to educate, policies could not be enforced. At the same time, education was assigned the role of developing conservative leaders who would accommodate themselves to the dominant white societies, namely, as 'coordinators' of the inter-racial relationship.

On the one hand, British colonial officials and missionaries at the core of the global discourse realised the difficulty of applying the American strategy of race management to the African context. They also saw the problems in Jones's oversimplified prescriptions for these issues. On the other hand, they applied the same frame of reference as Jones when they made judgments about 'good' and 'bad' Africans. Here is the ambivalence in the minds of British participants in the discourse regarding race issues and educational adaptation.

These actors *selectively* used and referred to American models, even though official statements – especially those in American archives – suggest there was a *wholesale* transfer. Aggrey was appointed as an Achimota staff member because of the Anglo-American appreciation of his skill of inter-racial mediation. However, this fact does not mean that Achimota's 'adapted education' followed the Hampton-Tuskegee model of black industrial education.

4-3 Educational transfer and politics of discourse

In this chapter, I have focused on the politics of educational transfer, the process of selling and buying educational ideas between parties with different interests. To establish a collaborative relationship with the government in the field of education and to protect the sanctity of religious education from government intervention, missionary societies attempted to exercise their influence in the formation of colonial education policy in British Africa. At the same time, American philanthropists actively promoted their own black industrial education model in Africa. The idea of agricultural and industrial education itself was not new in Europe. There were homegrown models of vocational education and mass education. What the British found special about the US was its experience in linking agricultural and industrial education with the management of racial issues. Strictly speaking, no one knew how much the experience of educating American blacks was relevant to Africa. The racial preconception and the collective desire to believe in its relevance made the whole exchange of ideas possible. Colonial officials and missionaries were in need of some authoritative assurance with respect to what they were doing.

In analysing the discourse, I paid greater attention to the motivations and psychology of main figures in the discourse than has been done by the conventional analyses of British colonial education policy. This actor-oriented approach helped me to grasp the real nature of the discourse, despite its appearance on the surface. The skilful appeal of American actors succeeded in leaving the impression that American influence was enormous. However, at most, their position remained that of external advisor who had not and would not be involved in the actual colonial administration and management of an increasingly confrontational relationship with the colonial subjects. It would be more accurate to say that it is part of the strategy of negotiation to show up the impact of certain ideas over others. Oldham, Jones and those key individuals who wrote the scenario of the whole process knew the rule of the game well. In fact, that was the capacity which put them in the position of mediators among interest groups, namely, mission societies, the Colonial Office and American philanthropic organisations in the metropole and their counterparts in the colonies. Although Aggrey was praised as a good black mediator and took part in the Phelps-Stokes missions to Africa, he was not involved in policy making at all. There were hardly any room for Africans, even the 'good' ones according to the white man's perception, to take part in this process. The lack of African perspectives in this whole process is also related to the neglect of contestation between Booker T. Washington and W.E.B. Du Bois, or the promoters of industrial education and liberal education for the blacks. W.E.B. Du Bois allied with African nationalists through the series of Pan-African Congresses. Still, despite that he was vocal on the issue of education in the US, because of most likely intentional avoidance of reference to him and his argument in the colonial education discourse, there lacks an overt influence from him on this matter.

The strong undercurrent which pushed through the process was the mission societies' demand for favourable partnerships with the government both in the metropole and in the colonies, so that they could gain financial and administrative support, while preserving room for religious education. The Colonial Office also needed a partner to operate schools and share the civilizing mission with them, in a cost-efficient manner. Therefore, the principles of multi-party partnership and systematisation of educational administration were key concerns. Also, because of the heightening political tensions in the colonies, the management of inter-race relations was a tacit but significant agenda. Particularly on this last point, the British looked for the model elsewhere. In other words, the British policy makers had already decided *before* inviting the American input that 'mission boys' education in Africa was futile and harmful as it took natives away from 'their place' (Jones 1925: 249). A preference already existed among colonial administrators for a practical education adapted to the African social background, even without American input. What was needed was the legitimisation that only an external source could provide.[34] However good Americans were in managing racial issues in the field of education, their expertise was still in an American context, not an African one. The US had considerably less presence in Africa than most of the European powers, outside of Liberia. Why then did Europeans look to Americans for advice? Arguably, it was because the Americans were safely distant from any British political or economic interests in Africa.

Also, educated Africans tended to have less aversion to American black education than to existing systems of education for the European working class, because of the impression their words gave. There was a curious tendency to praise American industrial education as a model for the self-help of Africans, as the Principal of the Institute, Booker T. Washington, was a black himself. The explanation that it was a self-help effort by the blacks enabled the Tuskegee Institute to gain support from the African elite. Edward W. Blyden, a West African ideologue (see Chapter Seven), visited Hampton Institute twice as early as 1879 and 1882. He praised it to be a 'noble monument' to black enterprise, which demonstrated 'what the African [could] do for himself' (Blyden 1903: 372). For him, it was important to educate Africans 'among the circumstances where they [were] expected to live' and to avoid the aloofness that separates the educated from the uneducated. From this perspective, Blyden thought, the Hampton method was ideal because it would avert the danger of creating Africans who were 'walking on their heads'.[35] Considering his consistent argument for higher and more education in West Africa, it is puzzling how he could support an educational institution for its role to avoid 'aloofness of educated blacks'. Unless it was a praised model in the US, he would not have made this kind of statement.

Similarly, Casely Hayford, a Gold Coast nationalist a generation younger than Blyden, described Hampton as 'one of the finest seats of learning in America'. According to him,

> [Hampton was] the work of Samuel Chapman Armstrong (the founder), a name which [would] ever be remembered with honour and veneration among cultured [blacks] throughout the world, for it was left to him to point the way of freeing the souls of Africans in America after Abraham Lincoln and his stalwart men of iron had freed their body. (Casely Hayford 1968: 161)

Also, Casely Hayford sent a letter to the International Conference on the Negro, held at Tuskegee Institute in 1912, explaining,

> We here feel that the great work that is being done at Tuskegee is a mighty uplifting force for the race.[36]

As such, even the African nationalists, who harshly criticised the colonial governments for political dominance and imposition of lower-class education, commented on Tuskegee and Hampton in appreciative terms. The British government could not lose anything by asking Americans for advice on education in Africa. At the same time, to enforce a comprehensive educational policy in Africa, the British needed some outside reference point. Some scholars suggest that the transfer of educational policy occurs when policy makers want to legitimise a policy that they already favour, in the eyes of the constituencies. This transference serves a symbolic role in the political discourse, which is, according to these scholars, more significant than the particular characteristics of the policy (Halpin & Troyna 1995: 307–8; Robertson & Waltman 1993: 29).

This drive for externalisation also existed on the American side of philanthropy. At home, the schools and programmes which use education as a means to discourage the blacks' aspiration for white collar jobs and equal rights were facing severe resistance. Northern philanthropic organisations such as the General Education Board, the Jeanes Fund, the Slater Fund and the Phelps-Stokes Fund devoted a lot of money and energy to promoting agricultural and industrial education for Southern blacks. Basically, these were the package of vocationally oriented programmes and moral training for the blacks to be equipped with the skills and values to appreciate the jobs available to them in the American South. The movement to resist the racial segregation and disenfranchisement of the blacks was rising. It was not only Du Bois and his National Association for the Advancement of Colored People (NAACP), but also many black ideologues opposed industrial education and demanded liberal education. In this context, despite their conviction of the importance of promoting industrial education, they recognised the necessity of re-authorising it to gain a high reputation overseas. Without considering this background, one cannot fully understand the motivation why those philanthropists were so enthusiastic in inviting study tours to the American South and exporting this model to Africa.

One point I have left undiscussed in this chapter is the aspect of exchange and the production of educational ideas and philosophies that rationalised and framed the educational practices in the field. As I demonstrated, the discourse was highly political in its nature. In fact, many people who discussed colonial education were not necessarily specialists in it. The exchange and production of knowledge on education occurs independently of the political sphere, although they are linked closely. Having this in mind, in the next chapters, I will shift my discussion to the educational philosophies which have inspired the actors who discussed and developed the colonial education policies.

Notes

[1] For example, see CBMS–IMC Box 219; Minutes of Board Meeting, the Phelps-Stokes Fund 1920–21.

[2] Fraser to Harcourt April 3, 1914, CBMS-IMC Box 263: West Africa.

[3] Minutes of the Committee of Reference and Counsel of the Foreign Mission Conference of North America, 28 February 1919, Archives of the Division of World Mission and Evangelism, Inter-Church Center, New York.

[4] Financial contributions came from Baptist Church, North (2,000 dollar); Methodist Church, North (2,000 dollar); Disciples Missionary Boards (2,000 dollar); Congregational Boards (1,500 dollar); Presbyterian, North (2,000 dollar); Presbyterian, South (1,000 dollar); Episcopal Church (1,000 dollar or 2,000 (uncertain)); and United Brethren (500 dollar or 1,000

(uncertain)). Minutes of the Board Meeting, the Phelps-Stokes Fund, 17 January 1920, the Phelps-Stokes Fund Collection, New York.

[5] Ibid.

[6] Oldham to Wilkie, 22 March 1920, CBMS-IMC Box 265.

[7] See also, private journal of Thomas Jesse Jones during his trip from West to South Africa, CBMS-IMC Box 263.

[8] Sir Gordon Guggisberg. 'Review of the Events of 1922–23' speech made at the Legislative Council, Gold Coast Government, 1923, PRO, CO 98/45.

[9] 'Educational Policy in Africa: A Memorandum submitted on behalf of the Education Committee of the Conference of Missionary Societies in Great Britain and Ireland', CBMS-IMC Box 219.

[10] Oldham to Ormsby-Gore, 9 May 1923, CBMS-IMC Box 219.

[11] H.Q. Cowell for the Under Secretary of State to Oldham, 14 May 1923, CBMS-IMC Box 219.

[12] 'Constitution and Functions of Advisory Committee', CBMS-IMC Box 219.

[13] W.G.A. Ormsby-Gore, speech at the dinner for Thomas Jesse Jones, 26 March 1925, Folder 2987 Box 286 Series 1-2, General Education Board, Rockefeller Archive Center.

[14] The memorandum by the Conference of Missionary Societies in Great Britain and Ireland reports that as of 1923, five of the British colonial territories, including the Gold Coast, had Boards of Education (Natal, Nigeria, Uganda, Kenya and the Gold Coast) (CBMS-IMC Box 219: Africa General Education).

[15] 'Recommendations and Resolutions of the Conference on Christian Mission in Africa', held at Le Zoute, Belgium, 14–21September 1926, CBMS-IMC Box 217.

[16] Minutes of the Board Meeting, the Phelps-Stokes Fund, 19 November 1924, the Phelps-Stokes Fund Collection, New York.

[17] Minutes of the Board Meeting, the Phelps-Stokes Fund, 28 May 1926.

[18] The General Education Board, one of the Rockefeller organisations, sent a group to investigate the educational conditions in Africa in 1942.

[19] The Phelps-Stokes Fund devoted 232,000 dollar in the 20 years between 1910 and 1930, which was about a quarter of its total expenditure on education. Compared to the actual impact of the Fund in determining policy, its financial contribution was modest.

[20] Letter of Thomas Donohugh to Anson Phelps Stokes, 22 March 1933, presented at the Board Meeting, the Phelps-Stokes Fund, 5 April 1933, the Phelps-Stokes Fund Collection, New York.

[21] For example, see the lecture by Ralph Linton, an anthropologist in W.E. Holt (Superintendent of Education, Nigeria), *Memoir of a Conference on Negro Education and tour in U.S.A 1937*, Rhodes House Library, Mss Afr.s. 914.

[22] Jones to Oldham, 11 October 1920, CBMS-IMC Box 214.

23 Hardaker to Oldham, 8 August 1923, CBMS-IMC Box 263.

24 Vischer to Oldham, 8 April 1 May and 23 May 1924, CBMS-IMC Box 219.

25 Oldham to Jones, 23 March 1923, CBMS-IMC Box 219.

26 For example, A.G. Fraser, Oldham's brother-in-law and the first principal of Achimota School, wrote from the US that he met Monro, 'Dean of Education Faculty', at Columbia University, who summarised for Fraser the latest theory of practice-oriented education suited to students' needs (Fraser to Oldham, 25 July 1919, CBMS-IMC Box 214).

27 'Phelps-Stokes Tribute', *East African Standard*, 3 March 1924, Folder 155, Box 11, Series 1, Rockefeller Foundation Archives No. 26, Rockefeller Archive Center.

28 Ibid.

29 'The Education of the African: Personalities & Principles of the Phelps-Stokes Commission', *East African Standard*, 25 February, 1924, Folder 155, Box 11, Series 1, Rockefeller Foundation Archives No. 26, Rockefeller Archive Center.

30 'Phelps-Stokes Tribute', *East African Standard*, 3 March 1924, Folder 155, Box 11, Series 1, Rockefeller Foundation Archives No. 26, Rockefeller Archive Center.

31 Ibid.

32 Thomas Jesse Jones, quoted in 'The Education of the African: Personalities & Principles of the Phelps-Stokes Commission', *East African Standard* 25 February 1924, Folder 155, Box 11, Series 1, Rockefeller Foundation Archives No. 26, Rockefeller Archive Center.

33 'Subject that Bristles with Difficulties: Governor Addresses Missionary Conference', *Rhodesia Herald*, 2 June 1924, Folder 155, Box 11, Series 1, International Education Board, Rockefeller Archive Center.

34 King named it 'Seal of international approval' (1971: 97). See also, Berman 1971: 142.

35 Blyden to Coppinger, secretary of the Colonization Society, USA 20 November 1879, cited in *The Southern Workman*, February 1880.

36 'The Negro in Conference at Tuskegee Institute', *The African Times and Orient Review*, Vol. 1 No. 1 (1912): 10–12. Folder 155, Box 11, Series 1, International Education Board, Rockefeller Archive Center.

Chapter 5

Philosophical sources of inspiration for African education

In terms of philosophical influence, there were a few educational philosophies which fed some ideas for the discussion on the contents of African colonial education. Unlike Chapter Four, which focused on the politics of educational transfer, this chapter will examine the sources of the educational ideas that fed the imagination of colonial educationists and became part of the philosophical framework of African education, which was vaguely shared among people involved in the discourse on colonial education. Utilisation and appropriation of educational ideas tend to be discretional and partial. Ideas picked from different sources are also mingled so as to support certain policies. Further, policy makers are more interested in attending to the perceived issues in front of them, rather than to know about any theory or philosophy deeply and precisely. Therefore, theories and philosophies are referred to only to the extent that they seem to be in line with the policy measures they intend to promote. Such an administrative and political demand for theories and philosophies causes two types of challenges for the examination of their origins. First, the references are patchworks of ideas from different sources but presented as if they are a single coherent set of ideas. Even when the policy makers cite a name of a specific philosopher, still, some part of idea is presented as if coming from the same person, but may actually come from elsewhere. Therefore, one has to cautiously differentiate what the policy makers wanted to believe, or wanted the audience to believe, as the authoritative view of famous philosophies, from what they actually are. The analysis of discourse will reveal the former but the latter has to be examined through a careful reading of the original works, which policy makers claim to be relevant. Second, sometimes, some fashionable terms walk by themselves, being given the meanings or changed from the original usage in the source philosophies. For example, 'learning by doing' was one of the terms frequently sprinkled in the reports and documents of this period. It originated from John Dewey's experientialist theory of education, but was used much more freely and in more creative ways than Dewey had probably meant by the people who cited it. In this sense, the meanings of the popularly used 'philosophical' terms cannot be taken on their face value, but have to be examined by comparing their usage in the discourse and the originals. By doing so, it becomes possible to understand the organic relationship between the normative sources of inspiration available at a certain historical point and the political discourse which refer to them albeit sporadically and unsystematically. The philosophies which I will review in this chapter are: American progressive educational philosophies, American black industrial education and British Victorian moralism in education.

5-1 Progressive education philosophies: 'learning by doing'

The early 20th century saw the emergence of various progressive educational philosophers represented most prominently by John Dewey (1859–1952), a professor at the University of Chicago and later at the Teacher's College, Columbia University. While mainstream educational philosophies at the time were still concerned with developing children to be good followers of authority, the progressive philosophers saw students as social transformers (Baker 1955; Curti 1978: 499–541; Howard and Scheffler 1995; McClure et al 1985: 25–30). Dewey thought that education should contribute to the growth of individuals by encouraging them to think about the solutions to actual problems rather than merely absorbing textbook knowledge. To change a society into a truly democratic one, he argued that it was not enough to teach the concept of democracy; students need to learn what democracy is by actually being in a democratic setting at school. Therefore, he stressed the importance of 'learning by doing'. He believed that the experience is the important condition for learning. According to his conception, learning happens through interaction of learners' internal motivation and preliminary knowledge with external influence, namely the environment. Since the interaction of the self and environment is the learning of itself, inquiry is an important objective of education. At the same time, it will be the basis of more learning. Therefore, education is a means and an end in itself. Because of such an attitude of valuing the process of learning and experience, Dewey and many progressive educationists in the early 20th century were called 'experientialist'.

Another characteristic of progressive education is that it highlights the intrinsic motivation of learners as the basis of education. Dewey argued that the content of education has to be provided according to the curiosity of learners. For this to happen, education should not be a process which is pre-designed according to the curriculum by the subject experts, who are away from the sites of learning. Instead, it has to be flexible to respond to the interests of learners. Broadly, this kind of approach in education has been called a learner-centred approach. In sum, for Dewey, experience is important because that is the process for the learners to subjectively link their motivation and previous knowledge with new stimulants.

Therefore, the practicality of education which Dewey envisioned was far from vocational education. Firstly, he did not support education which was designed to prepare a learner for a certain occupation, because the outcome of education depends on the motivation and process. The objective was not supposed to regulate the contents and process of education. Also, he was suspicious of providing the segregated tracks of vocational and general education. For Dewey, vocational schools would lead to the reconfirmation of the older division between the master and the labour class, and such a division was contrary to the values of democracy: social and economic mobility, and the wide and varied distribution of opportunities regardless of an individual's parents' status (Howard and Scheffler 1995: 27–41). It is a stark contrast to the black industrial education model at the Hampton and Tuskegee Institutions. While Dewey's philosophy was oriented toward social transformation, industrial education was to maintain the status quo in the American South. Also, while the former was learner-centred, the latter was to equip the learners to do the manual work which was available to the black population.

Dewey's experientialism also led to the rejection of traditional moral theories which clearly separate the moral virtues and natural phenomena, and to represent ethics in metaphysical terms. He considered that, in the constantly changing world and with multiplicity of personal experiences, no fixed ends or moral rules could be adequate (McClellan 1992: 62). This philosophy of ethics is also a characteristic difference of Dewey from other popular educational philosophies discussed in this book. Whether it is the religious morality of Christianity, of British society with Victorian morality, or for the American blacks, other philosophies basically assumed the virtue based on which practices of individuals were approved or disapproved, judged to be right or wrong.

In spite of this fundamental difference, one can see a shade of the progressive educational philosophy in the line of argument of black industrial education. 'Learning by doing', which progressives propounded, was frequently used as a catch phrase by advocates of the Hampton-Tuskegee type of education. The progressives' concept of a problem-solving approach to education, which was seen as an alternative to instruction in subjects that were artificially separated from each other, was adopted by Booker T. Washington, the first Principal of the Tuskegee Institute (Gardner 1975: 509). The Hampton and Tuskegee Institutes meant to make school a little world where education was to be identical with actual living. School was considered, in the spirit of Dewey, a social centre for solving problems (Curti 1978: 290; McClure 1985: 29; Peterson 1971: 154.). The difference was that industrial schools were to make black communities fit into the larger social structure, rather than to change the structure itself.

For progressive educationists, 'Learning by doing' would have a meaningful effect on students only when the curriculum was adapted to students' backgrounds and needs. In order to bring about such adaptation, teachers should first familiarise themselves with the societies and environment in which schools were located. When the progressive educational philosophy was exported to foreign soils, for instance, to Africa, the study of anthropological findings was encouraged so that educators could better understand and adapt education to a country's particular needs. In fact, progressives' conception of adaptation was to find the link of environment with the learners' interests, instead of selecting elements of local culture and customs to be incorporated into a curriculum transplanted from elsewhere.

In its original form, progressive education was not connected to any social class or specific type of curriculum. Rather, its aim was to break down the barriers of class and race, and to create a curriculum flexible enough to fit students' needs. However, there is a tricky point to all this, which makes it difficult to attempt to deconstruct the discourse on African education – namely, that the practical education promoted by progressive educationists was congenial to vocational education, which included black industrial education. Even though the progressive theorists intended to transform the class society through practical education, the dominant belief of the time was to link a specific form of education to a class. Therefore, the majority of people thought that elite education was to acquire knowledge rather than life skills and that practical education which encouraged students to learn from experience, whether it was vocational or not, was for the lower classes. This misleading proximity of progressive and vocational forms of education was conveniently used by promoters of black industrial education, which, by applying some of the catchy phrases of the progressive philosophy such as 'education for life' or 'learning by doing', made the worn-out idea of vocational training look new.

5-2 Vocational education in Britain and America

Vocational and adaptive education itself was not original to the US. In Britain, the emergence of an urban working class in the 19th century raised concern among the bourgeoisie, who felt the lower classes needed to be trained to be disciplined workers – and also to avoid social unrest by keeping the youth in schools. Primary and vocational education for the working class expanded in the 19th century, especially after the Elementary Education Act of 1870 (Lewis 1982; Rubinstein 1969; Davin 1996; Young 1984). In Europe, it emerged with the systematisation of public education and class conscious moralism. The British model of vocational education was developed to control the social issues caused by the influx of the rural population to work in urban factories in the face of rapid industrialisation. While the parents worked in the factory, children and adolescents stayed idle and were pointed out for the delinquency and crimes. Therefore, the school system was established to provide training in minimum skills to work in the industry with significant emphasis on morality to be good workers: discipline, punctuality and obedience. As I will demonstrate in the next section, in Britain, there was the educational philosophy for the elite, which was typically practised in public schools. Before industrialisation, schooling was exclusively for the elite. However, because of the socio-political demands to fit the emerging urban working class into the social structure, the ruling class invented the school system for the masses. The model of education with one teacher facing many students and providing modularised units of lessons, which John Lancaster developed at the end of the 18th century, spread widely and became the basis of the public education system. As this history suggests, education in Britain was clearly segregated by class and not only the contents to be taught, but also the ideal personalities to be cultivated were clearly different. Those who knew such contrast in the educational provisions in Britain, including African intellectuals, would rarely miss the strata inherent in the system, in which the vocational, mass education was ranked lowly.

The paternalistic attitude of the bourgeoisie, although well-meaning in many cases, determined conceptions of what kind of education was appropriate for the subjected people both in Britain and in Africa. Also, there had been several missionary attempts to provide vocational training in one way or another in Africa earlier than the first Phelps-Stokes Commission in 1920. The Basel and Bremen Missions, German Presbyterians, for example, were known for their strict discipline and agricultural or industrial training at schools. In the last decade of the 19th century, industrial education became fashionable among missionaries. Schools established along this line were the Lovedale Industrial School (1893) in Cape Colony, and other industrial schools in Freetown (1895), in Brass (1897) and in Onitsha (1898) (King 1971: 47). Lovedale was publicised in America as 'a Hampton in Africa', although there was no direct input from Americans to this school (Ludlow 1904; Editorial, *The Southern Workman* December1895: 199). Since schools were not run with abundant funds, there were local self-help efforts at various educational sites to raise income or feed themselves. These efforts began to be interpreted as the educational adaptation or industrial training around the turn of the century (Bude 1983: 343). Whatever it was named, the theories and practices of vocational education existed before the Hampton and Tuskegee model.

The education model promoted by American philanthropists was a type of vocational education, which tracked learners not only by race but also inherently by class. Racial conflict was explicit and severe between the white working class and the freed blacks after the Civil War in the American South. Social and economic advancement of the black population would threaten the job security and social status of the lower-classed white population. Therefore, education to fix the black in the current social and economic position was, in other words, to draw the line between these two groups whose interests would conflict. For this sake, black industrial education was to restrict the aspirations of black people on the double fronts of race and class.

Therefore, the advocates of this type of education were particularly cautious about filling the brains of students with book knowledge and fostering aspirations for white-collar jobs – they did not want to detach black students from the society in which they lived, with prescribed social and economic roles. Their primary concerns were that the content of education should have a practical application and be adapted to local conditions. For example, Thomas Jesse Jones, the educational director of the Phelps-Stokes Fund, repeatedly stressed the following 'four essentials' of education: (1) sanitation and health; (2) agriculture and simple industry; (3) the decencies and safeties of the home; and (4) healthful recreation (Jones 1925: 245–51). To relate every phase of education to the sanitation, housing, home and economic life of the student's environment – in effect, to 'socialize the teaching subjects'[1] – was, according to Jones, the fundamental part of education.

This emphasis on a practical education that was adapted to students' backgrounds, which became popular from the last few decades of the 19th century, was not originally linked to conceptions of racial differences between whites and blacks. However, when black slaves in America were liberated and began expressing a strong desire for an education, southern whites quickly emphasised the necessity for an agricultural and industrial education for blacks. Northern philanthropists devoted large amounts of money and energy to promoting this type of education. Among the active philanthropic organisations in this area was the General Education Board, one of the Rockefeller organisations specialising in education. In 1962, a half century later, R.B. Fosdick, in *Adventure in Giving*, a Rockefeller-funded review of the General Education Board's work, wrote that it was largely due to the demand of the Southern whites for a 'non-objectionable' form of education which pushed northern philanthropists to fund agricultural and industrial education:

> Certainly the kind of education which [the GEB] stressed was less objectionable to the South than the so-called classical type. If the White Southerners had to permit the Negro to obtain any education at all, they wanted it to be of the sort that would make him a better servant and laborer, not that which would train him to rise out of his 'place'. (Fosdick 1962: 85)

Although agricultural and industrial education for blacks generally acquired active support from both Northern and Southern whites, some models of it in particular were earnestly promoted. One was a form of vocational training at the secondary level which incorporated a course in training teachers for black primary schools. This model was first developed by Samuel Armstrong, who founded the Hampton Institute in Virginia in 1868. Armstrong was a Northern white who first came to Virginia as a soldier and settled as an agent of the Freedmen's Bureau, the governmental organ that promoted the welfare of the freed slaves, before starting Hampton Institute. Another agricultural and industrial institute for the black people was established in Tuskegee, Alabama in 1881 by Booker T. Washington, an ex-slave who himself was a graduate of Hampton.

Hampton's and Tuskegee's educational philosophies were strongly influenced by the racial views of the founders. Armstrong proclaimed that the political and economic subordination of blacks was justified by their lower stage of moral development than that of whites. According to him, only the habit of labour could save blacks from complete 'moral ruin' (Engs 1999: 70–86). Ideas about black industrial education flourished in the 1880s and were practised by various bodies, especially religious ones, but the Hampton-Tuskegee model was peculiar in its emphasis on manual labour as a moral foundation for black leaders and teachers. At Hampton and Tuskegee, an extensive routine in manual labour was established because the schools' faculties believed that a particular combination of handwork, political socialisation and social discipline would appropriately mould conservative black leaders. Literary education was given a minimum amount of attention, and it barely exceeded the 3R's that were taught in primary school. Students were expected to learn the 'dignity of labour' through practice, rather than by filling their brains with needless knowledge, and were strictly disciplined. As a matter of course, then, classical studies such as Latin and Greek were excluded because the school faculties believed that such literary knowledge would stimulate 'vanity' in black students. As Thomas Jesse Jones, who once taught social studies at Hampton, noted, subjects such as 'political economy, civil government, moral science and general history' were given an important place in Hampton and Tuskegee, which aimed at teaching 'the "right" ideas of citizenship, the duties of laborers, and the history of race development' (Jones 1906). Students were taught to believe that the position of blacks in the South was not the result of oppression but the natural result of the living together of two races that were at different developmental stages, and the performance in the examinations of these subjects determined teachers' evaluation of students. For the purpose of effectively developing character and cultivating 'civilized manners', a majority of students were boarded at school although there were night courses for non-boarding students. According to Armstrong, the boarding school setting enabled teachers to 'control the entire twenty-four hours of each day – only thus can old ideas and ways be pushed out and new ones take their place' (*Southern Workman* 10 September 1881: 91, cited in Anderson 1988: 46.) Because of its strictness in its character training in the 19th century, Hampton expelled many students for their bad work habits and 'weakness of character' and passed only one-fifth of its students (Anderson 1988: 54).

Another model which philanthropists actively promoted was that of the Jeanes School, a system for community development, centred on local primary schools. The Anna T. Jeanes Fund, established in 1907, developed and promoted this system in the South, and beginning in 1909, the Jeanes Fund cooperated with Southern public school authorities in its effort to employ supervisors of industrial teachers. A group of supervisors called 'Jeanes teachers' were trained in hygiene, home improvement, farming, etc., and they regularly visited village schools where they supervised the industrial work and development of the community around the school. Behind this system was the philosophy of self-help. Anderson reports that the largest proportion of Jeanes teachers' time was consumed by raising money for new schoolhouses and equipment (1988: 153). After the reduction of state funds for the Common School movement, the initiative to establish schools at the community level, [2] black communities had to collect small amounts of money from households and established schools. The Jeanes School system contributed towards accelerating this movement of self-help by providing necessary skills for building schools. The model of the Jeanes School was also transplanted to Africa. However, unlike the Hampton-Tuskegee model, the Jeanes School lost a large part of its racial connotation. Rather, it was accepted as a primary education programme that was adapted to social conditions accompanied by various activities for the self-help of the community (Dougall 1928).

The common characteristic of Hampton-Tuskegee and Jeanes School models was their stress on community transformation through teachers and leaders who were trained in their systems. In other words, Hampton-Tuskegee graduates and Jeanes teachers were seen as missionaries of 'civilization' and industrial work ethics. In this sense, one might argue that it is as 'transformative' as progressive education. However, American black education was to transform the black community and the minds of the blacks to fit into the white dominant society, instead of expecting the students to be the transformers to create a democratic society. In fact, this converging reference to the transformative role of education, albeit the contradiction of its actual meaning, allowed policy makers on colonial education to mix these fundamentally different philosophies as if they are along a seamless continuum.

Adaptation for Hampton-Tuskegee promoters meant, unlike the progressives' efforts of linking education to the innate curiosity of learners, to connect education to the context to which the learners were to be contained without aspiring for more. Another commonality of the educational philosophies of this period was the emphasis on moral education, in other words, 'character training'. Here again, moral education in the Hampton-Tuskegee model has less to do with developing personal strength than the sense of appreciation of things available to them and to the white society which allowed them to enjoy their current lives.

5-3 British Victorian moralism in education

5-3-1 'Public school': masculinity in elite education

The penetration of British public school morality throughout the British Empire was wider and deeper than generally assumed. When recruiting new officials, colonial administrators gave strong preference to the products of the old elite universities of Oxford and Cambridge, especially those who were trained at distinguished public schools before entering these universities. The public school experience was taken as a sign of well-preparedness as to the morality of its products. In some instances, this preference for Oxbridge-public school was extreme. Mangan reports that among 393 recruits to the Sudan political service in the 57 years of its existence (1899–1952), 281 (72 per cent) were Oxford and Cambridge graduates and 332 (84 per cent) were from the public school system (1986: 79–84).[3] Hubbard reports a similar situation in Northern Nigeria. Of the 60 education officers recruited for the Northern Province of Nigeria between 1900 and 1940 whose information about secondary education is available (the total number of recruits was 107), 31 (51 per cent) attended institutions that were considered public schools. Another 11 (18 per cent) went to schools not usually listed as public schools but that were 'probably modeled after them'. Five more attended great day schools, which 'shared many Public School characteristics'. Therefore, according to Hubbard's calculation, depending on the definition of a public school, 51 to 77 per cent of the education officers whose background is known received a public school education (2000: 29). While colonial administrators preferred recruiting Oxbridge-public school products, from the perspective of the products of these schools too, colonial services were good places to find employment. As Ranger notes, 'younger sons, well-born orphans, the sons of the clergy had experienced the "traditions" of the Public School [and] ... the university, but were not guaranteed secure advancement [in the British establishment]'(Ranger 1983: 215) so they found their way into colonial services, army and missions, and were often deployed in Africa and other parts of the Empire. Based on the information above, one can safely state that the majority of colonial officials and missionaries had direct exposure to the public school style of secondary education and educational ideas, and thus they spread the value of the public schools throughout the Empire.

Recruiters for the colonial services placed special emphasis on public school experience, because, as Sir Ralph Furse said, they believed that while 'English universities train the mind, the Public Schools train character and teach leadership' (Sir Ralph Furse, cited in Ranger 1983: 216). It was widely accepted that the foremost point of a public school education was not brains but character. Character, in the public school context, meant the ability and confidence to act as a member of the elite. Besides acquiring the proper manners of a gentleman, a list of virtues that the public schools installed were: truthfulness and honesty, the spirit of self-negation, self-discipline, loyalty (to institutions, class and country), esprit de corps, perseverance, courage, respect and obedience (Hubbard 2000: 31; Mangan 1987: 139–41; Rosenthal 1986: 90–91.). Though vague, the kind of person that the public schools were to form was the faithful follower of British upper-middle and upper class 'tradition', a person who behaved properly and would fit himself into the existing social structure. The peculiar methods of public school education were, therefore, a means to effectively and efficiently socialise students to a school's values and norms. The system of residential houses and prefects was considered useful for the practice of exercising leadership in the real world. Students learned to discipline themselves while obeying the greater authority of the school and masters (teachers). A uniform style of dress and a body of school traditions and customs also contributed to the development of a sense of obedience and to the internalisation of public school values. Among various points of public school education, one can hardly neglect to mention the obsession with team sports, which were then called 'games'. They were a feature of the educational philosophy of the late Victorian and post-Victorian eras and stressed the role of physical activities in character training.

The physical activity introduced for the working-class schools was military drill. In the middle of the 19th century, drill exercises were given to boarding students of six primary schools for 'paupers' 'so as to introduce regularity into the movement of so large a body of children, to secure prompt obedience to the direction of the teacher, and to maintain personal cleanliness and propriety' (Poor Low Commissioners' report, cited in Hurt 1977: 169; see also, McCann 1977). By the last quarter of the 19th century, drill had become an established part of the curriculum in both voluntary and Education Board primary schools. Via the 1871 Education Code, the Gladstone administration allowed a maximum of 40 hours' drill a year to count as school attendance for the purpose of earning grant-in-aid (Hurt 1977: 176–9).

Unlike schools for the working class, however, public schools were to enhance boys' capacity to govern and control others, and to enjoy freedom within an established order. Educators and policy makers widely believed that sports in the playing fields, rather than in the barrack square, would help to form the qualities mentioned above in public school boys. An educationist of the early 20th century called public school boys' attention to the importance of 'games' as follows:

> Realise the importance of games. It's in football and cricket and rowing that Englishmen get that splendid moral training which no other nations gets. ... None of [German and French boys] get that magnificent sporting instinct which is the real foundation of our great Empire. So what I want to say to you boys is: 'Play up and play the game'. Be proud of your reputation for efficiency in games – it is the

source of … higher imperial efficiency. (Duckworth 1912: 68, cited in Mangan 1987: 138)

The player who demonstrated the spirit of sportsmanship, perseverance and unconditional loyalty to the school or the boarding house he represented was highly honoured. *Tom Brown's Schooldays*, a widely read novel describing the public school life of a fictitious character, Tom Brown, provided the ideal image of the public school boy.[4] Schools were keen on producing episodes of Tom Browns of their own. For example, a schoolmaster of Harrow, one of the great public schools wrote:

> How often have I seen boys going in to bat without a murmur in a bad light at the close of a long summer day's play, or playing a losing game with almost heroic determination! The boy who thinks little of himself, and much of his Eleven or his school, has not spent his Public School life in vain. It used to be told how, in the days when the ring around the field at Lord's was less scrupulously kept than it is now, a Harrow boy's nose began to bleed when he was fielding; his mother, seeing his plight, ran out from the ring to comfort or relieve him; but the captain of the Eleven bade her retire with the solemn words, 'Madam, a Harrow boy must be prepared to shed his last drop of blood for his school'. (Welldon 1915: 180, cited in Mangan 1986: 38)

McClellan (1992) notes that in the US of the similar time period, discussion about moral education flourished, in which similar methods to those used in British public schools were promoted as useful for character training, such as school clubs, scouts and elected student leadership. Although American moral education was not connected with elitist chivalry as it was at public school, it should be noted that the idea of students' character training and the set of methods for fostering it were shared across the Anglo-American world.

5-3-2 Boy Scout movement: elitist moralism translated to a mass programme

The class-conscious and ethnocentric paternalism of the British upper-middle and upper classes made the graduates of the public schools believe in the virtue of diffusing certain elements of an education programme meant for the privileged few to 'less favoured people'. The Boy Scout movement, which was started by Baden-Powell in 1908, was a manifestation of this upper-class benevolence. The late 19th and early 20th centuries saw the mushrooming of various youth movements, which organised leisure activities for the working-class adolescents, and which legitimised control over them by the middle and upper classes (Springhall 1977: 14–18). Among these youth movements, the Boy Scouts were typical in the sense that Baden-Powell had a clear idea that the movement should follow the model of the public school. He declared that one of the main reasons for establishing the Boy Scouts was to provide a substitute for 'the Public School life which [was] only open to the comparatively few whose parents [could] afford it, and to give the mass of our rising generation some of the spirit of self-negation, self-discipline, sense of honour, responsibilities, helpfulness to others, loyalty and patriotism which [would] make "character"', and he claimed the Boy Scouts would provide character training which was not available in any schools for the working class.[5] Being educated in a public school (Charterhouse) himself, Baden-Powell was a firm believer in the public School's philosophy of character training. The tricky issue with character training in the Boy Scouts was that the working class was meant to be led, a different goal from that of the leadership training in the public schools. Rosenthal observes that Scout Law allows very little room for the development of the individual, except a development of the sense of absolute submission to authority (1986: 109–30). Putting that aside, the Boy Scouts have followed the public school tradition in the sense that they stress character training through physical activities, uniform dress, rituals and peer influence.

The enthusiasm for spreading the public-school type of education to the lower social classes and colonial subjects was not unique to Baden-Powell but was shared by a large number of people who experienced it. Therefore, it was understandable that the Boy

Scouts spread across the Empire very quickly. As early as 1920, only 12 years after the establishment of the movement, the Gold Coast government, the earliest among British colonies, officially recognised the Scouts and encouraged their school-based activities. Contrary to its stated universality and its supposed fairness to different sexes, races and religions, the ideas the Boy Scouts had were clearly orientated toward the public school ethos of 'muscular Christianity'(Springhall 1977: 53). The sex-specific nature of the movement is apparent when one compares the Law of the Girl Guide movement, which stressed the domesticity of girls, with that of the Boy Scouts. Moreover, the inconsistency of headquarters' attitude towards the racial controversy of the Boy Scout and Girl Guide movements in South Africa demonstrates the inherent contradiction in the policy statement of universality (Gaitskell 1984; Proctor 2000; Rosenthal 1986: 260–63). What we should note here, however, is the appeal of the Scout movement and its character training to the colonial administrators. Putting aside the incongruity of the policy at the practical level, the Scout movement was a source of imagination for moulders of colonial education in Africa.

5-3-3 Girls' education: wives of the classed men

As the model of education established for the masculine character development, there also emerged the idea of educating girls as their counterparts. It took shape in the mesh of the class stratification and gender differentiation. Bourgeois women were assigned different gender roles from working-class women and were educated accordingly. Regardless of the class, women were commonly expected to take charge of the households' domestic matters.

Such class- and gender-segregated idea of education was also brought to Africa through colonisation. In Africa, there are communities which are traditionally matrilineal and women actively take part in social activities including decision making. Also, even in the patrilineal societies, women often take charge of work outside of the household, particularly in agriculture or trading. However, the European culture brought the idea that productive activities outside of the household belonged to the men's world, while domestic activities to the women's world. Such values and the 'civilizing' interventions overturned the labour divisions between two sexes and domesticated women. In school, along the contrasting axes of the elite–masses and the male–female, women's identity was formulated.

What was most emphasised in girls' education was the role of women as the vector for transforming the family. It was often said by the promoters of girls' education that education for boys can only change individuals, but girls' education would contribute towards changing families and, in extension, the whole society, because they protect families and bring up children.

The mass education for Africans aimed to stop traditional customs which were considered immoral in the eyes of Europeans, and to teach the minimum 3Rs necessary for agriculture and simple manual work. What was particularly taught to girls were hygiene (cleaning, maintaining toilets and garbage disposal), health care (prevention and cure of simple diseases), child rearing, cooking and other household affairs. For the masses, even though it was school-based education, transmission of academic knowledge was secondary, but the main objective was for girls to learn from experience the skills to improve life in the given environment. Also, to stop immoral custom was considered to be an important 'civilizing mission' of mass education. What Europeans considered 'immoral' were not only rituals and arts like music and dance. Practices particularly discussed in relation to the girls' education were relationships and the division of labour between women and men. Polygamy was prohibited as immoral and insanitary.

Meanwhile, education for the elite girls aimed to develop the role models whose intellectual level was as high as that of the Europeans but also to maintain the sense of belonging to African society. Girls were expected to learn the way to maintain the bourgeois household properly. Similar to the British bourgeois women who did not take part in humble productive work but spent time growing flowers and knitting lace, African elite women were educated to be modest, thrifty and gentle partners to the elite men in their married lives. Unlike the working class, the household management expected of the elite women was not the kind of labour of a maid, but the overall decision and wisdom to protect the family. When necessary, they would hire a working-class maid. Symbolically, elite girls' schools in Africa made sewing classes compulsory. It was not because those girls were supposed to be seamstresses. Rather, the sewing represented the image of women who manage the household wisely, modest women who support elite males as spouses (Gaitskell 1984 and 2002; Barthel 1985).

Altogether, educational thoughts of Victorian Britain were characterised by strong emphasis on moral education to develop the personalities suited for the social class and gender of the learners. School activities, subjects and facilities were designed for students to acquire such characters through interaction with peers and teachers and taking part in activities.

5-4 Mélange of fashionable ideas to legitimise colonial education

5-4-1 Interchangeable concepts for educational adaptation

Across different educational philosophies and models, which were prevalent in the early 20th century, there were certain fashionable terms commonly used, such as 'learning by doing', 'adaptation' and 'character training'.

'Learning by doing' represented the general trend to value experience-based learning. Whether for the elite or for the masses, for boys or for girls, for transformation of society or for the maintenance of the status quo, it was considered important to acquire the knowledge and attitude suited to the purpose of education through practice. In the progressive philosophy, learning should happen centred around the motivation and interest of the learner, and the process of linking the knowledge and new experience itself was a significant part of education. For American black education, a large part of the time spent in the school was allocated to the agriculture or industrial training. Learners were expected to internalise the 'dignity of labour' through vocational practices. Also in a practical sense, work done by the students in these vocational or rural schools, both in the US and in Africa, yielded significant sources of income and materials for those schools and surrounding communities to be self-reliant. Meanwhile, for British Victorian educationists, participation in sports for the elite and regimental drill for the working class were an important part of the moral training to develop the sense of discipline, contribution to society and other personality attributes suited to the respective classes. Therefore, despite the differences of the objectives of education, these education theories of the early 20th century converged on their promotion of practice-based education.

'Character training', namely moral education, was another common concern of the educationists of this period. Sometimes, it was said that character training was even more important than knowledge acquisition. Being learner-centred, progressive education paid great attention to the personality of learners and related education to it. At the same time, this philosophy conceived the idea that the role of educated people was to transform society to be truly democratic. For this matter, the teacher was expected to guide the learners to acquire an attitude as responsible citizens of the democratic state and lead others to the betterment of society. In American black education, vocational practices and moral education were two sides of the same coin. To make the obedient black, devotion to manual work and formation of attitude to appreciate it were inseparable and the core of their education. With the Victorian moralism in Britain, it was not an exaggeration to say that character training was the prime objective of education. For the purpose of developing the personality, either of the ruler or the ruled, interaction with peer students and teachers at boarding houses or through school activities was carefully designed. Such character training also contributed to construct the collective identities of the Victorian and post-Victorian British. Particularly the graduates of elite public schools were proud to be trained as the truthful, courageous and self-disciplined delegates of British civilization to guide savage natives in the colonies and working-class population at home.

Finally, to achieve the perceived goals of respective educational thoughts, to 'adapt' the contents and mode of education to the learners' conditions were commonly considered to be important. Of course, the approach to adaptation differed significantly depending on the conceptions of the learners' conditions and the goals. For example, for the American black educationists, adaptation meant to maintain the status quo, while for the progressives, adaptation meant to align with the interests of learners. Except for the progressives, who valued the process of learning as much as the outcomes of it, most of the educational theories saw the preparation for future jobs and social roles as primary goals. In this sense, 'adaptation' was the way to adjust the educational practices to produce the graduates with the intended personalities and skills. Depending on the societal roles which would be expected of the graduate – leaders, workers, wives or colonial subjects – the mode of 'adaptation' would differ.

As such, actual meanings of the popular terms and their practical implications were diverse. Still, theories developed in the same time period shared a broad orientation. In the case of the educational ideas in early 20th century, they were all practice-oriented and highlighted moral education. Such converging terms and concepts connected theories and philosophies with fundamentally different natures. They served policy makers and practitioners to create their own mixture of educational ideas. In this sense, these terms were like revolving doors through which one can move across different educational thoughts freely.

5-4-2 The mixed model for the African colonies

While the Boy Scouts were an indirect transfer to colonies of a British public school education that had been adapted to British working-class children, there were people who actively promoted the direct transplant of the public school model to the colonies. One of the most influential among these promoters was Lord Frederic Lugard, who was not only known for his formation of the principle of indirect rule, but also for his innovative educational policy in Northern Nigeria, announced in 1915. Following the public school tradition, he advocated that 'the fundamental principle of [the Nigerian] education policy ... [was] that the training of character [was] more important than the training of the intellect' (Lugard 1925: 10). For him, the 'atmosphere' of schools was as important as the curriculum. Lugard described his idea of 'the central school'[6] for leadership training as follows:

> In ... the residential school ... the influence of the *British staff* can be brought to bear continuously. It is in *the play-fields and recreation hours* more especially that the public-school spirit can be evolved. The most effective method of training character ... is the *residential school*, in which the personal influence of the teachers and of the older pupils – entrusted with responsibility and disciplinary power as *'monitors'* – can create a social life and tradition, in which standards of judgment are formed and right attitudes acquired almost unconsciously through imbibing the spirit and atmosphere of the school. ... The Boy Scout and Girl Guide system may assist in [the object of character training].
> (Lugard 1925: 10; emphasis is added)

The instruments to be employed to achieve the goal of character training were (1) the residential school; (2) adequate British staff (those properly trained at public schools and ancient universities); (3) the delegation of responsibility for discipline to student monitors; and (4) the encouragement of games. Furthermore, a Nigerian regulation of 1915 stated that government grants should be allocated partly according to 'tone, discipline, manners, and character as exemplified by the virtues of loyalty, respect, and obedience'(Mangan 1987: 141; see also, Lugard 1922: Chapters 21 and 22).

The enthusiasm for transferring the character training of the British public school was not peculiar to Lugard but was widely shared by colonial officials, missionaries and educationists at home and in the colonies. Being predominantly the products of public schools themselves, they had a common belief that a public school education was the most sophisticated and effective way of training the youth. This belief interplayed with the ethnocentric paternalism of the time. As 'temporary' rulers who were helping colonial subjects until they would achieve the maturity of self-government, they did not doubt the virtue of diffusing the English upper-class system of education to 'less-favoured' people. The set of instruments used in public school moral education, namely, a British staff, boarding schools, the monitor (prefect) system and games, was frequently mentioned in the discourse on African education. Thus, it was not necessarily used only in the context of elite education, but in technical 'boarding' schools and so on.

The following passage from Guggisberg, Governor of the Gold Coast, is indicative of how educational ideas from different sources were mixed and presented as a coherent educational philosophy that was matched to a particular social context. Referring to the moral education instilled in the junior trade schools, which were vocational schools at the upper-primary level, Guggisberg wrote:

> The establishment of these Trade Schools is an attempt at producing ... educated artisans, wherein the trade or artisan instruction is valued as equal to literary knowledge and *both subordinated to character formation*. They are *boarding or residential institutions* where the pupils are kept under strict discipline ...
>
> The basis of Character training is the application of the *Scoutlaws* [sic] and Scouting principles combined with *organised games* for the development of the collective spirit, physical exercises for the improvement in physical health and mental alertness in the pupils, and *drill* for the creation of a proper school discipline, all of which when combined lead to the formation of a proper *School spirit*, the essential part of any well conducted school.[7] (Emphasis is added)

Although Guggisberg's argument does not look like the straightforward application of the public school model to Africa any more, the tendency to attach more importance to character formation than to skill or literary education was typical in the educational discourse of the time. Either in the philosophy of American industrial education or that of the British public school, character training was the topmost goal of education. Residential schools, the stress on games and school spirit were characteristic of the public school model. At the same time, the Hampton and Tuskegee Institutes also stressed the importance of the boarding setting for moral training. The Scouts and military drill, which Guggisberg listed alongside sports ('games'), were the physical activities originally devised for the working-class lads but not used in the public schools. Also in the US, the regimental drill was used at the Hampton and Tuskegee institutions as a means to discipline students. In Guggisberg's mind, the differentiation between methods for the leaders and for the masses had melted down. They were all put together in the category of physical activities, a set of tools for character training. Finally, Guggisberg applied the public school model, which was originally upper-class education, to trade schools, which were to turn out 'educated artisans'. David Williams argues that there were three criteria for Guggisberg in evaluating the 'character' of students. The first was whether the students participated in activities that Guggisberg thought desirable (such as playing games and joining the Scouts); the second was whether the student had a proper love of country; and the third was whether the school inspector approved of the 'tone (atmosphere)' of the school (Williams 1964: 296).

Guggisberg's educational idea implies that to people in the field, whether they were administrators, policy makers or school operators, it did not matter much which were the original sources of ideas or how precisely they understood them. Guggisberg referred to the British public school or Phelps-Stokes Fund, from time to time, to justify his educational policy. These educational ideas were, in a similar manner to the global discourse I examined in Chapter Four, used as external reference points. However, what Guggisberg basically did was to mix them together and created his own model of education for the Gold Coast Africans.

There is a divide between scholars who look at the influence of British upper-class education on African leadership training (Hubbard 2000; Mangan 1982, 1986 and 1987; Ranger 1983; Rich 1991; Rosenthal 1986) and those who focus on African mass education, which was started by missionaries and was later influenced by American black industrial education (Berman 1971; Brown 1964; Bude 1983; Hunt 1984; D'Souza 1975; Kallaway 1996 and 1984; King 1971; Lewis 1971; Marah 1987; Peterson 1971; Sivonen 1995). The former tend to place more emphasis on idealism, on a moralistic ideology supported by various forms of rituals accepted as 'tradition'. In contrast, the latter group of scholars is more interested in the pragmatic reasons for promoting a racially segregated form of education. I do not mean that these scholars have not paid attention to other philosophical sources of inspiration for African education than the one with which they are primarily concerned. The problem is that, too often, these scholars assume that different ideas had distinctly separable influences on the philosophy of African education, without any mixing or confusion in the process of transfer, and that one could single out the process of an idea transplanted to an African environment.

For ordinary missionaries or colonial officials involved in educational practice, the differences between educational philosophies were not extremely important issues. They were not obliged to follow a pure form of one model and reject all others. The same would apply to policy makers. What was important for them was to find a workable mixture of the ideas that were floating around. For instance, American black industrial education took some ideas from progressive educational theories. Certainly, Thomas Jesse Jones's theory of educational adaptation was a fusion of the Hampton-Tuskegee model of industrial education, the Jeanes School and his idea of managing inter-racial politics. The British policy makers in London remixed Jones's version of black education with the public school moralistic ideology. Further, in each colony, district and school, this cut and paste process of creating educational ideas continued. In sum, educational models and ideas were all floating around and cross-fertilising each other.

The question of educational transfer is largely a matter of politics and administration. At the political level, people negotiate developing a policy framework which would satisfy different interests in a compromised way. In the global discourse on African education, British officials and missionaries confirmed with American philanthropists that American models of industrial education were adaptable to Africa. However, this fact of political consensus does not necessarily indicate either that the American models were the sole philosophical source of influence on education in Africa or that the British policy makers believed in the virtue of American educational ideas without reservation. Policies formalise and fix the results of the negotiation of power and ideas at a certain time and in a certain place. Once they are written down, policies are fixed but ideas constantly flow and mix with each other. Therefore, one should be cautious about assuming that what was written in policy documents was what people believed and did. Moreover, terms used in such a document tend to be vague and seemingly neutral, which allows various interpretations according to the interests of people who use them.

In the following chapters of Part III, the focus will be shifted to the discourse and practice on the Gold Coast Colony. Against the peculiar local context, I will closely examine diverse ways of interpreting two common terms: 'character training' and 'adaptation'. The analysis of these terms demonstrates that people mixed and remixed the educational philosophies which were globally popular so that they could make these philosophies fit to their own interests. Then, I will also investigate how these mixed philosophies were implemented by educators and experienced by students at Achimota School.

Notes

[1] Thomas Jesse Jones to Sadler, 17 March 1933, Rockefeller Archive Center (RAC), General Education Board Series 1–2, 286/2984.

[2] Most US educational historians consider the period between 1820 and 1860 to be the period of the Common School movement. However, this only occurred in the North and West, not in the South. Common Schools were established in the South following the Civil War, i.e., in the 1870s. These schools were very popular with newly-freed slaves; in many Southern counties, the enrolment rates of blacks exceeded those of whites in the 1870s. However, when Reconstruction ended in 1877, Southern states began to restrict funding for black education. Thus its continued expansion depended upon community contributions and Northern philanthropy.

[3] The ratio of public school graduates to non-public school graduates is even larger (91. per cent), if one takes the number of recruits whose secondary schools are known (332) as the denominator, instead of total number of recruits. Mangan, *The Games Ethic and Imperialism: Aspects of the Diffusion of an Ideal* (1986: 79–84).

[4] The school was based on Rugby, one of the great public schools (Hughes 1971).

[5] British Scout Archives, Box D, Cadets 1910–16. Article on Cadets and Cadet training, 1916, cited in Rosenthal 1986: 90. See also, Springhall 1977: 53.

[6] The education system he imagined was a ladder with three rungs. The lowest was the village school or the bush school, which catered to the educational needs of the rural masses. The next rung was the intermediate or middle school, which more or less specialised in some form of vocational

training. And the topmost rung was the central school, which provided the secondary level education for the selected few. Lugard thought Tropical Africa had not advanced to a level that required higher education.

[7] Sessional Paper VII, 1923–4 "'Junior Trade Schools of the Gold Coast Colony". Ordered to be printed by His Excellency the Governor', Gold Coast: Government Press, Accra. 1923. PRO, CO98/38.

Part III

National discourse on education and struggle over hegemony

Once the *Memorandum on Education Policy in Tropical Africa* was developed in the metropole, the agreed principles of colonial education were brought to the colonies for application and practice. The national education system was institutionalised with regulations, mechanisms for supervision and quality control of schools, and standardisation of the curriculum. In this Part III, I will follow the process through which education policy was formulated in the Gold Coast and Achimota School was erected as the model of African leadership training. While Achimota served the population in the Gold Coast Colony, the teaching staff who were invited to found this school were from all the British territories and were considered to be the best suited to produce good results in this innovative school. Therefore, to discuss Achimota is not only to untangle the educational history of the Gold Coast Colony, but also to see how the British discourse on colonial education was translated to the practice with the best available inputs. The fact that the economy of the Gold Coast was lucrative and had a strong paternalistic governor made it no coincidence that this colony was chosen as the site for the model school.

Despite the global enthusiasm and interest in Achimota, the actual negotiation for adopting educational Ordinances, allocating budget or any other issues related to the education system, happened among the stakeholders in the Gold Coast: in the Legislative Council, in the meetings of the Department of Education or in the form of opinions expressed in the newspapers. In this sense, to analyse the discourse and practices in the Gold Coast is not to examine the way the global policy brought in a top-down manner was accepted by a colony passively. It was, in fact, a dynamic process involving actors not only within the colony, but also those outside. While the ideas brought from outside were accepted, they were transformed and were fed back to the global discourse.

The organisation of chapters in Part III follow suit in Part II. First in Chapter Six, I will provide the background for the readers to understand the context of the discourse. The historical development of school-based education along the coast of the Gulf of Guinea will be reviewed. Particular focus will be given to the period during which education was gradually systematised as a part of colonial administration. Then, I will discuss the political economy of the Gold Coast during the governorship of Guggisberg, which overlaps with the period of economic boom in Europe before the Great Depression.

Against the background presented in Chapter Six, Chapter Seven will discuss the politics of the educational agenda setting and Achimota, in relation to actors involved in it. In addition to the missionaries and colonial administrators, at the colony level, there was strong pressure from African nationalists and traditional authorities. In a crude sense, there was a controversy between Europeans' 'civilizing mission' and Africans' revivalism of tradition. However, African's reliance on the language of revivalism was as ambiguous as the Europeans' language of civilization, and the interests of educated nationalists and traditional chiefs often conflicted.

After examining the different arguments of actors and the motivations behind them, Chapter Eight will narrow the focus on the ways diverse opinions were negotiated in policy making and designing the education of Achimota as the experimental school. Two key terms, which were commonly used in the global discourse, became the nodes of discourse again: 'character training' and 'adaptation'. They were as if the grid to locate diverse views on the types of personality schools were to develop, the balance between Europeanisation and maintenance of African tradition and customs, and on the educational methods utilised to achieve the perceived goals of education.

While the large part of this book deals with the norms, actors and politics of discourse, Chapter Eight, the last chapter of Part III, will be on the practices of Achimota education and the experience of students who learned there. In addition to the archival sources, I will use the interviews with people who went to Achimota during its early years. After the long process from the development of policy framework on colonial education in the metropole to the establishment of Achimota, how did the norms change that were applied to the reality on the Gold Coast? How did the philosophy of Achimota education influence the life of students during and after their time in this school? By comparing the experience of the students and the ideas discussed away from them, one can consider the real implications of colonial education and the discourse about it.

Chapter 6

Political context on the Gold Coast

6-1 Prehistory: education until early 20th century

6-1-1 Castle schools

The earliest contact the area later known as the Gold Coast Colony had with Western education was through the coastal forts erected by the European slave traders. The first recorded attempt to teach children to learn reading and writing was in 1509 at Elmina castle, one of the coastal forts, by the hand of the Portuguese. However, this venture in education came to an end with the seizure of the castle by the Protestant Dutch in 1637. The Dutch West India Company established its headquarters at Elmina and a few years later opened a school for mixed blood (mulatto) children. Apart from a short-lived attempt by some French missionaries to found a school between 1638 and 1641, there were no more Catholic schools until the White Fathers re-entered Elmina in 1880. The first school run by the British was the one of the Society for the Propagation of the Gospel (S.P.G., Anglican), established in 1701. In 1765, Philip Quaque became the first African to be a Church of England minister; he was appointed schoolmaster on the Gold Coast and occupied this position until his death 50 years later. In 1821, the British government abolished the Company of Merchants and its forts were placed under the government of Sierra Leone. The merchants revived the school at Cape Coast after Quaque's death, and under the new government, it was renamed the Colonial School. This school produced the first generation of English-educated Africans.

6-1-2 Mission schools: a root of vocational versus literary education controversy

The Basel Missionary Society, whose education was looked upon as a model of education applied to the African background, first came to the Gold Coast in 1828. It was a German Presbyterian society with its headquarters at Basel in Switzerland, and at the request of the

Danish Governor de Richelieu, it sent out four missionaries to be stationed at Christiansburg, Accra. The Basels lost all four of the missionaries within three years from disease. Out of three volunteers who replaced them, two again died shortly after arrival. The sole survivor, Andreas Riis, moved inland to Akropong and opened a station associated with a school for converts. The Basel Mission opened the first boys' school in Akropong in 1843, and five years later, as soon as pupils with some education were available, a seminary was started for the training of catechists and teachers. The Basel Mission's education was characterised by its strict discipline, its inclusion of vocational and agricultural activities, and its use of vernacular as the language of instruction. As a way to accommodate the Christian teaching in the local context, Basel missionaries were very committed to developing the orthography of Ghanaian languages and translation of the Bible to them: Ewe, Ga and Twi. The Basel missionaries, who were from Germany or Switzerland, did not have any incentive to use English at school, although it was the *lingua franca* in the coastal area. Also they found it more effective to teach in the languages used by people (Martin 1976). Some historians suggest that Basel Mission's vocational bias in education was due to the resistance of the inland people, among whom the Basel Mission worked, to Western culture and Western educational institutions. Therefore, according to these historians, to avoid any opposition to sending children to school, the Basel mission oriented its curriculum toward skills training, unlike other missions whose education was almost exclusively literary (Foster 1965: 50).

However, other historians who looked at skills training at mission schools in Africa in general claimed that it was often the missionaries' need for survival that made them use students as a workforce at a school farm or workshop (Bude 1983: 343–4). Either it was Basel-Bremen or Wesleyan type, but in these early mission schools students were often viewed as a useful workforce to till the land, to manufacture some products and to run errands to maintain the Christian communities, which were considered as parts of the educational system. Even so, classroom instruction was exclusively literary. From the functionalists' point of view, however, literary education of mission schools had been equally 'vocational' as manual training, in the sense that it served the manpower needs of mission posts.[1]

Regardless of the original reasons for devising such approach of education by the Basel Mission, to the colonial officials of contemporary and later generations, who tried to promote 'adapted education', this model looked promising. Therefore, Basel Mission, together with its brother mission Bremen, received favourable treatment from the government. The Bremen Missionary Society operated in the German colony of Togo, bordering on the eastern side of the British Gold Coast, and it was not until the First World War of 1914–18 that part of Togo, and consequently its schools, came under the Gold Coast government's control. The Bremen education was run along basically the same lines as the Basel mission, practical education using the vernacular.

The first Wesleyan missionary arrived at Cape Coast in 1835. Like the Basel Mission, the Wesleyan Mission also lost some of its earlier missionaries. However, its educational work spread rapidly. By 1841, the Wesleyans had 165 students, and there were also 40–50 students in Cape Coast and Accra respectively (Foster 1965: 50–51). In contrast to the Basel Mission, which limited the access to school to converts' children and to the preparation of its catechists and teachers, the Wesleyan mission opened its schools as often as demanded by people. They used English as the medium of instruction and taught the three R's in English. Yet, even though its primary education expanded rapidly, the Wesleyan Mission was late to start secondary education. The first secondary institution opened by Wesleyans was the Wesleyan High School in Cape Coast, started in 1876.

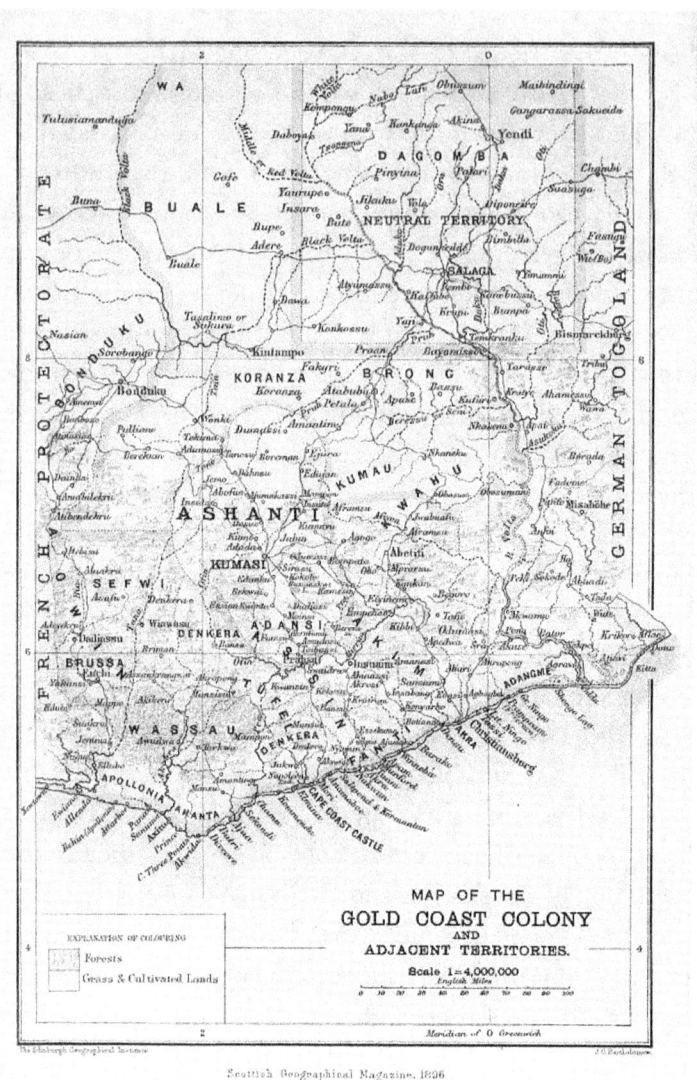

Map of the Gold Coast Colony (1896)

6-1-3 Involvement of the colonial government in education

Today's Ghanaian education system can trace its origin back to the 1880s when the British established their rule in the Gold Coast territories that mostly corresponded to current southern Ghana. While missions had been and kept being the main providers of education, the British introduced a colony-wide system of educational administration and rules. The Educational Ordinances of 1882 and 1887 were primarily attempts to reproduce the structural characteristics of British education (Antwi 1992: 32; Foster 1965: 81). The 1882 Ordinance was applied to the whole of British West Africa. It provided for both government-run and mission schools receiving grants-in-aid. Grants-in-aid were provided according to the efficiency of each mission in its school management. One inspector of schools was appointed and his territory covered all the British West African settlements. The subjects which had to be offered as conditions of grant-in-aid were not only reading, writing and arithmetic but also English language, and in the case of girls, needlework. English grammar, English history and geography were optional. Although the colonial government in the early 20th century was keen on adaptation, in the 1880s, the mandatory subjects to teach were the three R's in English, not agriculture or manual work. A new ordinance passed in 1887 made each colony an individual unit of educational administration instead of attempting to address the whole of British West Africa as one. A Director of Education was appointed for each colony. The 1887 Ordinance, with minor amendments, remained in force until the 1925 Ordinance. By 1901, there were 135 schools under the education system that were government run and assisted schools, excluding independent schools (Table 6-1). The total educational expenditure was 6,543 pound, which was less than two per cent of the total government expenditure (Antwi 1992: 33)

Table 6-1 : Educational Statistics of the Gold Coast: 1880-1945*

Year	Government Expenditure on Education		Primary Schools				Secondary (incl. Technical)				Teacher Training			
	Grants to Missions	Total	No. of Schools	Enrolment			No. of Schools	Enrolment			No. of Schools	Enrolment		
				Boys	Girls	Total		Boys	Girls	Total		Boys	Girls	Total
1880	425	1,325	**139			5,000								
1901	3,706	6,543	135	9,859	2,159	12,018								
1919	6,157	54,442	213	22,718	4,600	27,318								
1926	30,887	179,000	234	26,039	6,899	32,839								
1930		117,135	340	32,224	9,693	41,917	4	528	10	538	7	509	46	555
1940			467	46,631	15,201	61,832	5	1,114	85	1,199	6	384	198	582

(Unit: Sterling Pound)
*Figures only include government-run schools and assisted schools which were financed by the government.
** 1880 figures are approximate and include all schools, since no schools were 'assisted' until after the 1887 Ordinance.
Sources: McWilliam and Kwamena-Poh 1975: 141–2.

154

6-2 Issues of political debates and actors in the early 20th century

Before looking at the discussion on education on the Gold Coast during Guggisberg's governorship, it would be useful to review the issues of political debates and the actors who were involved in it. The gradual expansion of colonial administration was partly caused by the critical re-examination of the practices of missionaries in the earlier period. Civilizing mission, which was perceived as almost inseparable from evangelisation and Westernisation, drove missionaries' inland penetration. However, unrestricted transmission of literary knowledge and exposure to European culture, which was originally considered to be a useful strategy for civilizing the savage Africans, faced criticism. Colonial officials shared the sense of civilizing mission and never denied its necessity. At the same time, there was growing discussion to control Africans' aggression while assimilating them to a reasonable extent.

For African ideologues, land tenure and education were two major concerns, both of which were argued in close linkage with their rights of political representation. From the end of the 19th century, the British colonial authorities started to seize 'unutilised' lands and redistribute them to European settlers and private companies. Such was the practice which caused harsh resistance all over British Africa. In the case of the Gold Coast Colony, to prevent the Land Bill from being adopted in the Legislative Council, the educated elite formed a coalition with African intellectuals in other British West African colonies such as Sierra Leone and Nigeria. The educated elite raised their voices claiming to do so 'on behalf of' the illiterate masses. On the other hand, traditional chiefs, even though they also resisted European dominance, attacked the educated elite for the pretension of leadership. In fact, according to them, the educated elite were disconnected from the masses and used the card of 'representation' for their own interests.

There were roughly four categories of actors in the political discourse: missionaries, colonial officials, the African educated elite and traditional chiefs. Their interests diverged and converged on different issues and situations.

6-2-1 Civilising mission and rising criticism against mission schools

The motivation of missionaries to create a Christian community surrounding the church and school was based on their belief in the racial and cultural inferiority of Africans. There was a pseudo-scientific racism that Africans' mental capacity was less than Europeans'. Numerous serious scientific studies were conducted to demonstrate that the Negroid skull has less capacity than the Caucasian skull (Berman 1975a: 10). Along with these scientific studies, anthropological studies served to confirm the theory of racial differences in intellectual capacity and stages of human evolution.[2] Also, writings of European travellers, merchants and colonial administrators, which were often not based on serious research and were biased by their personal impressions, served to make up the common mythology that the African was a primitive, uncivilised man. These racial preconceptions about Africans framed the work of missionaries in Africa. They assigned themselves the mission of diffusing not only Christianity but also European civilization. In the mind of missionaries, the cultures which they were penetrating were not religiously neutral, but were 'heathen' societies controlled by the Evil One. All aspects of these societies, not only religion, but also economics, politics, morality, the arts and all that fell under the catch-all name of 'culture' were considered in need of repair. There was a widespread conviction in 19th-century Britain that it constituted the model of Christian culture and society that all societies should follow. This assumption was supported by racial evolutionism. The British considered Africans to be at the 'infant' stage of human progress, which demanded their altruistic effort to 'uplift' them to the European level of civilization (Stanley 1990: 155). According to this syllogism, evangelisation was closely associated with cultural transmission, and schools were considered to be centres of community transformation under the name of 'civilization'.

Another impetus to their African presence was, of course, to spread the gospel. To do this, missions needed teachers and ministers at outposts. They also needed educated African staff at central stations for Bible translation, administrative work, etc. A misconception often shared among recent scholars is that teachers at mission schools were all Europeans. There were far from enough missionaries to station at all schools run by missions. In the Gold Coast Colony in 1885, for example, the Wesleyan Methodist Society had three European missionaries, the Basel missionaries numbered 53, and yet each community had nearly seven thousand African members (6,855 Wesleyans and 6,800 Basels) (Mobley 1970: 32). Although there were some differences in policies between the two mission societies concerning the delegation of responsibilities to African ministers and staff, they both could not run their stations and schools without relying on Africans. Therefore, schools were indispensable not only for spreading the gospel, but also for supplying the manpower needed to maintain the structure of mission societies.

At the early stage of missionaries' inland penetration, to shield the converts from the influence of traditional authority, the missionaries segregated from the general population not only themselves, but also the African converts. The schools they established were either in these segregated communities or with boarding facilities, so as to limit the risk of converts/students returning to the 'heathen' practices and to maximise the Christian civilizing influence. These isolated Christian communities – 'Salems' as they were called – attracted hostility from the African populace (Berman 1975a: 31).[3] Earlier generations of African missionaries had to go through many hardships. When they converted, they were to detach from all their original social relationships and forced to live in Christian communities, only returning to their African friends and relatives to proselytise as Christian missionaries. The story of Nana Ofori Atta I's family would be telling about this point. His parents were from royal lineage, but they abandoned their place in the royal court and became evangelists of the Presbyterian mission. The family lived in a big house next to the church and the father confronted the royal court denouncing its 'heathen' practices. In 1886, the family was sent to evangelise at the town of Asuom and was 'roughly manhandled and then literally thrown out of town … [T]heir property was destroyed'. (Rathbone 1993: 29-30) When he was enstooled in 1912, regardless of his upbringing as a Presbyterian, Ofori Atta cut off his relationship with the church and its people at least in official places. As such, the location of traditional institutions at the time of rapid Christian penetration was an ambiguous and sensitive issue.

The culturally and socially uncompromising attitude of missionaries was criticised by Africans of the 20th century. Ephraim Amu, an African intellectual, questioned whether missionaries could have any intimate knowledge about African society while they intended to transform it:

> How many of our Missionaries are intimate friends of the Africans among whom they work as leaders? Can they speak with the average member of the Church in his own language? How often do they pay ordinary friendly visits to Africans? How often do they share their meals with them? (Amu 1940)

Casely Hayford, a leading nationalist of the Gold Coast, pointed out that as a result of such segregation missionaries did not know African culture and society. In his autobiographic novel *Ethiopia Unbound*, Casely Hayford explained, 'The fact is that you Christians have not taken the trouble to understand any other system but yours' (1968: 27–8). The missionaries criticised here were not necessarily Europeans. The majority of them were, in fact, Africans trained locally. What happened was that African evangelists internalised the Christian value system and assumed a great deal of missionary attitudes toward things indigenous. As Mobley observes, 'The result was a continued hesitancy in relating their messages to traditional worldview' (1970: 155).

A significant result of this uncompromising promotion of Christianity and European values was the transformation, even destruction, of traditional culture. Missionaries considered schools to be the efficient means to enlighten young people and let them break away from 'pagan practices'. The Principal of the Wesley College at Kumasi, where 'ministers, teachers and catechists [were] trained together', advocated this position, noting that:

> The champions of the Church must be champions of Education if they are to be consistent in profession and practice. ... [O]n the

Mission Field ... Churches and Church Schools are mightiest forces in breaking down barriers of fearful superstition and preparing the way for civilising influences.[4]

The criticism was raised not only from the Africans who opposed mission education from a cultural point of view (Pearce 1988). Mission education was also starting to be criticised by the colonial officials for producing Africans who were halfway westernised and uprooted from their traditional society. While colonial officers also shared the sense of the civilizing mission with the missionaries, facing the emerging economic and political situation in the colonies, they became growingly sceptical of educated Africans and mission education which were their cradles.

6-2-2 Saturating the labour market and scepticism of mission education

As the 20th century began, the Gold Coast economy had grown steadily owing to the export of agricultural and mineral resources. Cocoa farming and gold mining had developed on a large scale. As demonstrated in Figures 3-1 and 3-2, stimulated by the sharp rise of the international market price of cocoa, Gold Coast farmers increased their production capacity. Cocoa exports, which were only 230 tons per year during the period 1896–1900, rose to over 14,000 tons per annum in 1906–19, and 200,000 tons by 1930 (Foster 1965: 126).

This economic development brought not only increased revenue to the government, but also a large demand for manual labour. The labour migration to mines and cocoa farms in the eastern and central regions caused drastic changes in traditional social systems like land tenure.[5] Also, while the cocoa production capacity of the colony was constantly growing, the public began suffering from the fluctuating international price of cocoa and gold in the beginning of the 1920s. The labour demand, which had absorbed a great number of migrant workers, reached saturation point by the mid-1920s. For example, in the mines, employment fell from 15,000 to 10,000 during the late 1920s (Holmes 1972: 337). The labour situation of the Gold Coast changed from labour scarcity to labour surplus.

The colonial government tried to deal with some of the problems that plagued the educational system. Growing unemployment among school leavers was perceived by the Europeans as the negative effect of Western education which focused on three R's in English. They thought such education made students aspire to clerical work using the English language and develop a disdain for manual work and traditional society. Looking back, missionary education was criticised in that there had been little attempt to adapt the method and contents of education to local conditions.

Colonial officials regretted that missionary education allowed bringing up 'mission boys', Africans who mimicked European styles superficially. At the same time, racial evolutionism itself was not thrown away. Instead of direct exposure to European 'civilization', the Europeans promoted African's self-help effort of ascending the racial hierarchy while maintaining their African pride. This change of rhetoric explains in part why the government officials and missionaries seemed so double-tongued. On the one hand, they encouraged breaking down superstition. On the other hand, they tried to control the encounter of Africans with the Western people and knowledge, as it would uproot Africans. Mission education was blamed not only for uprooting educated individuals but also delaying racial advancement.

The role of schools in the communities was also reconsidered. Dougall, a mission educationist and a frequent writer on the issue of religious education, stressed the need to strengthen the relationships of church, school and community, because 'it [was] only through schools that the African villages in their worship and work and play [could] be won for [Christianity]' (Dougall 1937: 208–9). The idea to enhance the linkage of church and school with the community developed in close relationship with the avoidance of 'denationalising' educated Africans and to 'adapt' education to the context of learners.

Both Sir John Rodger and Hugh Clifford, who preceded Frederick Gordon Guggisberg as governors of the Gold Coast, recognised the country's educational needs, and both, accordingly, appointed educational committees to make recommendations for the improvement of the educational system. In fact, although many scholars attribute the educational reform of Guggisberg to his own initiative, he drew on the outline of the plan sketched by his predecessors.

Not so much for the economic reason of preparing the workforce, but because of the political reason to halt the Africans' aspiration for white collar work and political representation, the government's education policy favoured vocational training over literary education throughout the period. Government officials expressed, publicly and privately, that Africans should be educated to follow the African tradition and take up agricultural and manual work available to them, instead of being 'denationalised' by acquiring western education. The suspicion of the educated elite on the part of the government was widespread. As the government increased its presence in the education sector, the number of schools increased. However, the curriculum, which was biased toward vocational and agricultural education, coupled with the moral education for African dignity, did not correspond to the economic realities of the colony. The workforce demanded in mines and farms, which were saturated anyway, did not require any formal education. Moreover, the curriculum 'adapted' to job prospects and traditional life was not what Africans wanted. Educational institutions functioned to transform the surrounding communities and made students aspire to depart from traditional society and manual labour, whether it was intended or not (Kimble 1963: 62).[6]

6-2-3 Struggle for political representation

The Gold Coast has been a slave to foreign powers for centuries. She has been buffeted, tossed about and ill treated. She has now realized the hardships and difficulties in slavery and has found by what means she will free himself [sic] from servitude. She has found out that her sons will never be made free citizens to enjoy freedom, if she lightly regards secondary education.

(J. Thompson, a nationalist leader, cited in Boahen 1996: 176)

We are flooding the market with semi-educated youths for whom, owing to their disdain of manual labour, there is annually less employment. The very fact that they are educated tends to separate them in thought and sympathy from their less advanced relations. ... Failing employment in an office, and strongly imbued with an unhealthy dislike to manual labour, they fall a natural victim to discontent and consequently to unhappiness.[7]

(Sir Gordon Guggisberg, Governor of the Gold Coast)

Educational institutions which were operated by missions created a new social group, the educated elite. By the end of the 19th century, those who had been educated in mission schools and had become professionals, such as lawyers and medical doctors, increased nationalist pressure on the government. They advocated for Africans' political representation, abolition of restriction on higher appointment in the government structure and higher education. Colonial officials were cautious about the advancement of nationalists and attempted to suppress them by raising the relative position of royalties of traditional institutions as parts of the indirect rule structure. Among Europeans, the dominant view was that the educated elite spoke for their own self-interests, claiming that they legitimately represented mass opinions, while losing contact with the native life.

Until the mid-19th century, the African elite were less excluded from higher appointment in the government. There was an African lawyer who was even promoted to lieutenant governor during the furlough of the governor, James Bannerman, between 1850 and 1851. However, during the latter half of the 19th century, the Bannermans, who all occupied higher posts, fell from favour, and some were even imprisoned on false charges (Agbodeka 1977: 15).

Conditions for senior appointment included a degree granted by a European institution; Africans without a degree were not eligible. In the medical department of the Gold Coast, higher appointment of Africans was restricted because 'there [were] no local candidates, who possess the qualifications indispensable for the posts' (Government of the Gold Coast 1921: 40). One of these qualifications was a medical degree from a European institution. At the same time, the colonists began to limit opportunities for Africans to get a foreign degree. For example, the Educationists' Committee appointed by Governor Guggisberg stated that providing scholarships for a few to acquire advanced degrees in Europe was not the priority of the government, which was instead developing education of equal quality to European institutions on the Gold Coast (Government of the Gold Coast 1920). Europeans symbolically referred to African doctors and lawyers as impertinent groups of people who were too Westernised and lost contact with traditional society, while a general disfavour of educated Africans was applied to a wider group of people, who had attained some degree of formal education.

The government's negative attitude resulted from two factors. First was the nationalistic pressure from educated Africans. In 1897, the Aborigines Right Protection Society was established by nationalist leaders such as J.E. Casely Hayford, Mensah Sarbah and E.J.P. Brown. The Society's aim was to prevent the Lands Bill from being legalised, for it intended to make all unused land government property, while these lands had traditionally belonged to chiefs. Nationalists consisted of important traders, lawyers and other professionals who assumed the role as spokesmen for the African public and argued that such government action was a serious interference in the customary land ownership system. The Society even sent a deputation to petition the Colonial Office in London to withdraw the Lands Bill; this petition was accepted (Edsman 1979; Holmes 1972; Kimble 1963.). After that, the Aborigines Right Protection Society acted as a strong pressure group on the government's policy making and administration. These same nationalist leaders together with intellectuals from Sierra Leone and Nigeria organised the National Congress of British West Africa in 1920. The purpose of the Congress was to '[bring] before the Government the wants and aspirations of the people so that they [might] be attended to as best they [might]'.[8] The presumption of these elite Africans to speak for the illiterate masses and the effort of developing African identity beyond the territorial boundaries was received with suspicion by the colonial government and sometimes also by traditional chiefs.

Another cause for the colonial administration's suppression of the educated elite was the principle of indirect rule. The Colonial Office in London promoted the principle of indirect rule, which had been tested by Lord Lugard in Northern Nigeria using the structure of Hausa kingdoms there. It achieved the British objective in the context of Northern Nigeria, which already had a pretty centralised Islamic structure and had a smaller Western-educated population to, in the eyes of Europeans, undermine the traditional authority. However, application of this principle to the Gold Coast was not a simple process. There was no corresponding central traditional authority on the Gold Coast. Each ethnic group had an independent political institution that functioned separately from other chieftaincies. Moreover, the educated elite on the Gold Coast, who acted independently of traditional institutions, obstructed the colonial government's attempt to govern through these institutions. At the early stages of missionary education, people hesitated to send their children to school. Therefore, educated ones were those who were seen as unimportant by the traditional authorities. Education created a class of people whose power originated from outside chieftaincy and who began to attack traditional governance as backward.

In essence, the government, the educated elite and the traditional chiefs all agreed on the desirability of establishing a representative legislative system. But the question was who the legitimate representatives of the masses were.

The government's preference for traditional chiefs over the educated elite was explicit. For example, a head of a department stated:

> I would rather see such a process of evolution whereby native institutions are consolidated as part of the administration and developed to meet the changing conditions of modern times than a scheme of substituting Native district Commissioners for European District Commissioners, a scheme which leads to compete with or oust the ... [traditional chieftaincy] system.[9]

Not only the government officials, but also traditional chiefs opposed the arguments of some of the educated elite who claimed that they legitimately represented the public. Nana Ofori Atta I, paramount chief of Akim Abakwa (in the present Eastern Region), for example, challenged their claim by arguing that the right of representation was not granted to those who gained their power merely from education. He claimed that traditional chiefs were the ones who truly represent public opinion because, unlike the educated elite, they discussed issues with their people before speaking in public (Kimble 1963: 394).

The opposition of some leading traditional chiefs to the educated elite was not groundless. The Aborigine Right Protection Society (ARPS), the stronghold of African nationalists, proposed that the government elect African members of the Legislative Council through the ARPS. On the other hand, the government was preparing the plan to establish the Provincial Council system under the national Legislative Council, which was basically composed of appointed traditional chiefs, not on election.[10] The argument of nationalist leaders against the governmental plan was that the Provincial Council would take away the people's power of election. When the ARPS made this appeal, the nationalist leaders did not talk in advance to the powerful chiefs like Ofori Atta, who were supporters of the Society's mission, and this made them angry.

At the same time, the government accused ARPS of having manipulated chiefs under their influence to shun the plan of the Provincial Council by providing them with false information. According to a record of a district commissioner's interview with some chiefs and sub-chiefs, those chiefs influenced by the ARPS levied money from sub-chiefs and villages, explaining that the money would be used to prevent the government from 'taking the people's cocoa land and also from its purported intention of taking every second child from its parents for military service or other work'. In the view of the District Commissioner who reported the case, the money was obviously used 'to oppose the Provincial Council of Chiefs and [to support] the Elective Legislative Council'.[11] Although it is difficult to decide whether this alleged act of the APRS was true or not, it is known from this case that the colonial officials were obsessed with the idea of educated Africans manipulating people against the government. Also one can tell that there was a constant fear amongst the African population that the government would extract land and people from them. Appeals to this fear had the potential to make the African people turn against the government.

Unlike the educated elite, traditional chiefs of the period were often illiterate. In the earlier generation, chiefs who were requested by missionaries to send children to schools did not trust them and sent children of the households whose positions in the hierarchy of traditional institutions were less important. Therefore, chiefs were the last people who were educated at mission schools. Chiefs like Nana Ofori Atta I, who could read, write and debate on the same ground as the educated elite, were exceptional. This fact partly explains the nationalist elite's argument that they played the key role in the creation of public opinion. Mensah Sarbah, a nationalist leader, explained the role of educated Africans as informing the masses and expressing the collective opinions on their behalf:

> For all practical purposes, definite public opinion about the acts of the Government and legislature emanates from the educated classes, and whenever the untaught masses study and examine political questions which directly affect them, such as the Lands Bill of 1897 … they gain a great deal of their knowledge and ideas from what their privileged educated brethren tell them. (Sarbah 1906: 239)

Meanwhile, although there were a few outspoken chiefs, it is also misleading to assume that they 'represented' the views of all the chiefs and the public. Since most of them were not educated at school, they did not collect information distributed in English or take part in the political debate in the public space. Therefore, whether they wore the cap of traditional chief or of educated elite, it was only those who acquired the language and modalities of debates with Europeans that had a chance to raise their voices in the discourse. The majority of Africans who did not have such means were 'represented' in one way or another with limited occasions to know the nature of debates. As much as African perspectives were neglected in the discourse in the metropole, colonial discourse also happened above the heads of the majority of Africans. In sum, although the controversy between the European and the African was severe in writing and speaking, it happened within a small circle of the coloniser and the colonised, who shared the terms of confrontation. In this sense, they mutually contributed to construct the colonial realities (Memmi 1965).

6-3 Political rivalry and accusation for 'denationalisation'

There was a term which was often used to accuse a group of or individual Africans for their lack of capacity for representation: 'denationalisation'. To demonstrate to his political opponents that someone was a legitimate representative of the public, a person had to prove he kept contact with 'the people' and honoured their values and social customs. While there was a lot of disagreement, participants of political discourse, both European and African, agreed on one point. They all thought the African people should maintain the sense of belonging to and respect for African traditional society and its institutions, while concurrently being 'modernised', or 'Europeanised', whatever it would have meant. Either to denounce political enemies or to justify themselves, political speakers argued about 'denationalisation' frequently. For example, Nana Ofori Atta I, a paramount chief, denied the representative rights of the educated elite because of their lack of sympathy for their less Westernised fellows and their disconnection from them:

> If the educated native is still going to look to his less-favoured brethren as a source of deriving wealth and revenue, rather than help them out of their difficulties in ... proper and sympathetic ways, if the educated native is going to be trained for him to look down on, or to tell his parents, relatives, or chiefs in that sort of the sarcastic language to which we have been accustomed 'you are not advanced and skilled as I am, you do not know the tricks of the civilized world, you do not deserve the leadership naturally conferred on you, etc.', and then, without any authority from the right source places himself in a position to which he has no claim, then I fear our path to civilization will have been badly made. If the educated native is not going to keep within the limit to which his birthright entitles him and if ... he constitute[s] himself, without the necessary mandate, a ruling or legislative body, it would be no wonder if our expensive educational schemes sustained a failure ... [12]

It was barely hidden in Ofori Atta's statement that he was specifically criticising Casely Hayford, Hutton Mills and other nationalists, who organised the Aborigines Right Protection Society and National Congress of British West Africa, and who advocated for themselves as political representatives. On the other hand, Casely Hayford himself was also busy criticising people who were foolishly mimicking Europeans by wearing 'elegantly cut-away black morning coat and beautifully-glazed cuffs and collar, not to speak of patent leather shoes, which he kept spotlessly bright by occasionally dusting them with his pocket handkerchief, tucked away in his shirt sleeves' (Casely Hayford 1968: 73). He claimed that the attempt 'to bring about a cleavage between the people and the Bar (lawyers)' was a mistake because 'their interests [were] identical. [And] in the native community the lawyers [were] supported'.

While nationalist leaders like Casely Hayford pressed strongly for the reform of the Legislative Council and demanded political and social reform along modern, Western lines, they were not necessarily non-traditionalist. To the contrary, these people were the first to write about traditional customs and political institutions. In 1903, Casely Hayford published *Gold Coast Native Institutions*. Mensah Sarbah wrote about the customary laws of a coastal ethnic group, the Fanti (Sarbah 1897 and 1906). Whereas Nana Ofori Atta I not only embodied the traditional authority but also strongly believed in the power of modernisation. Ofori Atta believed that by acquiring the technical and institutional merits of Europe, Gold Coast Africans could be self-sufficient and could defend traditional life (Rathbone 1993: 37–8.). During this period, then, it was difficult to draw a clear-cut distinction between the 'traditionalist' and the 'modernist'. This admixture of nationalistic sentiment and the desire for Westernisation were the undercurrent of the major political actors' controversial attitude about education.

Both for the coloniser and the colonised, the issue of education was fundamentally linked with various political issues. The criticism of mission education for producing 'denationalised' 'mission boys' was the reaction to the reality that the educated elite constituted the class of nationalists and became the threat to the stability of colonial rule. The intensifying confrontation of the African elite and the colonial government was also related to the economic and labour market conditions in which the employment opportunities for

Africans in the public sector had shrunk. On the political front, they were discussed as the issues of employment, political representation, land ownership or cultural dignity. However, the deep root of these debates was the fundamental issue of developing the African citizens with desirable personalities by means of education. What is desirable and how education can cultivate such personalities was another layer of issues. Still, people, either Africans or Europeans, looked for solutions to the problems and the prospects in education.

Notes

[1] Yates notices that 'Christian missions in the Congo (1879–1908) were not interested in training skilled artisans or agriculturists … [but its] vocational education concentrated upon the preparation of religious workers (Yates 1976: 193)'.

[2] Anthropology came to be closely enmeshed with colonialism. Anthropologists provided information about traditional institutions which the administration needed. Among anthropologists of Africa who provided the information for and rationalisation of colonial rule were A.R. Radcliffe-Brown, Bronislaw Malinowski and Lucy Mair (Hetherington 1978: 13).

The Royal Anthropological Institute sent letters to the then newly established Advisory Committee on Native Education in Tropical Africa, suggesting that the Institute should be officially represented on the Committee. One letter stated the value of having an anthropologist on the Committee was that he '[had] gained his knowledge of natives by actual field work in the continent concerned, for experience suggests that there are very considerable differences of outlook and of mental development between the various groups of black men'. C.G. Seligman, President of the Royal Anthropological Institute, to Ormsby-Gore, Chairman of the Advisory Committee, 13 May 1925, CBMS-IMC Box 223. See also the Institute to the Committee, 2 December 1926, CBMS-IMC Box 222.

[3] Boateng, a son of a Presbyterian priest, recalls that 'we lived in a section of the town known as the "mission"; in some towns the Christian area was known as "Salem". This area was populated by teachers from the school, the local Presbyters, catechists, and very elderly members of the Church' (1975: 81).

[4] Sanders, 'Report of the Sunday School Teachers Conference held in connection with Wesley College Re-union Courses, Sept 1928', WMMS West Africa Correspondence, Box 773 No 1456.

[5] See Holmes for the analysis of the development of cocoa farming and its relation to political movements on the Gold Coast (Holmes 1972).

[6] See Martin for similar observation in Nigeria in the same time period (1988: 76).

[7] 'The Post-War Gold Coast: A Review of the Events of 1923, with a Statement showing the Policy adopted by the Government for the Progress of the People and the Situation with regard to Trade and Finance', PRO, CO 98/44: Minutes of the Legislative Council 1925–6.

[8] Casely Hayford, inaugural address delivered during the British West African Conference held at Accra on 11 March 1920, cited in Sampson 1969: 62.

[9] Government, 'Report of Committee of Enquiry on the Native Civil Service', 40.

[10] Guggisberg's proposal for revision of the representative system, 4 March 1924, PRO, CO 96/645.

[11] Enclosure to Gold Coast Confidential of 10 Sept 1926, 'Collections of Money by Certain Chiefs who mislead their people by averring false reasons' from Winneba District Commissioner to Commissioner of the Central Province, PRO, CO 96/666/8.

[12] Letter to the Educationists' Committee dated 26 April 1920. Appendix to Sessional Paper I 1924-5 'Interim Report of the Educationists' Committee 1922 appointed by His Excellency the Governor, 23rd May, 1922', Accra, Gold Coast: Government Press, 1922, PRO, CO 98/ 41.

Chapter 7

Educational discourse and Guggisberg's administration

After overviewing the broad socio-political context, interests of major actors and their issues of debates, this chapter will narrow its focus on the educational administration and discourse in the Gold Coast Colony. As I discussed in the previous chapter, the issue of education was closely related to that of Africans' position in the colonial structure, in terms of their political representation and higher appointment, and sat at the crossroads of racism and cultural nationalism. While mission education was criticised, missionaries' presence as the school operators was an indispensable part of the systematisation of colonial education. Mission societies were also in need of governmental support for financing and administration of their schools. Therefore, the government–mission relationship in education was as significant an issue as civilizing mission and 'adaptation' of education to the African learners.

Since the educational discourse in the Gold Coast Colony parallels with that in the metropole regarding key concepts and logic, I will present my analysis in relation to the earlier discussion. While the processes in the metropole and the colony went in parallel, the demands for implementation and local politics caused some significant divergences. Therefore, instead of discussing the case of the Gold Coast Colony as a periphery which accepted the influence from the core, as assumed by the dependency theorists, I will present it as a more creative process to apply the global policy framework to their own needs.

Since I focus on the inter-war period in my analysis of global discourse, I will highlight the period of a visionary governor: Guggisberg. His period of governorship precisely overlaps with the positive post-war recovery period in Europe. This is when educational issues on the Gold Coast were watched with great interest in London and were debated and practised widely in the colony itself. Contrary to the widely accepted view that Guggisberg was the one who devised the educational scheme for the Gold Coast, what he did was to actualise the idea of his predecessor Clifford. As early as 1916, Clifford told his idea of a multi-denominational government secondary school privately.[1] He also appointed a committee to consider the establishment of a secondary school in 1918.[2] What Guggisberg had, which his predecessors lacked, was his strong personality and the economic prosperity of the colony. Kimble analyses, '[Guggisberg's era] was the age of paternal administration; much that was achieved through the Governor's personal initiative [which] might not have been politically acceptable a generation later, but he came at a time when the country needed exactly the kind of economic planning and leadership that he was able to give. It would be difficult to find a parallel among colonial Governors of any period for his combination of idealism, moral fervour, and shrewd practical foresight' (1963: 55).

7-1 Development of the colonial education system during the governorship of Guggisberg (1918–27)

Supported by abundant revenue and with the emerging need to control its colonial population, the government stepped forward to establish a thorough administrative system on the Gold Coast. During his governorship (1919–27), Guggisberg inaugurated innovative programmes in various public sectors to prepare the industrial and social bases for the Gold Coast to be economically self-sustaining. Supported by the abundant revenue from booming cocoa exports, Guggisberg inaugurated the construction of the first general hospital in Kohle Bu and of a deep-water harbour in Takoradi. Education was among the programmes which earned Guggisberg's greatest attention, for he regarded education as 'the first and foremost step in the progress of the races of the Gold Coast' (1927: 202). The government expenditure on education grew steadily, backed by the country's economic growth and the government's initiatives: it jumped up from 54,442 pound to 179,000 pound between 1919 and 1926. In addition to that, during the same time period, the government had spent 395,000 pound on the construction of new schools (ibid: 200), most of which was spent on the Prince of Wales College and School at Achimota. From the beginning of the century to 1926, the number of government-run schools and government-assisted primary schools nearly tripled, from 135 schools to 340.[3] The proportion of government and assisted schools in the total number of schools also steadily increased (135 out of 255 schools in total in 1901, 213 out of 463 in 1919 and 234 out of 534 in 1926)(Guggisberg 1927: 198). Expenditure on the grant-in-aid for assisted schools had been a large continuous part of the governmental expenditure on education. In 1901, it amounted to 57 per cent (3,706 pound) of total expenditure (6,543 pound). In 1919, it grew to 6,157 pound (11 per cent) out of total 54,442 pound, and then 30,887 pound (17 per cent) of 179,000 pound in 1926. The reduced proportion of grant-in-aid in the total expenditure between 1901 and 1919 did not mean the decrease in the actual amount of money spent on grant-in-aid, but indicated the overall increase of the allocation to education. The expenditure on education was nearly30 times more in 1926 than at the beginning of the century (See Table 6-1).

In order to articulate a comprehensive education policy, Guggisberg created the Board of Education in 1920. The Gold Coast Education Board was headed by the Governor and attended by the Director of Education, by representatives from missionary societies (Wesleyan Methodist, Scottish Presbyterian, Roman Catholic and Anglican), by traditional chiefs and by African professionals. The formation of an education board in each colony was among the instructions of the Advisory Committee on Native Education in Tropical Africa of London, and it was meant to adapt the standard educational policy devised by the Advisory Committee on Native Education in Africa (ACNETA) to local contexts. The renowned Guggisberg's Sixteen Principles, announced in 1925, were drafted by the Gold Coast Education Board and parallels the general framework of the ACNETA. At the same time, it was more than a mere copy of the ACNETA's guideline. These Principles were expressed in the words of Guggisberg, who was truly convinced of the value of his own educational ideas. They provide a handy list of the issues that European educationalists and administrators were concerned about and attempted to address in their educational practice. *The 1925*

Education Ordinance passed by the legislative council included these Principles as the basic rule and philosophy of educational administration. They read as follows:

- *First Principle* – Primary Education must be thorough and be from the bottom to the top.
- *Second Principle* – The provision of Secondary Schools with an educational standard that will fit young men and women to enter a university.
- *Third Principle* – The provision of a university.
- *Fourth Principle* – Equal opportunities to those given to boys should be provided for the education of girls.
- *Fifth Principle* – Co-education is desirable during certain stages of education.
- *Sixth Principle* – The staff of teachers must be of the highest possible quality.
- *Seventh Principle* – Character-training must take an important place in education.
- *Eighth Principle* – Religious teaching should form part of education.
- *Ninth Principle* – Organized games should form part of school life.
- *Tenth Principle* – The course in every school should include special reference to the health, welfare, and industries of the locality.
- *Eleventh Principle* – A sufficient staff of efficient African Inspectors of Schools must be trained and maintained.
- *Twelfth Principle* – Whilst an English education must be given, it must be based solidly on the vernacular.
- *Thirteenth Principle* – Education cannot be compulsory nor free.
- *Fourteenth Principle* – There should be co-operation between the Government and the Missions; and the latter should be subsidized for educational purposes.
- *Fifteenth Principle* – The Government must have the ultimate control of education throughout the Gold Coast.
- *Sixteenth Principle* – The provision of Trade Schools with a technical and literary education that will fit young men to become skilled craftsmen and useful citizens.

(Guggisberg 1927: 204–25)

First of all, the Ordinance was the official announcement that the government would have a firm grip on educational administration (Fifteenth Principle), while co-operating with the missions who had been the main providers of education (Fourteenth Principle). The Ordinance authorised the government to inspect all schools and to register teachers, so that it could weed out unqualified teachers and substandard schools (Sixth and Eleventh Principles). In terms of the provision of educational opportunities, Guggisberg was ambitious enough to state that all levels of education should be provided: namely, primary (First Principle), secondary (Second Principle), tertiary (Third Principle) and technical secondary (Sixteenth Principle), though he knew that it was not feasible to make education compulsory and free (Thirteenth Principle). The other Principles were about educational practice rather than administration. As I discussed in Part II, two major concerns of people involved in the global educational discourse were 'adaptation' and 'character training'. That orientation was maintained by Guggisberg in this colony. Instead of following the same syllabus as European schools, Europeans believed that the education in African schools should be adapted to its environment, social background, culture and the needs of students. 'Special references to the health, welfare and industries of the locality' (Tenth Principle) and use and teaching of vernacular at school (Twelfth Principle) were the approaches of adaptation which had already been widely appreciated in the international arena and were still being experimented with in different parts of Africa. Girls' education was another topic of trend (Third and Fourth Principle). Another distinctive feature of British colonial education, 'character training', was highlighted, of course (Seventh Principle). As I demonstrated earlier, 'religious teaching' (Eighth Principle) and 'Organized games (sports)' (Ninth Principle) were viewed as tools for character training and were integral parts of colonial education.

By comparing the principles presented in the *Memorandum* by the ACNETA and Guggisberg's Sixteen Principles, there is no doubt that he followed the basic framework of British colonial education. However, one can see a clear departure from Guggisberg's Sixteen Principles in the British framework. The Gold Coast administration placed more emphasis on non-vocational and leadership education, while the ACNETA's aims were to systematise educational administration to provide vocational and technical education especially for the masses. This difference in the emphasis along the continuum of vocational–liberal education was largely caused by the unique political context of the Gold Coast. Unlike in East and Southern Africa, where the conflict between white settlers and African masses was severe, there were limited numbers of Europeans in West Africa. Because of the severity of living conditions and the risk of diseases, permanent migration of Europeans did not progress much. The majority of white residents in West Africa were either missionaries or colonial officials. To supplement the shortage of manpower to maintain the European offices and posts, the relative positions of the educated Africans were elevated. Therefore, despite the African confrontation and the arguments to break the 'denationalising' effect of education, colonial governments in West Africa were more tolerant of the demands for higher and literary education from Africans. They were also in need of educated leaders to mediate between Africans and Europeans.

7-2 Mission societies' dilemma

Before the government stepped into the field of education, missions were the major operators of schools in the Gold Coast. However, the change of environment in the early 20th century put them under pressure from various sources concerning school operation. The first source of pressure was from the government. An increased government presence in the field of education forced the missionaries to find ways to cooperate with the government and, to a large extent, comply with various regulations. For want of financial assistance, mission education was gradually dragged into vocational education, which was preferred by the government. At the same time, missions faced the strong demand of the Africans for increased access to literary education. Missionaries were placed in a dilemma between meeting the demands of Africans and cooperating with the government. With the meagre financial support from the home offices and the demands of their evangelising mission, they were vulnerable to pressures from both Africans and the colonial government.

7-2-1 Government–mission relationship: forces for alignment

When the government proceeded to seize control of education in the early 20th century, these missions faced the challenge of deciding to what extent they had to modify their educational practice to comply with government policy and to what extent they could maintain their own practices. When the Educational Ordinance of 1925 was enacted, all the schools, whether financially assisted by the government or not, became under the supervision of the government. All the teachers were to be registered and, to do so, teachers needed to comply with certain qualifications. Whether a school was to be added to the list of government's grant assistance was determined by the reports of inspectors who visited schools regularly.[4] Therefore, inspectors' comments on the general curriculum and on the specifics of school activities had a strong influence on a school's destiny.

Vocational education

Increasing control by the government affected mission schools in roughly two ways. One was to force the school curriculum in the government's favoured direction. As was the case with other British colonies, the Gold Coast government preferred a type of education oriented towards vocational skills training. The government's grants-in-aid for schools were not evenly distributed among different missions. Mission societies that were known for vocational education, such as the Basel and Bremen Missions, tended to receive more grants than other missions. Coupled with denominational rivalry, the government's grant-in-aid policy and its very particular awarding criteria often became a cause of discontent.

While the government took initiatives in secondary education and some model vocational schools, primary education was considered to be the responsibility of mission societies. At the same time, the government's preference for practical and vocational education surfaced in various educational funding programmes. For example, the King Edward VII Memorial Scholarship changed its scheme to limit its assistance to students studying 'the industrial arts and crafts'.[5] Alerted by the narrowing of educational opportunities, Casely Hayford, a leading African nationalist, stated that 'the Scholarships Scheme should be made ... general so as to include: Junior Scholarships and Intermediate Scholarships; Industrial Scholarships, and University Scholarships'.[6] Vocationally oriented Basel and Bremen Mission schools benefited more from government grants than any other missions. In 1911, out of 199 pound 10 shilling 6 pence grant-in-aid for industrial and agricultural work, three-quarters went to two German Presbyterian missions (Basel: 59 pounds 19 shilling 6 pence; Bremen: 87 pound 2 shilling 0 pence). Basel mission received five out of seven prizes for the best school plantations. According to the Report of the Education Department, 'the [carpentry] work in ... the Basel Mission Schools [was] far in advance of that done at the other schools where [the same] subject [was taught]'.[7] Rev. R.A. Lockhart, the headmaster of Mfantsipim (Wesleyan) School harshly criticised the government for withholding funding based on its preference for vocational and lower-level of education:

> Our Government grant will be doubled IF MFANTSIPIM BECOMES AN ELEMENTARY SCHOOL. It is not easy to believe that [the] Government intends to treat us like this, for such a policy is an invitation to leave the secondary school field of labor. ... If the intention of Government is to discourage the flooding of the country with youths unable to get a job, and therefore likely to become the disaffected element in the community, we submit that the danger lies in the elementary school rather than in Mfantsipim. Our boys are mostly in good employment. ... Turn to the elementary schools and you find a breeding ground of disaffection. Hundreds of boys receive a seventh standard certificate – for which certificate there is little justification in modern educational practice – and having what they regard as a passport to the world of the intelligentsia they become in very many cases the unemployed candidates for the black coated professions. Here lies the real danger of disaffection – a danger which is within the power of government to remove. ... To force a school

like ours on to a lower level of efficiency is not going to avoid disaffection.[8] (Capital letters are original)

While all missions, desperate for funds, worked to meet increasing government demands, they complained of government inspectors' interference, of government requirements that demanded professionally trained teachers and of the government's emphasis on vocational over religious values. Even so, they accepted the governmental control and regulation as legitimate.[9] Missionaries used various channels for their voices to be heard by the educational administration. For example, they coordinated pressure from missions through home offices and through official channels in the colony, such as the Board of Education and the Legislative Council. However, there was a tacit understanding that the confrontation was within the existing structure, not to overthrow the framework itself. It is because, largely to protect the mission interests on the ground, their home offices took part in the development of the general framework of colonial education and managed to include the 'government–mission partnership' as one of the key principles.

Religious education

Another cause of headache for missionaries on the ground was the government's control over religious education at school. The British government at home and in colonies welcomed religious education so far as its content was not narrowly denominational. *The Memorandum on Education Policy in British Tropical Africa,* issued in March 1925 in London, 'recognized in a very explicit way the importance of religion in the education of the African people'.[10] However, this acknowledgement of the value of religious education did not mean that missions were given free rein. Rule 25 of the Gold Coast Education Ordinance of 1925, which laid down the subjects of instruction for primary schools, did not specify religious instruction as a compulsory subject. Although the introduction to a booklet *The schedules for managers and teachers* stated that religion was essential in education, no indication of suitable schemes was given in the schedules.[11] In fact, the curricular requirement of the government for assisted schools were too tight for missions to set aside as much time for religious instruction as they wanted. Therefore, it was always a matter of concern for missionaries whether religion was given 'due recognition' in government-run and government-assisted schools. Although the government appreciated religious education in general as a means of moral uplift of Africans, missions were to give up denominational contents if they received the government grants, which often contradicted the missions' principal goal of education: evangelisation. The statement of Rev. Oettli, the Basel Mission Inspector, shows this dilemma felt by missions:

> The Government grant grew larger and larger ... but against this we must set the subtle difficulties which arose from this time and which had never been felt before. The Mission had to fight to keep up the missionary character of their schools and this fight grew more and more serious with the growing demands of the Government.[12]

On one hand, there were people who believed that Bible lessons were the essential part of religious education. According to Price, an educational missionary, a firm knowledge of the Bible would provide a basis of judging the difference between doctrines and would teach students to appreciate the denomination to which he/she belonged (1938: 235–8). Meanwhile, the majority of missionaries and government officials were of the opinion that religious education was important as a way of developing character in students, but the knowledge of the Bible of itself was of secondary importance. For the sake of character training, the majority of Europeans considered classroom instruction as merely one of various forms of religious education. It was a typical way of considering the moral effect of education in experientialist term, which was prevalent in the early 20th century (see Chapter Five). They imagined school as a whole to be a miniature Christian community, in which students learn the Christian way of living through various school activities and interactions with teachers. The atmosphere of a school was more important than instruction in Bible knowledge as a subject. The line of argument of this latter view was widely shared by both mission societies and the government (for example, Lugard 1933: 5; Oldham & Gibson 1931: 31). However, the question of whether or not schools provided a sufficiently Christian environment always provoked debates.

Denominational rivalry and increasing control by the government

Denominational rivalry was heated in Africa even more than in Europe. T.A. Beetham, a Wesleyan educational missionary, who taught and later became principal of Wesley College, Kumasi, Gold Coast, reported that he was surprised by the *Asantehene* (paramount chief of the Ashanti) when he said his own sons left in England went to a non-Wesleyan school. Given the situation in his territory, it was unimaginable for the *Asantehene* that the British did not have schools for each denomination within an accessible distance.[13]

The 'conscience clause' (section 25) of the 1870 Elementary Education Act in Britain was applied to schools in Africa too, which said that 'religious instruction might be given in State-aided schools, with the assurance that parents have a choice whether or not to let their children receive religious instruction'. Missions argued that so far as there were followers of their denomination, even if there were schools nearby operated by other missions, they needed to establish a school 'to meet parents' demand.[14] According to the school inspectors' reports, denominational rivalry caused the dramatic increase in the number of schools, which coincided with local pressure for more educational opportunities. The competition resulted in the lowering of teaching quality and the opening of schools too close to each other from the viewpoint of geographic distribution of educational access.

The government was concerned with the quality of education. One of the aims of the Education Ordinance of 1925 was to control the quality of schools by inspection and teacher registry. When a school could not fulfil the requirements of grant-in-aid, mission societies had to bear the cost and the salaries of teachers. Moreover, even the teachers of non-assisted schools had to have a certain level of qualification and be registered, although the qualification standard was lower than that for assisted school teachers. Within two years from the Ordinance's coming into effect, 136 schools had to be closed down 'voluntarily' by missions themselves, largely because of the inability to fulfil the quality requirement of the government and, at the same time, short of their own funds to continue operation.[15]

7-3 African demands for more and better education

7-3-1 Demands from the general public

Missions faced not only the necessity of negotiating with the government for control over internal affairs of schools, but they were also sensitive to African opinions. Such sensitivity of missionaries to African pressures placed them in a vulnerable position. Even though there was general agreement between the government and mission societies about government control in exchange for the grant-in-aid, that could not stop the public demand for education. During the few years after the introduction of the Education Ordinance of 1925, African representatives raised the same question repeatedly in the Legislative Council: how did the government think to meet its responsibility to satisfy the educational demand while closing down schools?[16] Newspapers covered this topic in almost every other issue.[17] The government kept responding that the bill was 'unanimously' approved by the Council members, including Africans. However, the cry for education seemed not to calm down until the government provided some remedy. A sub-committee was appointed from the Education Board to consider the problems caused by the closing down of schools in 1928. The sub-committee's analysis about the cause of the problem was the shortage of qualified teachers, and it proposed to set lower standards for 'rural' schools' teachers and to establish pre-service crash training courses for rural teachers.[18] This proposal of dual standards for teachers invited another big debate.

Some people asked if there was any difference in the educational needs of rural and of urban communities. As 'rural bias' of primary education practically meant increased vocational instruction sacrificing the time for academic subjects, many Africans opposed this idea.[19] In any case, the tug between government control and Africans' demand for educational access continued throughout the period this book is concerned about. Since this debate involved the issue of money granted to school operators, missions were tossed about from here to there.

Those who were educated at mission schools at first were from lower social classes. However, as people came to see the pragmatic value of education from the example of the earlier generation, the demand for education spread like a fire fanned by wind. By the mid-1920s, chiefs came to want schools in their villages and towns, because otherwise they could not keep young people who would work and pay taxes to them.[20] Chiefs considered having a school to be a sign of prestige: 'A village chief who [could] boast of a school [felt] that he [was] of a much higher standing than the one who had no school. ... The higher the educational opportunity, the higher the social prestige.' (Amissah 1947).

For most of the Africans, religion was not the main reason for attending mission schools. Their spiritual needs were well provided for through traditional belief systems and they did not feel much contradiction to let practices of Christianity and traditional belief co-exist.[21] What they appreciated were, in addition to the economic incentive of education, the external symbols such as European clothes, books including the Bible and a 'civilized' manner that came with this education (Berman 1975c: xi-xv; Mackenzie 1993: 55; Yates 1971: 165). Any suggestion that the educational system should be specially tailored for colonial subjects with the exclusion of contents that were considered irrelevant was fiercely resented. The Africans' enthusiasm to learn classics, Latin and Greek, was remarkable. Robert Cole recalls his school life in colonial Sierra Leone in his autobiographic novel:

> I liked Greek even before I had started it, just as I had liked the idea of studying Latin. ... To my mind the knowledge of Greek is the crowning mark of a liberal education. (Cole 1960: 168)

According to an old professor who graduated from Mfantsipim School in 1948, as a student, whether he could join the class of Latin was a matter of grave importance:

> In my time, if you [were] not selected for Latin, you felt you had failed in life, almost. ... [T]he only group in my class who felt as if they [didn't] quite belong were those who didn't do Latin. If [students] were

not good [at academic work], they were put in a particular class where they were saved from doing Latin. (Interview in July 2002)

Missionaries knew the fact that Africans were largely attracted by the European air which schools provided them with, and not necessarily by religion. However, it was not among their options to stop operating schools. If they did so, they thought that Africans would develop an impression that 'Christianity [was] an affair of the uneducated peasant and [had] no message for the modern man'.[22] Therefore, given their primary goal of evangelisation, the last thing missionaries could do was to cut the link between Christianity and education in the African imagination. Africans constantly protested any action to halt their educational aspirations. This strong desire even often influenced the government's educational policy making. And mission societies not only refrained from withdrawing educational work, but also occasionally established elite institutions like Mfantsipim or Adisadel in the hope of gaining more converts and in response to anxiety over the support of influential Africans.

7-3-2 Nationalists' demands for higher education

The higher a man's education the more he becomes imbued with race pride, and the less will be the tendency to break away from immemorial customs.

(E.J.P. Brown)[23]

The higher a man is educated the higher he is able to think and reason; it also promotes the growth of the moral sense ...; and nothing gives the mind clearness and distinctness of thought [more] than a high education ...

(E. Mate-Kole)[24]

The above quotes, one from an African lawyer (Brown) and another from a paramount chief (Mate-Kole) demonstrate how deeply they desired higher education for Africans. For African intellectuals, advanced education seemed the medicine for all wounds. It would enhance not only intellectual capacity but also national pride, morality and access to higher employment. This desire for education was shared among both African professionals and traditional chiefs. Nana Ofori Atta I, paramount chief of Akim Abakwa, was very keen on his children's education. Virtually all of his more than one hundred children were enrolled at a local Presbyterian primary school, and the well-performing ones were sent to secondary schools and sometimes even to England to continue their education (Rathbone 1993: 47). Africans, either nationalists or traditional chiefs, desired more and better education. However, when it came to the building of consensus, there were political rivalries that restricted them from working hand in hand. While most of the politically active people of the time expressed their opinions about education in one way or another, the most vocal ideologists were Edward Blyden and Casely Hayford.

Blyden, born in the West Indies but 'a pure African Negro', was a leading figure in the educational scene in West Africa from the mid-19th century until his death in 1912. He taught and later became principal of Liberia College, a well-known grammar school. He published his opinion frequently in the newspapers and he had personal connections with influential colonial administrators who had power over educational policy making (Livingston 1975). Blyden was a strong promoter of the idea of a West African university. He was of the opinion that Africans deserved a degree-granting university affiliated with a British university, and he believed that it was the government's responsibility to provide such an institution. According to Blyden, 'an African institution of higher learning should provide for the full and free development of the African race'.[25] He called for an African-controlled institution with special emphasis on African values and ancient history, and he questioned the teaching of a Western curriculum without adaptation. While rejecting modern European subjects, he recommended the curriculum retain the study of the classics, Greek and Latin languages and literature. For him, the degradation and proscription of the black had taken form during the period of modern European civilization. Therefore, learning modern European subjects would mean swallowing racial preconceptions developed by Europeans. Interestingly, none of the African speakers during the period rejected learning 'the Classics', which, from the eyes of a later-generation researcher, seems equally European and foreign to African tradition. Blyden also promoted students' wearing of African clothes and eating of African food in order to erase notions of Europeanism as compatible with Christianity which had been imprinted in African minds. Although Blyden himself did not give up his strictly European lifestyle, and although he was not himself free from the European value system prevalent during the period, he was the first to have presented the idea of an African higher education for African leadership.

The person who took over Blyden's ideal of a West African university was Casely Hayford. He stepped far ahead of Blyden in terms of Africanisation of the university in his imagination. He placed special emphasis on the learning of local languages, on using the vernacular as the medium of instruction and on learning local history. At variance with Blyden, Hayford kept completely silent about the place of Western learning in the West African university (Ashby 1966: 177–80). Another difference between Casely Hayford and Blyden was the former's vocal rejection of the industrial training that was widely promoted by Europeans as an appropriate form of education for Africans. Probably due to his scarcity of allies and the bleak prospect of successfully confronting the colonial government, Blyden allowed his scheme to maintain the industrial features to gain official support. In fact, as I have demonstrated in Chapter Four, he visited the Hampton Institute known for black industrial education and praised it as a 'noble' effort of the black's self-help (1903: 372). Casely Hayford, on the other hand, was a politician for whom education was an important but ancillary part of his more general appeal for African political rights and cultural nationalism. For him, emphasising the fact that Africans had a tradition to build upon to develop African leadership was as important as establishing a West African university itself. Industrial training, which was often referred to as *the* adaptation of a European curriculum to an African environment was, for Casely Hayford, a totally different thing from Africanised education under the leadership of Africans with pride in their traditional culture. To Africanise schools, he considered that Africans had to control the curriculum and the administration. Africans had to decide what was important for their youth to learn, which was totally different from accepting a 'peculiar kind of education' designed by Europeans to be appropriate for Africans.[26]

As discussed in Chapter Three, African nationalists admired and followed the news of black activism. The key African nationalist leaders including Kwame Nkrumah of the Gold Coast took part in the Pan-Africanism Conference which was launched in 1919 by W.E.B. Du Bois, an American black promoter of enfranchisement and liberal education. While it is difficult to determine how far or how directly African intellectuals were influenced by these American black race ideologies, this transcontinental solidarity was an important source of inspiration for them. As the colonial government carefully screened the information from America, colonial subjects did not have 'official' access to any black activism, except for that promoting industrial education. Even so, in 1920, Governor Guggisberg requested the permission of the Colonial Office to ban the importation of 'violently "aggressive", "intensely racial" and "dangerous" 'American magazines to the Gold Coast, because of 'the pernicious influence such [magazines] exert on the mind of the impressionable "educated" West African'.[27] The request was denied in consideration of people's right to access information. However, the fact that the government attempted to control the circulation of ideas indicates that African intellectuals actually had such vexing.

7-4 Secondary schools as the sites for producing African leaders

7-4-1 Prince of Wales College and School at Achimota

The Prince of Wales College and the School at Achimota were established in 1927 by the Gold Coast colonial government. At the time of its establishment, the School had branches of kindergarten, primary to secondary school and a teacher training college. It also granted degrees in engineering, which served only a handful of students. The original plan of the government, which had been fostered from the time of Governor Clifford, was to establish a secondary school which would be the stepping stone for a degree-granting university. It owed not a small part to the demand of African intellectuals for a West African university. When Governor Guggisberg came in 1919, he publicised the plan widely. Then, A.G.

Fraser was selected as the first principal in 1924, and he altered the plan in a drastic way. He imagined that a really satisfactory system of secondary education could only be established on the basis of a system of primary education much in advance of anything then in existence on the Gold Coast. Therefore, he pushed his idea that Achimota should include a model primary and kindergarten to provide a nucleus of well-trained children to feed the secondary school of Achimota (Fraser 1925).

The core founders of the School, Governor Guggisberg of the Gold Coast, A.G. Fraser, the first principal and James Aggrey, assistant vice principal and sole African member of the teaching staff, meant it to be the model school at which education was adapted to the needs and background of African students while providing the highest level of education 'such as the wisest parents in Europe would feel to be satisfactory for the education of their own children'.[28] It was an experimental site of finding the ideal mixture of things African and European with the purpose of developing leaders who were not uprooted from their African society but who acquired European intellect and sophistication. For the founders, Achimota was the site to realise all their educational ideals. To achieve the ideal of 'adaptation', it provided a wide variety of courses including handwork, agriculture and vernacular languages. It also emphasised extra-curricular activities such as sports, tribal drumming, play acting, singing (African and European songs) and social service. Achimota intended to provide an all-round education, not just academic, so as to develop in students balanced characteristics that were suitable for leaders.

On the day of Achimota Inauguration (1927)
Governor Guggisberg, sitting in the front centre, was sided by A.G. Fraser, first principal, to the left. The third from the left in the front row was James Aggrey.

As for the facilities, in addition to classrooms and dormitories, it had a pumped water system, a swimming pool, a hospital, a farm and a model village. It even intended to serve the surrounding communities with medical dispensaries, distribution of innovative agricultural techniques and comprehensive community support at the model village. The initial estimate of annual cost was 48,806 pound, and the cost of the building was to be 258,000 pound. At this point already, the estimated cost summed up to be a half of the government's educational budget. As it turned out, the building cost grew to more than 600,000 pound, leaving some construction unfinished. The original idea was to make Achimota financially independent except for an annual governmental subsidy of 48,806 pound. However, at the time of the School's opening, the amount of subsidy was raised to 68,000 pound, which still could cover only one-seventh of the total cost.[29] Obviously, Achimota was financially unstable.

Despite that Achimota started with sections other than the secondary school, in this book, I will focus on the secondary school. The reason for this focus is that, as I explained in Chapter One, other sections were short-lived and were additional to the original purpose of this model school.

7-4-2 Other secondary schools (Mfantsipim and Adisadel)

Two secondary schools preceded the Achimota School on the Gold Coast, Mfantsipim and the Adisadel. The Wesleyan High School, established in 1876 in Cape Coast, was the origin of Mfantsipim School. The Adisadel College was started in 1910, also in Cape Coast, by the Anglican Mission. Both are boys' schools until today, while Achimota was co-educational. Also, these schools provided highly academic education exactly following the European curriculum. Subjects they taught included Scripture, History, English History, Arithmetic, Algebra, Geography, English Grammar, Physics, Chemistry, Greek and Latin (Boahen 1996: 31). They have enjoyed the reputation for a good number of their students passing the Cambridge Certificate Examination and proceeding to higher education in Europe. The purpose of missions' operation of secondary schools was to train African ministers to serve respective churches as transmitters of the Christian message to the African masses, and to inform the church about African customs and belief. To attract Africans' support for the church was a primary motivation for operating schools. For this very sake, education of mission secondary schools placed heavy weight on academic education, which Africans at the time strongly demanded. While Achimota, the government secondary school, made much of agriculture and manual work as a part of its all-round education, such activities were nil in Mfantsipim and Adisadel.

In the following chapters, I will use Mfantsipim as a contrast to Achimota. The reason for the reference is not so much because Mfantsipim was a mission school as because it was the stronghold of African nationalists. African nationalists who actively participated in educational discourse, such as Casely Hayford, Mensah Sarbah and E.J.P. Brown, were listed as members of the Mfantsipim School Committee, the steering body of the school. In the case of Casely Hayford, he was also on the Achimota Committee. The contrast between the Mfantsipim School and the Achimota School is a contrast between the official statements of nationalists and their educational practice, or between what the British officials wanted and what the nationalists wanted in terms of education.

Mfantsipim School was the pioneer of academic secondary education on the Gold Coast. However, the serious shortage of funds and lack of support from the home committee forced the Wesleyans to shrink the scale of its education. By 1910, the school was nearly dying off. What revived the school was the European missionaries' rivalry with the Anglican and African nationalists' zeal for higher education. The establishment of Adisadel College (then called S.P.G. Grammar School) by the Anglicans in 1910 boosted the engagement of the Wesleyan home committee and the Gold Coast District office out of the fear of losing the support of Africans to the Wesleyan High School and, by extension, to the Wesleyan church. In the meantime, African members of the Wesleyan Synod proposed to support the school financially. Since the Wesleyan mission had the longest presence among the missions in the coastal area, and since they maintained a policy of delegating authority to African members of the church, by the beginning of the 20th century, the Wesleyan Synod had a camp of educated Africans at the centre of its decision making. Mensah Sarbah, the President of the Aborigines Right Protection Society (see Chapter Six), was the central force which stimulated the synod and African nationalists to revitalise Mfantsipim. In 1909, Mensah Sarbah prepared the site to construct a new school building and proposed a loan of 200 pound for construction. In addition, the school alumni and nationalists formed local committees to collect voluntary donations. Because of its rehabilitation process, the school after 1910 came to reflect the zeal and educational view of nationalist leaders. What they wanted was, similar to the Achimota founders, better and more education for leaders who maintained pride in their African heritage. The difference was that nationalists sought to have control over the school administration and a higher academic education no different from that of European schools, while Achimota was a European attempt to adapt the European curriculum to African soil.

In 1934, Mfantsipim School had 206 students, whereas Adisadel had 183.[30] Together with Achimota and the Accra Technical School, the number of secondary enrolment in the 1930s was only a little more than five hundred (see Table 6-1). On the other hand, according to census data in 1931, the total population of the Gold Coast Colony, Ashanti and the Northern Territory totalled 3,160,000, 39.7 per cent of which, roughly 1.25 million people, was under fifteen years of age (Kay 1972: 310–11). Against the total under-fifteen population, five hundred secondary students constituted a very small group. In this sense, discussion about secondary education on the Gold Coast of this period, either at Achimota or Mfantsipim, was that of education for the selected few who were meant to be leaders, not for the masses.

7-5 Ambivalence among actors

As was made clear in the *Memorandum* agreed in the ACNETA in London and Sixteen Principles on the Gold Coast, there was basic consensus that mission societies and the government work in partnership. Mission societies relied on the government for grants to maintain their schools and mission posts, while the government needed mission societies as the school operators to maintain its education system. Despite this mutual dependence, the standard applied for schools to qualify for the grant-in-aid restricted missions from maintaining religious education. Not only were religious subjects to be provided outside of the core curricular time, denominational contents were banned. The government inspections and the criteria for assessing the quality of education effected by mission-run schools were to conform with the line of education preferred by the government, which was vocational education.

Even with these difficulties and restrictions, missions did not have a choice but to continue operating schools. Unlike earlier periods when the general public was suspicious of mission schools, by this period, there was strong and constant pressure from the public to establish more and better schools. Missions were even concerned about losing followers to other denominations because of the failure to meet such expectations of education. Missions were in limbo between the governmental requirement to increase the vocational content of education and the public demands for higher and literary education.

Not only the general public, but the educated elite were pressing strongly on the government for higher education. Independent of the nationalist plea for higher education, the Gold Coast government had been preparing a scheme for a government-run secondary school and a higher education institution since the governorship of Sir Hugh Clifford (1912–19). Governor Guggisberg, Clifford's successor, announced his scheme of a secondary school and teacher training college at Achimota in 1924, which was welcomed by African intellectuals, the nationalist elite and traditional chiefs. Achimota, in its original plan, was assigned the role of preparing the road to higher education, which was clearly stated in governmental documents and was agreed to by the Colonial Office in London.[31] The nationalist leaders assumed that the Achimota scheme was a sign that the colonial government accepted their proposal of a West African university. Casely Hayford stated at the third session of the National Congress of British West Africa:

> It is satisfactory to note that almost all the recommendations have met with the serious and favourable consideration of almost all the Governments of British West Africa, and nowhere more pronouncedly than in the Gold Coast where some £500,000 is earmarked for educational purposes in carrying out the magnificent programme of the Prince of Wales' College, Achimota. (Sampson 1969: 81.)

It was a bold assumption, however, considering the colonial administration's suspicion and caution against educated Africans. Hostility to the nationalist group was uncompromising in the Guggisberg administration and the plea of the National Congress of British West Africa for a West African university met with scant support in official circles (Kimble 1963: 181).

The educational discourse was thus complicated by political rivalry. Even the issue upon which political rivals seem to have agreed was contradicted frequently because of the fact that it was promoted by a group's political opponents. Without considering this political climate, one cannot understand the inconsistency of people like Casely Hayford and J.E.P. Brown, who were, on the one hand, members of the Achimota Council and praised Achimota School's

Africanised curriculum and, on the other hand, who were involved in the re-formation of the Mfantsipim School, whose curriculum was least adapted to the local environment. And contrary to the nationalists' avowed pride in things traditional, the attention paid at Mfantsipim to the teaching of African culture, history and language was minimal. Mfantsipim's education indicates the ambivalence of nationalists' attitude towards African tradition and European culture. The intellectuals propounded equilibrium between the pragmatic demand for Westernisation and cultural nationalism. According to Tony Martin, to gain privilege in traditional society, the African intellectuals 'had to boost their past institutions without ... introducing their study into schools to affect academic programs which constituted yet another instrument for restoring their privileges in Afro-European society'.[32]

As Martin rightly pointed out, promotion of African traditional values was a tactic for African intellectuals to position themselves in between the African masses and Europeans. Naturally, in their political debates and personal lives, the boundary between tradition and Western values was constantly redrawn to fulfil different requirements. For example, Adelaide Casely Hayford, wife of J.E. Casely Hayford, was the pioneer of female education in West Africa. She was born into a family of very high class and detested life in Africa. As much as her husband did, she promoted African pride and a return to the traditional values. Still, she spent most of her life in Britain. The girls school she established in West Africa was for African girls to develop exactly the same high class values as their British bourgeois counterparts and she herself was called African Victorian feminist (Cromwell 1986). It indicates that promoting African culture and being married to a nationalist could comfortably co-exist with behaving like a Victorian bourgeois lady.

The ambiguous line between the traditional and European values not only allowed room for manipulation but also provided the common ground for political actors with seemingly opposing positions. Although there was distrust between Africans and Europeans, it is a mistake to assume that Africans were excluded from educational policy making in all but their exerting external pressure as the National Congress of British West Africa or in the press. They were always right at the heart of the educational policy making body, the Gold Coast Education Board, established in 1920. The Board was chaired by the Governor and attended by the Director of Education, by representatives from missionary societies (Wesleyan Methodist, Scottish Presbyterian, Roman Catholic and Anglican), by traditional chiefs and by the educated elite. Among African representatives, Nana Ofori Atta I and Casely Hayford were active participants. These two were also listed as members of Achimota Council, the policy-making and administrative body of Achimota School. Seeing further that these people were also the unofficial members of the Legislative Council, one can hardly say that Africans were excluded from policy making as a whole. Governor Guggisberg did not hide his distrust of educated Africans, but he did not exclude them from educational policy making. Ofori Atta attacked the Aborigine Right Protection Society and its leaders openly but sat in councils and committees with them side by side. And all these political rivals agreed on one thing: the Gold Coast needed to develop African leaders who fostered African values and were not aloof from the masses.

Notes

[1] Sneath to Goudie 20 July 1916, Wesleyan Methodist Missionary Society Archives (WMMS): Correspondence.

[2] PRO, CO 96/601.

[3] Graham 1971: 160; Kay 1972: 370; and, Report of the Education Department for the years between 1919 and 1927, PRO, CO 98.

[4] The insufficient number of inspectors had always been the problem for the colonial government. In 1920, there were only five inspectors covering all the Gold Coast colony and Ashanti. In 1922, the Educationists' Committee, which was appointed by Governor Guggisberg, proposed to employ at least 28 inspectors (Sessional Paper I 1924–5 *Interim Report of the Educationists' Committee 1922 appointed by His Excellency the Governor, 23rd May, 1922*, Accra, Gold Coast: Government Press, 1922 (PRO, CO 98/41). However, as of 1930, there were only 20 inspectors including both European and African (PRO, CO 98/57 Minutes of Legislative Council Meeting on 26 February 1930). Since the passing of the Education Ordinance of 1925, not only governmental and government-assisted

schools, but all schools were visited and reported upon by inspectors. Also, the number of schools was increasing dramatically during this period. Considering the reliance of the education system on school evaluation and quality control by inspectors, inadequate capacity of inspection was considered to be a critical drawback.

[5] Gold Coast Leader, 25 November 1911.

[6] Ibid, 30 May 1912.

[7] PRO, CO 98/20.

[8] Lockhart, Mfantsipim School Records, Annual Report, 1931, cited in Boahen 1996: 266–7.

[9] Summers indicates that the situation in South Africa, the 1920s–30s, showed a similar pattern (1999: 77).

[10] Oldham to members mission societies of the CBMS, 28 April 1925, CBMS-IMC Box 219.

[11] PRO, CO 98/55 Report of the Department of Education 1929–30: 62.

[12] *Allgemeine Missionszeitschrift*, September 1915 8, cited in Gyang-Duah 1996: 263.

[13] Rhodes House Library, Oxford University, Mss Afr. S. 1755 (Oxford project on the development of education in pre-independent Africa).

[14] Lionel Bruce Greaves, 'Educational Freedom Overseas', the Church Assembly Overseas Council (28 August 1951), Rhodes House Library, MSS Afr. S. 1755.

[15] PRO, CO 98/50 Report of the Department of Education 1927–28: 31.

[16] For example, Glover-Addo and Nana Ayirebi Acquah III in the session of 1 March 1928; and K.A. Korsah in the session of 26 February 1930 (PRO, CO 98/51, 57).

[17] The *Gold Coast Spectator*, weekly paper established in 1927, was the apparent vanguard in this issue. It backed the Assisted School Teachers' Union and reported about long waiting lists for children to be accepted at schools, delayed payment of teachers' salaries, government's misallocation of educational budget, etc.

[18] Sessional Paper XXI 1928–9 'Report and Recommendations of the Committee appointed by His Excellency the Governor in March 1928, to consider the problem created by the closure of Inefficient Schools', Accra, Gold Coast: Government Printing Office 1929 (PRO, CO 98/51).

[19] For example, Appendix E, Nana Sir Ofori Atta's Dissent, Sessional Paper XXI 1928–9 'Report and Recommendations of the Committee appointed by His Excellency the Governor in March 1928, to consider the problem created by the closure of Inefficient Schools'. (Accra, Gold Coast: Government Printing Office 1929). Minutes of Legislative Council, 29 July 1924 (PRO, CO 98/41).

[20] For the similar reaction of chiefs in Southern Rhodesia, see Summers 1997.

21 Boateng remembers his grandmother, being a firm Catholic, had no hesitation about observing many of the traditional customs and holidays (1975: 82).

22 Oldham and Gibson, *The Remaking of Man in Africa* 25. Boateng's claim based on his own experience at a Presbyterian secondary school in Odumase-Krobo, the Gold Coast supports this view (1975: 87).

23 Legislative Council Debate 4 February 1921, PRO, CO 98/35.

24 Mate-Kole to the Director of Education, 7 October 1915. Attachment to Sessional Paper V, 1916–7: Papers relating to Secondary Education, PRO, CO 98/27.

25 Inaugural address as the President of Liberia College, 'The Aim and Methods of a Liberal Education for Africans', (1881), cited in Okunor 1991: 111.

26 Presidential address delivered during the second session of the National Congress of British West Africa, held in Freetown, Sierra Leone, January 1923, cited in Sampson 1969: 73.

27 Guggisberg to Viscount Milner, Secretary of State, Colonial Office 15 October 1920, PRO, CO96/616.

28 A.G. Fraser, 'An address delivered at the fifth meeting of the Achimota College Council on Nov. 17th 1931 by the Rev. A.G. Fraser, Principal of Achimota' Achimota Pamphlets No 5 Achimota: the College Press 1931, Achimota School Library.

29 Newlands 1932; 24 August 1929. *Gold Coast Times*.

30 CBMS-IMC Box 263.

31 After all, Achimota School never gained the status of university. The first degree-granting state universities in British West Africa were University College of Ibadan, Nigeria, and University College of the Gold Coast, both opened in 1948. University College of the Gold Coast took over a part of the teacher training college and the engineering course of Achimota. As for private universities, Fourah Bay College in Sierra Leone, run by the Church Missionary Society, was the first to grant degrees from Durham University, UK. Fourah Bay was opened as a seminary in 1848 and launched university studies in 1876.

32 Tony Martin, 'Garvey and Pan Africanism' Second Dubois Memorial Lecture, W.E.B. Dubois Center for Pan African Culture, Accra, 12 January 1990, cited in Agbodeka 2002: 17.

Chapter 8

Achimota School as an experiment

The major concerns of colonial education in the early 20th century can be summarised in two terms: adaptation and character training. These were terms which were widely used in educational discourse but not necessarily with consensus about their meanings. The main point that Thomas Jesse Jones and the Phelps-Stoke Fund made was that a curriculum and a way of teaching should be adapted to an environment and students' needs. As I pointed out earlier (Chapter Five), American progressive educationists were also promoters of 'adaptation'. The difference between them was that, whereas black industrial education was meant to prepare students to accept the existing socio-political structure and the low position of the blacks in the capitalist economic hierarchy, the progressives saw education as the site of self-motivated learning which would lead to transform society to become more democratic. In either case, however, school was seen as a microcosm of the real world. Both promoters of industrial education and progressives thought students should be prepared for life after school ('education for life') either for the sake of change or conformity. The emphasis on the closer relationship between schools and surrounding communities, and on the school environment and contents of education being well connected to life outside of school were the common characteristics of educational thought of this period.

'Adaptation' was also promoted in the Gold Coast Colony. Mission education in the 19th century was criticised for the lack of 'adaptation'. Not only Europeans but also Africans supported the value of 'adaptation'. Cultural nationalism spread among members of the educated elite, some of whom authored books about customary laws or traditional institutions (Casely Hayford 1903; Sarbah 1897 and 1906). The term 'adaptation' was too broad to suggest any particular course, except that it suggested a difference from any conventional educational practice in Africa. In a way, it was because of this ambivalence that at least temporarily all parties with different interests secured cooperation among each other under the cause of advancing African education.

During this period, the concept of 'character training' was inseparable from that of 'adaptation'. One feature of the educational thoughts of this period was their departure from mere knowledge transmission to the formation of personality. The goal of adaptive education was, after all, a formation of character that fostered what were considered as 'traditional' or 'native', whatever it would have meant. All the instruments of adaptation were used to make the educational setting effective in forming the characters of those who were not alienated from the society they should belong to. So far as early 20th century Africa is concerned, there was virtually no advocate of education as a mechanism of social transformation. Even the African nationalists, who argued for political advancement and increased educational opportunities for Africans, did not think of overthrowing the framework of the social structure itself but advancement within it. Therefore, for the majority of people who were concerned with African education, school was the site for socialising students with the norms and values which operators of schools wanted them to internalise.

Differences of opinions arose about which norms and values students should be socialised with so as to be a properly 'educated people'. This question is directly related to another question about the ideal type of character to be developed at school. For example, to develop a Christian character would have meant to train someone who embodies the Christian values of altruism, thriftiness and faithfulness. Accordingly, to socialise students with Christian values, one should think of turning the school into a microcosm of the ideal Christian society. The more the emphasis was placed on character development, the more the atmosphere of the school was considered important as a site for character development. In other words, adaptation was a concept which changed its practical meaning according to a particular perception about the type of character that was to be developed at a school. To adapt education to the students' needs and background, one had to define the needs and social norms to which students were expected to conform.

In this chapter, after a long process to untangle the norms, actors, context and structure of discourse on colonial education from the metropole to the Gold Coast Colony, I will finally focus on the debates over education to be conducted in the model school for leadership education – Achimota School. First, I will demonstrate how diverse views were expressed in terms of 'character' to be developed on the Gold Coast. There were roughly five character traits promoted by key actors, namely: efficient workmanship; leadership; Christian character; the holder of a sense of citizenship; and the follower of African traditions and customs. Despite varying expectations as to the type of personality to be fostered in school, actors unanimously agreed that education on the Gold Coast had to be linked to the traditional society and the values in it. Then, the next part of the chapter will untangle the opinions expressed in the process of defining 'tradition' for designing Achimota education. I will also discuss popular educational means for character development in the early 20th century, and the ways they were adapted to Achimota. A great deal of such educational arrangements had to do with character development. I will discuss various extra-curricular activities, vocational subjects, location of 'tradition' in school and co-education. The last part of the chapter will introduce the stories of students who experienced Achimota in its early days, based on interviews with them.

8-1 Type of character to be developed at school

The inclination to emphasise character training in education had brought educationists to the extreme of stating that it was the primary objective of education and that the acquisition of knowledge or skill was subordinate to it.[1] Missions and the government agreed on the need for character training on the Gold Coast (Anim 1966: 81–3). Africans were no less committed to this role of education. Mensah Sarbah, a leading nationalist and a steering member of the Mfansipim Secondary School, declared the school's character training aim in the school magazine, *Mfantsipim Edwindzi*:

> The Mfantsipim School is not a cramming establishment but a place where it is sought to impart sound learning and religious education; and the Principal with his assistants endeavors to train the boys in the habits of thoughtfulness and foresight in relation to the life one has to live in West Africa. ...[2]

However, even though they accepted the value of character training, Africans never wanted to give up the more realistic benefits of education, namely, a better chance of earning money, and access to European knowledge and culture. Thus, the following comment, which appeared in the *Gold Coast Leader*, indicates this subtle stance of African intellectuals on the matter of education:

> Education [should aim] at the development of the highest type of manhood and womanhood for the best social efficiency. This aim does not make one's earning capacity less, nor does it limit the educated man as a scholar or make him deficient in knowledge or wanting in culture and proportional development of his faculties; but it puts manhood at the top and gives to all these other aims a larger significance.[3]

As the term 'character training' became popular among people involved in education, they began to use it to legitimise their own educational practices or ideas without serious consideration of its actual meaning. A.G. Fraser, principal of Achimota School, pointed out in his regular mail to his friends:

> Wherever one goes in the school world, here as elsewhere, one hears the word 'character training'. Often the most disreputable school, with no sense of honour in its treatment of teachers, boys, or finance, shouts loudest of its 'character-training' aim. Indeed we are all inclined to be rather vague about character-training. Perhaps it is because we do not first make up our minds about what character we want to create, in which case we would naturally be rather vague about the training required.[4]

For an analyst, this abuse of the term 'character training' is a source of headache. Since too many meanings were attached to a single term, and since it often looks as if the users of the term did not themselves closely examine the practicality of what they were talking about, it is difficult to segregate the different types of character which were meant to be developed. However, most of the attributes of the personality of character seem to fall into one of the following areas: efficient workmanship; leadership; Christian character; the holder of a sense of citizenship; and the follower of African traditions and customs.

8-1-1 Efficient workmanship

The type of character which was discussed in the most apparent way and, therefore, caught the most attention of the historians, was the idea of efficient workmanship. According to this idea, education is a means of producing useful and obedient workers who meet the demands of the labour market. Putting it differently, this is the perspective which considers 'adaptation' as a way of fitting education to the existing economic structure, rather than a way of making it culturally relevant. The colonial administrators' distrust of educated Africans led them to view education as a mechanism through which the African child would acquire a bit of a polished manner, obedience and discipline, and skills useful to make the student employable right after leaving school. The good workers, trained properly, were thus not supposed to develop political aspirations. This logic of training useful workers echoed a large part of the logic of American black industrial education, but it also reflected elements of British working-class education.

As I have noted earlier, African intellectuals were suspicious of workmanship training because they thought it was being imposed as an inferior form of education (Bude 1983: 353; Marah 1987: 462; Setse 1974: 23; Ward 1991: 171). At the same time, it would be misleading to deny the supportive voices of Africans for the vocational aim of education. First, there were the utilitarian Africans who supported it, using the expression in a newspaper article, the 'Bread-and-Butter' object of education.[5] For them, to earn a living in the new economic structure, an African youth needed mental, as well as physical skills, as preparation to be a worker. The following quotation from S.D. Tetteh represents this view:

> Those in high educational circles came to the realization years ago that the aim of elementary and secondary education was not solely to prepare for College, that the great majority could never hope to attend a higher institution of learning, and that something serviceable must be done for those who could not hope for the higher education.
>
> Education, therefore, is coming to be regarded more and more as a preparation for life – one of the most essential duties of which is to earn a living. It is not that the schools have failed in doing their work, but that business procedure has become so systematised that without training in its customs and usages a young man aspiring to a career is handicapped.[6]

While the first type of African voice justifies workmanship training in a utilitarian term, there was another group of Africans who stressed that the respect for manual labour should be the basis of national advancement. This type of argument overlaps with that of Booker T. Washington and James Aggrey, who were appreciated by the Europeans and Americans as 'good' black mediators (Chapter 4). An article that appeared in the *Gold Coast Leader* stated:

> As a Race we can never rise, until we pay more respect and have more regard for manual labour, unless we do away with the contempt we usually have for manual labour. What this country lacks, and lacks most miserably, is independent men, and to see the rush which our young people make for the merchant's desk or for the Government offices, or for the professional garb, makes one ... groan within himself, that all is lost for our Fatherland. What this country wants are Agricultural Schools.[7]

One thing which needs to be noted here is that the agriculture which the above writer mentioned was not subsistence farming but cash cropping. As I have mentioned in Chapter Three and Six, the Gold Coast Colony saw a dramatic increase of production and export of cash crops, the primary one of which was cocoa.[8] Cocoa production changed the existing social structure which was based on subsistence agriculture. The mention of agriculture in the article is, therefore, not a call for the return to 'traditional' agriculture, but for the acquisition of the latest technology of agriculture to increase the productivity of cash cropping.

This attitude of returning to agriculture was supported by many traditional chiefs who thought that the youth who acquired literary education would be attracted to urban life and salaried work, abandoning rural communities which were the basis of the chiefs' authority. In this argument, there was slippage between 'adaptation' as cultural relevance and as *assimilation* into the capitalist economic structure. Not only among Europeans but also among Africans, there was a mistaken notion that an education that prepared Africans for the jobs accessible to them (manual work) was interchangeable with the concept of culturally sensitive education. It has been widely said that British adaptation was a contrast to French assimilation, which attempted to make Frenchmen out of Africans, instead of 'adapting' education to the context and letting Africans develop on their own terms. However, in practice, there was no simplistic dichotomy between 'assimilation' and 'adaptation'. The British curriculum was as much assimilationist as the French (Mangan 1987: 158).

8-1-2 Leadership

At the other end of the continuum from the idea of workmanship training was that of leadership. The latter strongly reflected the British public school philosophy of leadership training although, as usual, it was not the only influence. One of the advocates of leadership training was A.G. Fraser, the founding principal of Achimota School. He had been the principal of Trinity College in Ceylon for nearly 20 years (1904–22) before coming to Achimota (Ward 1965), and was an active ideologist on colonial education. Fraser was similar to Lord Frederic Lugard, who was a firm believer in the value of a British public school education. Naturally, as the principal of Achimota, which was meant to be the model secondary school for leaders, he was a promoter of leadership training that followed the spirit and methods of the British public schools. In a letter to the prayer helpers, he defined his character training as a way 'to get the student up to his very best for the service of his land and people'.⁹ For the British, the memory of educational failure in India was fresh and bitter. They believed that, because they had allowed too wide an access to higher education to Indians, the educated elite became a strong nationalist group that threatened the stability of colonial rule. The lesson was inscribed in the British colonialists' minds: don't repeat the mistake of India in Africa. Thus, the training of leaders should be done very carefully so as not to make them rebellious but to make them leaders under colonial rule.

While some educational ideologists like Fraser and Lugard were advocating this idea of leadership training, there were people who were alert to placing 'too much insistence on leadership and high training'. J.E.W. Hood, an administrator in the Colonial Office, London, thus commented on a memorandum on 'education of African communities':

> There is one statement with which I do not agree and that is 'The general progress of the people depends on a steady increase of highly trained African leaders in all walks of life'. That is true, but it is only true as a goal to be aimed at, and what at the present time is wanted is not anybody highly trained, but an ordinary individual with some training, not too removed from the daily round and the common task to be unable to take part in local life and local habits of thought. In other words, I do not think that we have got anywhere near the stage of the highly trained African leader. We do not want the Divisional Commander nor even the Platoon Leader. What is wanted is ... The level of the Lance Corporal ...[10]

As for African intellectuals, leadership training was of the foremost importance in advancing education. The reason that nationalist leaders such as Casely Hayford, Mensah Sarbah and J.E.P. Brown advocated higher education was that they thought Africa needed more leaders who were as highly educated as Europeans (see Chapter Seven). For them, leadership education virtually equalled greater access to higher academic diplomas and degrees. They certainly talked about the importance of teaching African tradition and the avoidance of aloofness on the part of educated Africans, but differently from European ideologists, they were far from ready to compromise the academic standard of education for the sake of adaptation.

8-1-3 Christian character

As for religious bodies and missionaries, their primary concern in the field of education was to develop Christian character. Thus, while schools were considered the recruiting sites of new converts and of training catechists and teachers, there was a widely accepted moral notion of mission education, namely, the uplift of Africans from indulgence in pagan practice and superstition. Dougall argued that whatever content which was taught at school was useless unless moral principles were presented to students, which was only possible through religious teaching. He stated, 'Personality attains [mental] freedom and completeness only in obedience to God' (Dougall 1938: 105). Believing that only the teaching of Christian morality could lead Africans to civilization and to the abandonment of the pagan practice of polygamy, one radical promoter of religious education argued:

> Most important preliminary to civilisation – namely, education; and with secular education must go hand in hand ... moral education – the ideals of the Sermon on the Mount. ... Civilisation [and] education ... will in time bring [Africans] to the Christian ideal of one wife ...[11]

It was not only narrowly within the missionary community that the moral cause of Christian education was accepted. Rather, that cause was nearly unanimously accepted among Europeans concerned about education in Africa. The 'liberal' British ideologists believed that Africans were religious people and had the potential for moral uplift if their superstition was successfully replaced by Christian faith. Lord Frederic Lugard thus expressed his opinion that religious teaching should be added to every curriculum in Africa 'to replace the superstitious fears of the Supernatural which haunt the primitive savage from the cradle to the grave, and to assist in forming a higher ethical code'. He continued:

The recognition that 'the religious motive is the deepest and most abiding in the life of the African', and that his whole life is dominated and coloured by his belief in the ever-present Supernatural, forces us to the conclusion that as those beliefs become undermined and their rites proscribed, something must be supplied to take their place. We make 'witchcraft' a penal offence, and regard a death resulting from the poison ordeal as a case of murder. The exposure of twins to death, and human sacrifices, are regarded in the same light. Tribal authority and the maintenance of law, order and morality – such as they were – depended, however, in the last resort on the sanction of superstition.

And here the new policy differs from the old. 'The greatest importance must be attached to religious teaching and moral instruction [to fill the blank space left by banned practices of traditional belief].' (Lugard 1925: 6–7; see also, Lugard 1933: 5)

Traditional belief and practices were judged in the light of Victorian Christian morality and once they were labelled 'immoral', the British began to think of replacing them with European ones (Ocaya-Lakidi and Mazrui 1976: 282). In an atmosphere of government–mission cooperation, colonial administrators encouraged religious instruction, albeit non-denominational, at government-assisted mission schools. And the obsession with the moral purity and discipline of Victorian–Edwardian-Georgian Britain gave a central place to the development of Christian character in African schools.

Africans accepted the Christian education in their own light. Contrary to the suspicion of mission education in the earlier period, 20th century Africans were attracted to school, to no small extent, by the European culture and manners of acting that schools transmitted. Ordinary Africans did not distinguish between things Christian and European. To accept Christianity did not necessarily cause moral conflict for them, because Christianity did not replace traditional belief but co-existed with it in their lives. Not only the masses, but also the African intellectuals had no problem with Christian education. Having been products of mission schools, most of these intellectuals were pious Christians. Therefore, they criticised the practice of mission education for its ethnocentricity, but still accepted it in principle, for they were also convinced, similar to Europeans, that there were some African practices which were backward and needed to be removed.

8-1-4 Holder of a sense of citizenship

The next type of character training was to develop the sense of citizenship. To put it differently, it was an effort to develop the sense of belonging to a community. Of course, one person belonged to several communities – local, tribal, familial, national and imperial. This multiplicity of citizenship resulted in the conflicting messages that were sent from colonial administrators to African subjects. On the one hand, Africans were taught to live for the benefit of the African community, to share with illiterate neighbours, and not to use their education merely to satisfy self-interest. On the other hand, Africans were told to praise the British royalty and be proud of being a member of the British Empire. As evidence of the former expectation to develop commitment to African society, a paper presented at the Achimota Educational Conference in 1928 states:

> School life is a miniature world where we can see that the efforts of all are needed to contribute to the welfare of the whole. Laziness, selfishness and disloyalty bring loss not only to the individual but to the community. School training should lead to a right outlook on life as children realize the value of their own powers and their responsibility for using them for the good of others as well as for themselves.[12]

Meanwhile, school children were also expected to learn the proper attitude as British colonial subjects. Every year on 24 May, the birthday of Queen Victoria was celebrated throughout the British Empire. It was called Empire's Day and filled with events for African school children. In the morning, children of government and government-assisted schools gathered and saluted the Union Jack. Then, headmasters delivered addresses that praised the Empire and there was a national essay competition for senior children on 'How the Day was observed'. In Accra, the capital city, the Governor addressed 'the importance of the Day and the duties and responsibilities of every British subject'.[13] Also in Accra, there was a parade of school children, and the songs sung at the parade always included 'Rule Britannia'.[14] As an event, it seems to have been a merry one, especially the parade. *The Gold Coast Spectator* reported the excitement of people observing the parade:

> 'Rub-a-dub-dub! Rub-a-dub-dub!' People rush out to see what is happening. Children of twenty-seven schools are marching gaily to the old Polo Ground. They are neatly dressed, some in white with red or blue bands, some in khaki, others in tussore [sic]. They are all marching with a rub-a-dub-dub of their drummer boys. Many people, some of them parents and guardians, flank either side of the streets to see the little ones pass by with their rub-a-dub-dub. ... 'It is Empire Day', chimed in a lettered man. 'To-day, the Twenty-fourth of May, is the day on which good Queen Victoria of blessed memory was born'. More than that: Queen Victoria was named 'good', because she ruled well, always seeking the interest and happiness of her many people scattered all over the earth's surface, ordering that justice and fairplay [sic] unalloyed be extended to them all.[15]

It is imaginable that this cheerful mood of festivity was attractive enough for ordinary Africans to develop approbation for things British. It is ironic, however, that while the British were anxious that educated Africans should maintain their sense of belonging to traditional African society, they encouraged students to parade for the glory of the British Empire and sing the British anthem. Quite naturally, there arose criticism from Africans that it is disrespectful to African consciousness for children to sing the British anthem:

> [In the British national anthem], 'Our Nation' did not mean the Gold Coast Nation but the British Nation; 'Our race', our this and our that and the other things were all unblushingly English and to put such sentiments and assertions in the mouths of Native boys and girls without discrimination may spell loyalty of a sort, but it is dangerously demoralizing, because it is dangerously *denationalizing*. We want our children to be trained to think naturally and to realize that it is nothing derogatory to prize their own country above rubies and the things of their country above all other things.[16] (Emphasis is added)

8-1-5 Follower of African traditions and customs

Closely related to the above-mentioned sense of belonging to a society was the last type of character, i.e. the person who maintained respect for African customs and institutions. As I have noted, Europeans were keen on adapting education to the African environment so as to avoid 'denationalising' educated Africans. At the same time, African nationalists, if not all the educated elite, advocated for the training of African leaders, who had pride in their background and were self-sustaining, and who did not 'ask for elbow room from the white man'(Sampson 1969: 182). Last and more than anybody else, traditional chiefs had a strong desire to keep the educated youth under the influence of traditional institutions. For the chiefs, education had been a threat to their authority. Education provided a new route of social mobility for those who did not have the privileges in the traditional hierarchy of chieftaincy. Expansion of education resulted in the decline of the authority of traditional chiefs. Since chiefs could not stop the popular demand for education or deny the benefits of education, they advocated educating the youth to respect traditional customs and institutions. Omanhin Ababio II, the Paramount Chief of Aburah, said:

> Our youngmen [sic] must not be content to wear the clothes of their fathers. They must aim at being masters and leaders in the business and politics of their country. Above all they must be true citizens and patriots. The great need of the country is for a class of educated men loyal to the past, devoted in the present and determined for the future.[17]

It is indicative that Omanhim Ababio focused his discussion on the development of leaders who were 'loyal to the past' and never mentioned clerks employed in the lower stratum of colonial administration or commercial firms. Clerks were the targets of criticism from all parties – chiefs, African professionals and Europeans – for their superficial adaptation of Western lifestyle and customs and for their disrespect for 'African tradition'. Clerks were a class of people who did not get as high an education as professionals. At the same time, most of them were not from royal lineage or anything close to it. Also, they drew a line between themselves and the illiterate masses. Their very aspiration to be closer to Europeans and their lifestyle put clerks under attacks from various groups of people who argued for balancing Europeanisation with maintenance of African customs and institutions.

There was an issue which affected a person's perception about most of the five types of characteristics discussed above – efficient workmanship, leadership, Christian character, citizenship and rootedness in African society – and that was the problem of defining 'tradition'. An analysis of the different definitions demonstrates that even though people used the same term 'character training' to express their opinions, the qualities they meant were diverse, often conflicting with each other. Without defining African society and its culture, one could not think of the actual process and content of educational adaptation. No African or European believed that African tradition should be maintained as it was. In fact, they all thought that *some* part of that tradition was not worth maintaining or, in the worst cases, harmful. Then, there was the issue of what customs were worth maintaining and what part of European or Christian culture should be adopted. D'Souza argues that adaptation required a set of 'three R's': '(1) rejection of what was considered unscientific and obnoxious, like witchcraft; (2) retention of the best of indigenous culture; and (3) rejuvenation of the old by grafting an alien Western culture, preferably with a Christian bias' (D'Souza 1975: 35; see also, Armstrong 1926: 215; Ranger 1983: 211–53).

The types of characteristics reviewed above were not mutually exclusive. While they contradicted one another in some significant ways, still they co-existed in the imagination of the respective persons who took part in the discussion. Ideologists, either African or European, wanted leaders who fostered traditional norms and values while understanding and using the modern knowledge brought by Europeans. They wanted Africans to acquire Christian morality while being very cautious about 'denationalising' them. Moreover, they wanted Africans to have a sense of belonging both to traditional society and the British Empire. When the internationally accepted ideas of 'adaptation' and 'character training' were brought to the local level, the issue which was left untouched was pushed to the forefront: 'What is tradition?'

8-2 Definition of African tradition

Once Governor Guggisberg publicly expressed his will to establish a school, immediately after his arrival in office in 1919, there was much discussion about the curriculum and other aspects of education. Both in the metropole and in the Gold Coast Colony, the question of how to educate African leaders at this prospective government model school on a gigantic scale was a hot topic of discussion not only among educationists but also among politicians and bureaucrats. Despite differences of perspective, almost everyone involved in this discourse agreed that Achimota education was to be 'adapted' to the students' background by the teaching of 'African tradition and customs'. However, the students of Achimota had various ethnic backgrounds, and did not come from a single group which might be called 'Gold Coast Africans' (see Table 8-1). Similarly, their 'traditional' practices and customs were diverse. As the content of adaptive education began to be discussed, issues became prominent, such as 'What is tradition?' and 'How could Achimota adapt its education to such "tradition"?' These concerns are reflected in the conversation between two traditional chiefs, Nana Ofori Atta I and Fia Sri II, who later became members of the Achimota Council:

> Ofori Atta: How would you like boys trained – as in Europe or in accordance with Native Custom?
> Fia Sri: As in Europe.
> Ofori Atta: What do you mean by this?
> Fia Sri: To read and speak in English.
> Ofori Atta: Do you want them to forget their own Native Custom?
> Fia Sri: No! No!![18]

Fia Sri was no less concerned about maintaining 'Native Customs and Institutions' than Ofori Atta. What this dialogue implies is rather the ambivalence of both men on matters of 'Native Customs and Institutions' and Westernisation. The authority of traditional chiefs rested on traditional values and social structure. At the same time, chiefs like Ofori Atta believed strongly in the power of modernisation for African people's self-reliance. Thus, as a member of the Legislative Council and various education-related boards and councils, Ofori Atta advocated Africans' increased access to a better quality of education[19] as well as the social advancement of school-educated people.[20] More than anything else, however, he was an advocate of teaching local history, traditional customs and customary laws. Rathbone contends that Ofori Atta was one of the colonial government's most respected sources on 'customary law', one who 'both interpreted 'custom' and also 'invented' tradition and codified it for a grateful colonial government'(Rathbone 1993: 33; see also, Rathbone 1994: 6). To teach tradition at school required the redefinition of that idea and the reduction of flexible customs into fixed prescriptions. Ofori Atta, therefore, tried to stimulate the government and traditional chiefs to preserve 'native' artefacts and history for educational purposes.[21]

Table 8-1: Ethnic Backgrounds of Achimota Students (1932)

	Kindergarten /Primary	Above Middle School	Total
Twi	48	109	157
Fanti	27	72	99
Ga	42	85	127
Ewe	23	83	106
Northern Territories (Hausa)	2	5	7
Nigerian (Yoruba, Efik)	3	1	4
Total	145	355	500

Source: Newlands, Hussey and Vaughan 1932: 46

African nationalist leaders such as Casely Hayford, Mensah Sarbah and E.J.P. Brown were no less interested in teaching things African.[22] While calling for pride in tradition, nationalist leaders were not so keen on codifying native customs for the sake of education. By Africanisation, Casely Hayford meant a school run by Africans, not the localisation of the curriculum. He wanted the content of

African leadership education to be exactly the same as that taught in European schools, while placing importance on copying traditional African ceremonies at school.

In contrast, the British involved in Achimota devoted a great deal of time and energy to researching, recording and teaching traditional culture and history. The Achimota founders considered the School not only an educational institution but a centre for research and for setting educational standards for the whole colony, and even more widely, for West Africa. Therefore, they assumed the role of screening traditional dance, music, stories and so forth, adding to the curriculum only those which were '(morally) good' and worth transmitting to young Africans.

The effort to standardise the 'tradition' to be taught at Achimota started long before the foundation of the School itself. *The Interim Report of the Educationists' Committee 1922* made extensive recommendations concerning the planned government secondary school. Attached to the report was a record of interviews on the issue of secondary education with Africans and British of diverse backgrounds, including African intellectuals, representatives of missions and colonial officials. The interviews, half of which were conducted by Ofori Atta, covered a variety of issues regarding the location of tradition at the new government secondary school. What kind of food should be served in the School, 'Gold Coast food' or European? If both, how should they be eaten, with hands or with utensils? Was it necessary for students to be taught the customs of the country? Was there any objection to the students being taught drumming, dances and songs?[23] Everyone agreed that traditional customs should be taught but disagreed on the details. Chief Fia Sri II said that students should eat with their hands, whereas Casely Hayford, who was also actively involved in managing the Mfantsipim School, said they should use a knife and fork. J.E.P. Brown, another lawyer with a deep interest in education, said that teaching 'native songs' was fine but that dances were offensive. Casely Hayford agreed to all songs, dances and drumming. Therefore, at the stage of the preliminary survey of 1922, no consensus was reached on the exact content of the 'tradition' that was to be taught at Achimota School.

The task of defining 'tradition' was thereafter passed to the British staff of Achimota. The first members of the staff – Aggrey, Ward, Irvine and Fraser – arrived on the Gold Coast in 1924, three years before the actual opening of the School, and were continuously joined by more staff. The reason for their early arrival was Fraser's plan that they study the local languages, customs, history and traditions of the country. For example, in 1925, Sandy Fraser and Philip Brown were sent up-country to learn Twi, a vernacular (Agbodeka 1977: 41). Ward spent a great amount of time inland visiting traditional chieftains to record the oral history of different lineages. As a history master with a sincere enthusiasm to teach the history of West Africa as seen from African eyes, Ward put many orally transmitted histories, traditions and customs down on paper.[24] The Achimota staff also wrote scores for some traditional folk songs, to preserve them as closely as possible to their original form (Agbodeka 1977: 115; Irvine 1995, 34-36). However, the effort to standardise rendered the 'traditional' activities out of date, since, in practice, the form of the dances and songs changed flexibly over time.[25]

It was agreed among the African intellectuals and educators involved that Achimota School was in an authoritative position to 'eliminate what was objectionable in native customs, and preserve and elevate that which was good'.[26] Because of this mission of codifying 'tradition', Achimota allowed its staff the time to learn local cultures and languages before starting to teach. Staff developed teaching that was adapted to the defined 'tradition' and culture of Africans on the Gold Coast. The staff members were of the best quality in their respective fields, were specially selected by Principal Fraser and were equipped with the latest educational ideas. As such, they were authorised to decide just which 'traditions' were worth maintaining. Such exceptional treatment was facilitated by the formal and informal support of the ACNEBTA in London, the Gold Coast's stable financial basis, and the commitment and trust placed by Governor Guggisberg in Fraser's approach to Achimota education.

Although a variety of people had high hopes for Achimota's adaptive education, the School was generally unpopular among white residents, who considered it no different from the bookish, Eurocentric education of earlier generations, which they claimed had developed half-Europeanised Africans who were resentful of colonial rule. Nor was the School popular among colonial officials, who were irritated by Achimota's autonomy from the Gold Coast Department of Education and by the large part of the colony's education budget that was consumed by the School (Ward 1965: 204). Suspicion of Achimota was strong among Africans too, who thought that it was a tool of the government to impose a second class education on Africans to maintain their oppressed position. While the archives tell a positive story about Achimota, the public mood was far from supportive. In its early years, Achimota spent much energy gaining public support among Europeans and Africans on the Gold Coast.

Achimota School's Emblem

At the same time, the School did not forget to posture the peaceful inter-race relationship. For this, James Aggrey, the sole African founding member of Achimota and internationally renowned inter-race mediator, played his role. As much as Booker T. Washington used the metaphor ('Cast Down your Bucket') to remind

American blacks of humbleness and a cooperative attitude toward the white, James Aggrey often used metaphors to express his view about race relations. James Aggrey compared the relationship of Africans and Europeans to the black and white keys of a piano. This metaphor inspired the design of the Achimota School emblem, which has been passed down until today. Unless blacks and whites worked harmoniously together, there would be no music. At the same time, he pointed out, they were separate, not mixing with each other. This view of racial cooperation and segregation was expressed by Booker T. Washington too, who used the metaphor of five fingers of the hand, which work together but exist separately. Such echoes between two figures known as the 'good' mediators between the races, one in the US and another on the Gold Coast, presented the outlook that Achimota is not only based on the British model, but also the American successful example. No doubt it made American philanthropists content. Also, African nationalists appreciated it as much as the whites, because it suggested that the new school in Achimota was of global high esteem, having a renowned African educator on its staff whose education philosophy was parallel with another famous American black educator.

8-3 A public school in Africa

Achimota staff made extensive efforts to adapt the curriculum to West African students and to make them proud of their own African background rather than being 'denationalised'. But the School primarily followed the English public school model of leadership education, and Principal Fraser attached special importance to 'character training' in his conception of Achimota education:

> Character-training is much the most important thing. It must come in the thoroughness of work, *the spirit of team play, the religious teaching*, and in the training in *love of country and practical service for the people of the country*. It must be given by *a staff which lives with and for the boys*, and the Africans on that staff must be selected only when they are able to bear comparison with the Europeans on it. (Emphasis is added)[27]

The educational scheme of Achimota followed the educational line of the public school and echoed Lord Lugard's idea of leadership education for Africans precisely. Achimota's character training aimed to achieve all of the five types presented earlier. The primary goal was to develop the character trait of leadership, but it was closely linked with Christian character, sense of citizenship, rootedness in tradition and, surprisingly, workmanship too. As I will demonstrate later, vocational subjects were an important part of Achimota education to foster the sense of 'dignity of labour'.

To develop a sense of leadership, cooperation and service to the people, the School encouraged extra-curricular activities that included team sports and social service. Religious teaching was considered important for developing Christian character, and a great deal of emphasis was placed on the boarding arrangement and on developing a close relationship between students and teachers.

Fraser shared the popular belief of contemporary educationists that good character could not be developed by classroom instruction alone, but had to be acquired through experience and interaction with teachers who represented the ideal character.[28] Although it could not get public school masters, Achimota did recruit many from Oxbridge to its teaching staff, the majority of whom had public school experience and embodied British upper class morality (for the composition of the Achimota teaching force, see Table 8-2).

When the residential arrangement was adapted to the environment of the Gold Coast at Achimota, a new justification was attached to it, in addition to teacher–student interaction and the development of self-discipline under prefects. This was to bring students from different parts of the colony and from different ethnic backgrounds together, so as to help them develop a sense of citizenship on the Gold Coast and then to work in cooperation (Setse 1974: 34; Ward 1965: 126). The newly established colony lacked a sense of shared membership across ethnic boundaries. From the British perspective, leadership training was closely connected with the development of citizenship of a nation-state. Before independence, the justification for citizenship development was widely supported by graduates of secondary boarding schools on the Gold Coast; these graduates were firm believers in the virtue of residential secondary education.[29] Not surprisingly, the boarding houses of a few secondary schools and the University College of the Gold Coast, which were modelled on British boarding houses, contributed to the development of the nationalism that, in the end, removed colonial rule.

Table 8-2: Composition of Achimota Teaching Staff (1932)

		European	African	West Indian	Indian	Total
Senior	Male	22	2	1	1	26
	Female	10	2	0	0	12
Junior	Male	0	11	0	1	12
	Female	0	3	0	0	3
Total		32	18	1	2	53

Source: Newlands, Hussey, and Vaughan 1932, 47

The school day at Achimota was finely scheduled, beginning with the rising bell at 5:30 in the morning and lasting until the lights were turned off, a practice which followed the British metropolitan model precisely. Every aspect of school life was designed to develop loyalty to School, peers and country; esprit de corps; truthfulness; spirit of service to the public; self-discipline; and obedience. The School song is evidence of the desire on the part of the Europeans to mould Africans to fit the British image:

> From Kumasi or Accra, from the Volta or the Prah[30]
> We are brothers and our mother is the school.
> She will guide us all and each,
> So to learn that we may teach,
> So to subjugate ourselves that we may rule.
> Play the game,
> Shout her name,
> Spread her name afar.
> She's ahead of all the host,
> She's the school of whom we boast,
> She's the glory of the Coast,
> ACCRA-A-A.[31]

Just as in English public schools, Achimota publicised episodes of students whose behaviour embodied the School's spirit, the 'Tom Browns' of Achimota. For example, the *Report on Achimota College 1934* presented the story of Dogbatse, one of the competitors for Achimota in the inter-college cross country race. Although he grew very tired as the race went on, he believed that it would be a shameful act to give up, so he struggled on desperately till he fell and died. 'When he fell a member of staff kneeling down beside him said, "Twenty yards, can you finish?" He answered, "I can't – isn't it sad? Isn't it a disgrace – what will happen to my College?" With these words he bowed his head and died in anguish.'[32] According to the English public school morality adapted to Achimota, Dogbatse's act was considered a noble, self-negating act of loyalty to school.

8-3-1 Social services

Achimota also encouraged students to undertake social welfare activities – experiential learning about the leaders' duty to their people. On the Gold Coast, the government encouraged the establishment of a 'Junior Red Cross Link' in middle and secondary schools. Each of these links 'adopted' a village and the members of the link went there to help the villagers 'to clear away rubbish, to build their houses, markets, culverts, latrines, and roads. They also treat[ed] minor cuts and sores'.[33] The social service activities in which students participated were thought to bring about both community development and leadership training for the students. By means of social service, Europeans believed they could avoid alienating future African leaders from the masses and maintain their respect for traditional values and norms. Through interaction with European teachers, students were meant to internalise a sense of duty to the African people. The correspondence of one past student would suggest the School's social service programme developed the sense of the duty to the public in at least some of its scholars. 'I believe that one of the many vital contributions which Achimota can give to our country through her pupils is the "Spirit of Social Service" in other words the "Spirit of Service to others".'[34]

8-3-2 'Adaptation' to African 'tradition'

Although it followed the model of the English public school, Achimota's primary goal was to adapt its education to African 'tradition'. Teaching and research in African music were notable characteristics of Achimota which were not present in most other schools. Concerned parties in and outside the School hotly debated what was acceptable 'traditional' music to be taught at Achimota. Saturday evenings were reserved for tribal drumming by four ethnic groups: the Ga, Fanti, Twi and Ewe. The 'Negro spirituals' developed among American blacks were also introduced to Achimota's music education so as 'to duplicate some features of American Negro education in the Gold Coast' (Agbodeka 1977: 115). To draw parallels between American blacks and Africans was not unusual in the early 20th century; such parallels were frequently used to justify transplanting the Hampton-Tuskegee model of black industrial education to Africa. However, reference to the Hampton-Tuskegee model was carefully avoided by the Europeans involved in the foundation of Achimota lest it stir the suspicion of Africans that the School was to impose a second class education on Africans. At the same time, the model was not entirely unwelcome to African intellectuals, who saw an opportunity to learn from the practices of (or those designed for) American blacks if they could be beneficial in advancing Africans socially and politically. It seems that to teach American black music was not objectionable and accepted as part of teaching 'African tradition'.[35]

The European staff also attempted to write down African music in score form. In doing so, they tried to understand the composition of the music according to European musical theory and tradition. One of the staff believed he found that Gold Coast folksongs had 'strong musical resemblances to old folksongs in Britain and Europe'. He then thought that lessons should be organised so that students could 'understand the gradual development of European music' from the so-called lower developmental stage of African music (Wallbank 1935: 230–45). At the same time, Achimota staff made efforts to provide a good education in European music. There was a school orchestra that practised on Friday evenings and Saturday mornings, and some students who showed musical talent were given the opportunity to take private violin lessons.[36]

Drama was another extra-curricular programme active at Achimota. At first, a series of vernacular plays were performed 'with but little rehearsing ... with simple plots, rich in local colour: village scenes, scenes on farm, chief's courts, "fetish" ceremonies, humorously presented' (Williams 1962: 62). Later, drama became more 'sophisticated' with the help of the staff. In 1933, *Caesaris Incursio in Oram Auream*, a European script adapted to an African context, was performed in Twi, Fante, Ga, Latin and French. In it, Julius Caesar founded Achimota. Following this, the students of Achimota performed various European plays and musicals by Shakespeare and Gilbert and Sullivan, including the latter's *Mikado*, a satire of the European upper class, using the motif of Japanese emperor. On the one hand was the value of adapting European plays and performing them in local languages; on the other, an obvious tendency to see dramatisation of village life or of African ceremonies and rituals as less sophisticated than European plays 'adapted' to the African context. Though the criteria of selecting European plays for African adaptation does not seem very clear. Africanising the *Mikado*, a Japanese story written by a British writer, seems to be twisted in the eyes of today's observers.

8-3-3 'Dignity of labour' – handwork

A seemingly odd characteristic of Achimota education, given the elitist nature of the School, was its stress on handwork. To scholars who appreciate the influence of American industrial education, however, this part of Achimota education looked quite natural (Sivonen 1995: 108–12). Promoters of American black industrial education, such as Thomas Jesse Jones, repeatedly stated that Achimota was an offspring of the American model (the Hampton-Tuskegee model) (Jones 1924). As discussed earlier, there was noticeable caution on the part of British colonial administrators and educationists in referring to American black industrial education when they spoke publicly about Achimota. The School was a site of leadership education, while Hampton and Tuskegee were institutions meant to halt black aspirations for social mobility. Such discussion, however, was slippery because even the educators of Achimota did not think its graduates capable of advancing as far as the British ruling class. However well educated, they would, at most, be leaders of a subordinate race.

There was a wide range of non-examined courses called 'hobbies' that were provided since the inauguration of school in 1927 (see Table 8-3 for Achimota's curriculum). They included (a) woodwork, bookbinding, printing, weaving, art and music for two years; (b) tailoring, cobbling and basketry for one year; and (c) hair-cutting and racquet repairing for one term. From 1929 onward, other hobbies were added, including metal work, wood-carving, dyeing, pottery, house decoration, car repair, photography and botanical drawing (Agbodeka 1977: 82-3). There were also farm and commerce courses in which students could learn the theory and practice of each field.

The fact that these courses were named 'hobbies' indicates the stance of the school that Achimota students were encouraged to take these courses to learn the 'dignity of labour', which was a part of the character training to be leaders of African masses who live by handwork. American black industrial education emphasised the moral effects of teaching manual work. Through practice, it was considered that students would internalise the sense of appreciation of the handwork. Although Achimota did not expect students to take up the handwork as their occupation, the philosophy of providing such subjects shares the basis with that of black industrial education. Achimota students, who were considered the future leaders of the Gold Coast, were not obliged but were strongly encouraged to learn the 'dignity of labour' to understand the masses and lead them well.

Table 8-3: Core Curriculum of Achimota Middle and Secondary Schools*

	Middle School				Secondary School			
	Year 1	Year 2	Year 3	Year 4	Year 1	Year 2	Year 3	Year 4
Scripture	2	2	2	2	2	2	2	2
Vernacular	2	2	2	2	2	2	2	2
English	6	7	7	6	5	5	5	6
Arithmetic or Mathematics	6	7	6	5	5	5	5	6
History (Elementary)	2	3	2	2	2	3	2	3
Geography	3	3	2	2	2	2	3	3
Elementary Science				2	2	4		
Art	2		2	2	2			
Handwork (Hobbies)**	2	2		2	2			
Metal work (Boys)			2	2	2	2		
Music	3	3	3	3	2			
Physical Training (Boys)	2	2	2	2				
Domestic Science (Girls)	4	6	6	6	4	4	4	
Latin					3	3	5	6
Nature Study					2			
Hygiene						1		
Agriculture						3	7	7
Botany							7	7
Physics								7
Physics and Chemistry							7	
History								6

*Extra-curricular activities, which were the characteristic of Achimota, are not included here.
**Handwork (Hobbies) was sub-divided into various elective courses.
Source: Newlands, Hussey, and Vaughan 1932, 50

8-3-4 Co-education

Co-education was another characteristic of Achimota which was realised through the strong support of its founders, especially A.G. Fraser and James Aggrey. Although other aspects of Achimota education were picked from educational recipes more or less acknowledged in the international arena, the idea of having girl boarders on the same site and mixing boys and girls in the classroom was ground-breaking, at least in Africa. On the Gold Coast, co-educational schools had already been operated by missions at the primary level. And there had been girls' boarding schools. However, there had been no co-educational secondary boarding institution except for one senior school run by the Bremen (later Scottish) mission in Peki Blengo.[37] Achimota was the first government-funded boarding school to embrace co-education in the entire African continent. Fraser was clear in his conviction of the virtue of girls' education, but he was not so sure about co-education. However, since it was only at Achimota that Fraser could practise the kind of education he wanted African boys and girls to receive, he accepted Guggisberg's idea of co-education (Ward 1965: 199–200). Aggrey, the sole Gold Coast native among the Achimota founders, declared, 'When you educate a boy you educate an individual. When you educate a woman you educate a family'.[38] Aggrey also claimed that educated African men needed educated wives as 'helpmeets'.[39] 'Liberal' educationists of the time, like Fraser and Aggrey, began to see the role of wives as not merely maids but the equal partners of men in maintaining a civilized family life. At the same time, Fraser demonstrated the racist view that providing education for both sexes would effectively reduce the Africans' sexual activity, although in saying that education could change this behaviour, he must have meant to challenge the widespread view that Africans were genetically inferior. According to Fraser:

> Almost every observer of African life has remarked on the way the African brain ceases to develop after puberty. From my limited experience, I should say it does not cease to grow where it is given a reasonable chance through sexual purity. But this over-indulgence is so widespread and it has caused so much mischief that many have come to look on this stoppage of brain development in Africa as a natural law. To free our peoples from this is the first and greatest gift education [of both sexes] can hope to offer. (Cited by Ward 1965: 200)

The view that Africans were morally inferior was behind the British teachers' practice of recording only those African customs and practices deemed appropriate to teach African youth. The idea of girls' education to develop into the partners of educated men was, then, an effort to change the relationship between the sexes to be morally acceptable in the eyes of British teachers. This goal of girls' education seems to have been achieved at Achimota to some extent; the rate of marriage between Achimota graduates was quite high in its early years. For several Achimota female graduates the lifestyle of the married European staff also became the model of their married life. The European-style house, the way to clean it, European diet and cooking, and the way spouses interacted were among the things girls learned at Achimota. In other words, Achimota played a role in making educated women 'helpmeets' of educated men who would live a Westernised married life.

Achimota invited the criticism and hesitance of many Africans by making the School both co-educational and residential. Facing difficulty in recruiting female students at first, some measures were taken to attract girls, such as setting lower fees for girls than for boys and encouraging the enrolment of girls whose siblings or relatives were already at the School.[40] Regardless of the worries in the first few years, Achimota founders stuck to their ideal of co-education. In the Achimota Inspectors' Report of 1938, 10 years after the School's establishment, the female section of Achimota was firmly established as an integral part of the institution, which was no longer charging lower fees. Also, by the late 1930s Achimota was training more than 43 per cent of the women teachers in the Gold Coast (Williams 1962: 44). All things considered, Achimota's contribution to female participation in education, directly and indirectly, was significant for the Gold Coast and British West Africa as a whole. (See Table 8-4 for trends in enrolment at Achimota and Table 6-1 for educational statistics of the Gold Coast Colony of the period.)

Table 8-4: Achimota College and School - Number of Students

	1926		1927		1928		1929		1930		1931		1932	
	Male	Female	M	F	M	F	M	F	M	F	M	F	M	F
Kindergarten	6	0	36	23	86	26	109	0	81	74	31	16	26	20
Primary	0	0	0	0	0	0	41	0	86	0	64	24	57	26
Middle	0	0	0	0	0	0	42	8	76	0	71	34	79	32
Secondary	0	0	0	0	0	0	0	0	0	0	0	6	80	18
Teacher training	117	0	106	0	133	0	141	0	148	0	142	0	126	0
University Intermediate	0	0	0	0	0	0	0	0	4	0	5	0	17	0
Others*	0	0	0	8	0	5	0	10	7	12	1	15	3	16
Total	123	0	142	31	219	31	333	18	402	86	386	95	388	112
	123		173		250		351		488		481		500	

*Others include those who stayed at school as Student Teachers after primary school (all female) and those who went to specialized courses after secondary school.

Source: Newlands, Hussey, and Vaughan 1932, 44.

8-4 Experiencing Achimota education

While the School's founders, policy makers and educationists had discussed the ideal leadership education to be realised at Achimota before its establishment, how did students experience this education? How did students internalise the moralistic messages transmitted through various educational methods of character training? This is important because the moral influence of the School played a significant role in (re)shaping African cultures and identities in later years.

8-4-1 Social mobility

> I know somebody now who came from a small village near Keta. Our first day in the dormitory, I remember him, he was standing [by the electricity switch turning it on and off]. He'd never seen the electricity. But he, by the time we left upper [form] 6, had won all the prizes in mathematics, chemistry, and so [on] and so forth, became a brilliant gold medalist in London University for Medicine, became an orthopedic surgeon, and became a surgeon general for Barbados, and all that. I mean, by when he came, all he had was a very sharp brain. So if you had the image of somebody who did this on the first day at school, and turned out to be a really great scientist, then you understand what education can do to people.[41]

One of the most striking things in interviews with Achimota alumni is the dramatic scale of social mobility. Children of less-educated poor parents were able to move up the social ladder via scholarships to Achimota (see Figure 8-1 for parental occupations of students). Bowles and Gintis argue that in a capitalist society, factors such as class, race, sex and the socio-economic status of the family often work to reproduce the 'capitalist order' (1975: 81). According to Bourdieu's theory of cultural reproduction, educational systems assume familiarity with the dominant culture in a society, in which students from higher-class families have more advantages than those from lower-class families because of their exposure to highly valued 'cultural capital' at home (Bourdieu 1974: 32). In contrast to these theories of social reproduction, in the early days of Achimota, students from a less privileged socio-economic background gained the opportunity of dramatic social mobility by going to Achimota.

This social mobility was a result of Achimota's attempt to develop a new type of African leader; the idea originated from British suspicion of the emerging class of the African elite. In the early years, 60 per cent of the students at Achimota were on scholarship in one form or another (Newlands, et al 1932: 28–9). Even though the ratio was later reduced, throughout the colonial period, scholarship students constituted about 40 per cent of the total population of the students.[42] There were roughly two kinds of scholarships: one for academic excellence; another for students from remote areas with the potential to become leaders, with the children of pastors, teachers, ministers and chiefs often selected. At a time when educational opportunity was mostly limited to people in the coastal areas, Achimota scholarships provided access to education for those in inland and remote areas (Williams 1962: 120; for the ethnic composition of students, see Table 8-1). Several national leaders at and around the time of independence (1957) had attended Achimota on academic scholarships and were later sent on scholarship to Europe for higher education. These included Emmanuel Amfom, first dean of the University of Ghana Medical School; K.A. Busia, national president and political activist in exile; K.B. Asante, staff member of the first president, Kwame Nkrumah, and foreign service official; and A.A. Kwapong, vice-chancellor at the University of Ghana. For all these Achimota opened the door to upward mobility.

In colonial Ghana, it was only after the 1940s that the number of secondary schools increased to more than a handful.[43] Until then, there were only two boys' schools (Mfantsipim and Adisadel) in addition to Achimota. All in all, there were around five hundred secondary students each year.[44] No comprehensive data are available about secondary students' social backgrounds in the colonial period, but compared to the diverse backgrounds of earlier Achimota students, those of the Mfantsipim students were more uniform. Since it had a far weaker financial basis than Achimota, Mfantsipim could provide only a couple of scholarships each year. Thus, the majority of students were funded by their fathers or relatives. The fee was not too high, and was affordable for middle-class families, provided a family was conscious of the value of sending a child to school. In general, a parent who knew the value of education was himself educated to some extent. In the parents' generation of my interviewees, if a person completed primary school (Standard VII) or received private lessons on literacy and numeracy, they were considered educated. Mfantsipim never took the effort to go out and recruit students. Therefore, most of its students were from Cape Coast – where the school was located – and coastal towns.

Figure 8-1: Parental Occupation of Achimota Students (1932)

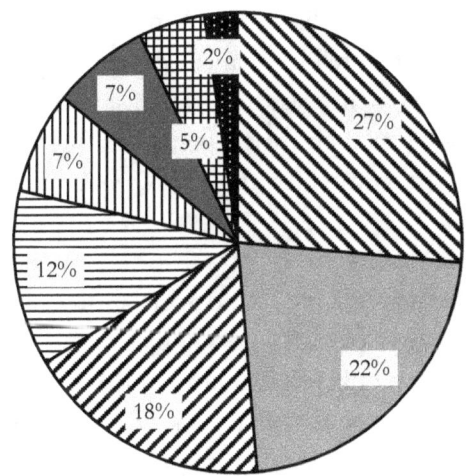

◪ Commercial (independent merchants, store-keepers and commercial agents)
▣ Agricultural (small or large holdings)
▨ School teachers
▤ Clerks and subordinate government officials
▢ Ministers, Clergymen
▨ Traditional chiefs
▢ Artisans and craftsmen
▪ Superior government officials

Source: Newlands, Hussey, and Vaughan 1932, 45-6

8-4-2 Boarding school life

As the founders of Achimota School emphasised, the boarding system framed school life. The great majority of students, both boys and girls, were boarders; there were very few exceptions. Most of the interviewees were unanimous over the benefit of the boarding arrangement: to live with and befriend students from different parts of the country who spoke different languages, were of a different sex and were of different family backgrounds. As noted earlier, unity was one of the most important goals of the Achimota founders. For the interviewees, Achimota 'brought the country together'; 'Everybody was treated equal[ly]. So you [forgot] about the differences. And what you [were] most aware of is that you [were] an Achimotan'; and 'Even when you leave, you have a feeling for the school. You know it's your Alma Mater, and you know that everybody who's gone there is your brother, whether he speaks Ga or Twi or Ewe'.[45] In all likelihood, students in the early days of Achimota were more closely exposed to the founders' philosophy than those in the later generations. Therefore, it is difficult to tell how much of the early students' trust in the boarding arrangement was the internalisation of the founders' views and how much was their own conviction. But old Achimotans consistently stressed the value of the boarding arrangement for its unifying role.

Achimota graduates of earlier days also mentioned the value of all-round training, which included handwork, sports, arts, social work and so on, in addition to academic subjects. According to one interviewee, if you were only good at academic work, but not on the sports field, 'you may [have felt] that you [were] not complete. You didn't run away from athletics or sports, just [burying] your face in the books all the time'.[46] This might be typical of an obsession of earlier students who were directly influenced by the School's original philosophy. But even in Achimota this concern for 'all-round education' did not last very long. George, an interviewee who left Achimota in the 1950s, claimed that he was among the best students, earning various academic prizes, but he admitted with no apparent regret that he was not good at sports.

Cultural influence was still another point raised by interviewees. Some of them came from villages and knew nothing about urban life or European culture. Still, the cultural influence was felt in more or less the same way by children who came from relatively better-off families. In its early days, Achimota School was filled with things that were not available outside: piped water, European teachers,

European food and European supplies. Although students were taught not to alienate themselves from their fellow Africans and there were African cultural activities like traditional drumming, the Western influence on them was enormous.

8-4-3 Co-education

While the male interviewees mentioned cultural influence in more general terms, women focused on the domestic aspects of European life, copying the lifestyle of the European staff, 'the way ... they kept house and the way ... the whites treated their wives'.[47] At least from this female interviewee's point of view, European men did not treat their wives badly, and she thought that this good impression of European married life made Achimota boys and girls want married lives like the ones white couples had. Female graduates also remembered that they were closely supervised in cleaning their boarding houses every weekend, which male graduates often did not mention, even though they were also supposed to have cleaned their complexes. After each inspection, the housemistresses announced which dormitory was cleaned the best. As a female graduate put it, 'It was a great jubilation when your dormitory was first'. One interviewee remembered that she was said to have committed an 'offensive' act when her group did not do a thorough cleaning job.[48]

Another lasting influence of Achimota education, which was mentioned only by female interviewees, was the attitude of humility and thriftiness. One can assume this was an aspect of female character training, and a message largely transmitted through mistress–student interaction in the boarding houses.[49] While there were female students who went to work professionally after graduation, the basic purpose of education for girls was to make them good wives. This message was absorbed by the female students.

Five female graduates whom I could interview had socially active husbands and sons. It was difficult to identify female Achimota graduates unless through the word of mouth of the successful males' network. The flip side of this fact is that these women internalised the female role of good and wise wife and mother of a high class family transmitted at Achimota. Their husbands were the elite who were a professor of University of Ghana, first president of Ghana

Chamber of Commerce, diplomat and accountant. Out of five couples I met, three husbands were also related to Achimota, either as a student or a teacher. Among these female interviewees, some had the experience of teaching at girls' schools for a short period before marriage. It seems that being a teacher in a girls' school was not a bad choice as an experience for an elite woman. After marriage, most of them devoted themselves to voluntary social services and church activities, but never did paid work. In sum, those Achimota graduates I met had created the class of elite women, replicating the Victorian-gender morality in Africa.

Although I could not meet them, there seem to be a few female graduates of the same generation, who turned out to be professionals. One of them acquired the undergraduate degree in nursing, on government scholarship, in the UK and became one of the first batches of nurses in Kohle Bu Hospital, the first general hospital on the Gold Coast. Since a nurse was female occupation then, she did not deviate from the stereotype of elite women. Still, this case can be considered as the one in which the girl developed her independent identity, without being a domestic partner of a successful husband. In fact, putting aside a few leading nurses who has overseas degrees like her, the majority of early nurses were from non-elite households.

Another female graduate whom my interviewees mentioned succeeded in her business of food processing and sales. There might have been some sudden change of family situation after graduation, but she started a small-scale trading venture using the confectionary baking skills learned at Achimota and expanded it to a level to be known widely in Ghana. This is a very exceptional deviation from the model of Victorian housewife which Achimota transmitted. At the same time, it is interesting to see that the baking skills she learned in the 'hobbies' class in Achimota helped her in a completely different way from the original intention to teach 'dignity of labour' to prospective leaders.

Both male and female graduates appreciated co-education. The ratio of graduates who found life-long partners at the School was quite high. One male interviewee said the marriage of two people who had shared the experience of equal friendship between men and women at Achimota was desirable. All the interviewees confirmed that female students were treated equally in the School, even though sports and handwork were things for which girls were considered unfit. They said the equal treatment contributed to making girls more confident about themselves and thus encouraged their emancipation.[50]

Achimota's co-education had the effect of transforming the relationship of married couples and the norms of family life among its graduates by promoting the European style of marriage and women's position in it as humble and thrifty helpmates of men. Overt and covert messages transmitted in various aspects of school life made both female and male students internalise the values of European married life, which co-existed with the message to maintain pride in African 'tradition'. This aspect of girls' education may be one of the examples in which Achimota's 'adapted' education was incongruous. Whereas it preached pride in 'tradition', Achimota transmitted to the girls European values of married life through various activities. Such transmitted values on marriage and families took root when they married men similarly educated at Achimota or other secondary schools; these values were then transferred to the next generation.

8-4-4 Cultural production under the name of 'adaptation'

It has often been said that British colonialism was adaptation, in contrast to the French model of assimilation. In fact, this analysis of Achimota School reveals that both efforts were made within a single school. While the School tried to *assimilate* Africans into English public school norms and European civilization, it stated its purpose as *adapting* its education to the African 'tradition', and devoted a great deal of energy to this effort. Furthermore, even though the School attempted *adaptation* and *assimilation*, what happened was, in fact, the *creation* of a new culture.

In its early days Achimota School was a site of cultural production. The School's students were from diverse social backgrounds. Achimota had several scholarship schemes and as many as 40 per cent of the students were on some type of scholarship, either for academic excellence or on the basis of their family backgrounds. Furthermore, Achimota was one of very few co-educational secondary institutions in Africa at the time. Therefore, Achimota students of both genders came from families of different socio-economic status, from various parts of the country, and from different ethnic groups. Achimota provided a gate for socially upward mobility. Students of various backgrounds were exposed to the Achimota founders' idea of new African leaders through classroom learning and various other aspects of school life. In this situation, the education at Achimota played a significant role not only in defining the characters of individual students, but in creating a class of people who shared the cultural traits learned at Achimota. They were inevitably influenced by their contact at the School with Western values in such matters as styles of living, married life, music and literature.

For students who came from places in which the practice of 'African customs' was a matter of daily life, the 'African tradition' codified at Achimota was itself foreign. These 'traditions' were not *adapted* to the students' background in any real sense; on the contrary, students were socialised to Achimota culture, which was invented by picking and mixing aspects from different sources. In this process of cultural production, not only the two 'traditions' – public school and African – were operating.

In addition, other educational philosophies had their own places in Achimota education. While denominational segregation was carefully avoided (there were also Muslim students), religious morality was considered to be an important building block of 'character training'. American black education cast its shadow in the elective courses of 'hobbies'. There was a wide variety of vocational courses in this category, although they were provided not with the aim of preparing future manual workers, but for moral training of future leaders to know the 'dignity of labour'. The very fact that James Aggrey was a founding member of this school reflected the strong interest in managing inter-race relationships. The reason that scholars have provided diverse views about early days of Achimota, as if they are looking at different institutions, is because of the School's almost excessively wide-ranging activities. Depending on which of its educational endeavours is considered the core of Achimota education, the results of analysis would vary. Still, despite the unique mixture of educational ideas and objectives of 'character development', British Victorian ethos in its education was hard to overlook.

Achimota opened a way to social advancement for many youths who might not have thought of leaving their home villages otherwise. After independence in 1957, Achimota graduates comprised a large number of the leaders in the political, economic and academic fields of the young nation, Ghana. In that sense, the goal of the Achimota founders to develop African leaders was achieved. However, the School was not very successful in making leaders who were 'Western in intellectual attitude towards life, but who remain[ed] African in sympathy'.[51] In fact, they were Westernised to a considerable extent – not only intellectually, but also culturally. Keeping students 'African in sympathy' turned out to be extremely difficult in a school filled with facilities, artefacts and activities deemed to be of the best quality by European standards.

Generally, people who were at Achimota before the early 1940s expressed a greater emotional attachment to Achimota than later generations. At that time, the School had much better facilities than any other secondary school on the Gold Coast, a wide variety of activities for students, the best teachers and house masters/mistresses who took good care of the boarders. Interviewees who were at Achimota after the mid-1940s were less attached, sometimes even critical.

Achimota extended its educational work into too many areas and its cost was disproportionately high for the revenue of the Gold Coast Colony. As soon as the economic recession began in the 1930s, Achimota suffered financially and was obliged to cut one aspect of its educational work after another. In the 1940s, the school gave up most of its extra-curricular activities and the effort of 'adaptation', and began to focus almost exclusively on academic subjects. The Achimota School today makes a totally different impression on people who study its education. It is not *the* School any more, but merely one of many academically high-performing schools. Many of the recent students do not even know about the ideals and practices of the earlier staff to adapt the best educational models of the early 20th century to Africa.

Notes

1 Specifically about agreement of missions and the government on the needs of character training on the Gold Coast, see Anim, 'Ghana', 178, 81–3.

2 *Mfantsipim Edwindzi*, June 1911, cited in Boahen 1996: 185.

3 'The Larger Life Education', in *Gold Coast Leader*, 11 May 1907.

4 A.G. Fraser, Letter to Prayer Helpers No 7, April 1925, Rhodes House Library, Mss Brit.Emp.s. 283 Fraser.

5 'The Larger Life Education', *Gold Coast Leader*, 11 May 1907.

6 S.D. Tetteh, 'The need for commercial education in the Gold Coast', 17 March 1934, *Gold Coast Spectator*.

7 'Wanted – An Agricultural School', *Gold Coast Leader*, 23 March 1912.

8 In 1920, the volume of major cash crop exports were: cocoa – 124,800 tons; rubber – 100 tons; palm oil – 2500 tons; palm kernels – 7,700 tons; and kola – 7,300 tons (Kay 1972: 336–7).

9 A.G. Fraser, Letter to Prayer Helpers No 7, April 1925, Rhodes House Library, Mss Brit.Emp.s. 283 Fraser.

10 Note by J.E.W. Hood, 1February 1934. PRO, CO 847/3/15.

11 Optimist, 'Missionaries and Education in Pagan Africa', *Journal of African Society* 23 (1923): 46.

12 Report of the Achimota Third Educational Conference held on 20 and 21 December 1928 (Accra, Gold Coast: Government Printing Office, 1929), 16, Achimota School Library.

13 Report of Education Department 1911, 20. PRO, CO 98/20.

14 *Memoir of Samuel Hanson Amissah*, Rhodes House Library, Mss Afr. S. 1755.

15 'Empire Day in Accra, 1934: Hear the Country's Cal', by E.W. Note Dowuona. *Coast Gold Spectator*, 9 June 1934.

16 'The Moral Lessons of Empire Day', *Gold Coast Nation*, 30 May 1912.

17 'Speech made by Omanhin Ababio II of Aburah. Mfantsipim School and the Wesleyan Girls' High School Combined Speech Day, Concert and Prize Distribution'. *Gold Coast Nation*, 25 December 1913.

18 Interview with Fia Sri II by Nana Ofori Atta, paramount chief of Akim Abuakwa. Evidence given before the Educationists' Committee, 5 July 1922. Appendix to Sessional Paper I 1924–5: *Interim Report of the Educationists' Committee 1922 appointed by His Excellency the Governor, 23rd May, 1922*, Accra, Gold Coast: Government Press, 1922. PRO, CO 98/41.

19 Minutes of Legislative Council, 29 July 1924, PRO, CO 98/41.; Appendix E. Nana Sir Ofori Atta's Dissent, Sessional Paper XXI 1928–9 'Report and Recommendations of the Committee appointed by His Excellency the Governor in March 1928, to consider the problem created by the closure of Inefficient Schools', Accra, Gold Coast: Government

Printing Office 1929; Minutes of Legislative Council, 29July 29 1924, PRO, CO 98/41.

[20] Minutes of Legislative Council, 29 July 1924 (PRO, CO 98/41), 14 March 1934 and 20 March 1934 (PRO, CO 98/63).

[21] For example, Minutes of the Legislative Council, 15 February 1929. PRO, CO 98/54. Also, Appendix VI, Letter from Hon. The Omanhene of Akim Abuakwa, *Educationists' Committee Report 1920*, Accra, Gold Coast: Government Printing Office 1920. PRO, CO 98/27.

[22] They were members of Mfantsipim School Committee. Also, Casely Hayford, together with Ofori Atta, was an African representative at the Gold Coast Education Board (established in 1920) until the early 1930s. Ofori Atta, Casely Hayford and J.E.P. Brown often attended the Gold Coast Legislative Council as non-permanent members, and remarked on various issues including education, PRO, CO98 Minutes of the Legislative Council.

[23] Sessional Paper I 1924-5: Interim Report of the Educationists' Committee 1922, PRO, CO 98/41.

[24] He wrote a draft of a history textbook that was sent to Oxford University Press for publication and stirred up controversy in the Colonial Office; officials thought the draft was prejudiced in favour of Africans and against British acts in Africa. PRO, CO 96/700/16. As for his contact with and interpretation of African life and tradition, see Ward, W.E.F. *My Africa*, Accra: Ghana University Press, 1991.

[25] *Report of the Achimota Third Educational Conference held on 20th and 21st December, 1928*, Accra, Gold Coast: Government Printing Office, 1929 30, Achimota School Library; Ward, *Fraser of Trinity and Achimota* 204.

[26] Ibid, p. 28 and p. 30.

[27] Fraser, A.G., with regard to the character training at Achimota, 146, cited in Guggisberg, Sir Gordon. The Gold Coast: A Review of the Events of 1924–5 and the Prospects of 1925–6, PRO, CO 98/45.

[28] Governor Guggisberg, cited in 'Training the Negro: Lessons from the Gold Coast', *The Times*, 25 April 1923, CBMS-IMC Box 267.

[29] Interview with graduates of Achimota and Mfantsipim in summer 2002.

[30] These are all names of places. Kumasi was the capital of the Ashanti tribe and was in the northern part of the Gold Coast Colony. Accra is the capital of today's Ghana and is 10 km south of Achimota. Volta is to the east, toward the border with Togo, and Prah is to the west.

[31] Williams 1962: 25. Today, the first and last parts of the song have different names of places, reflecting the enlargement of territory from the Gold Coast Colony to Ghana. It now reads,

    From Gambaga to Accra
    From Wiase to Keta
    …..
    Achimota-a-a.

[32] Report on Achimota College 1934, cited in Agbodeka 1977: 66.

[33] Report of the Education Department 1935–36: 47–8. PRO. CO 98/67.

[34] Cited in Fraser, A.G. *Letter to Prayer-Helpers No. 56, September 29th, 1930*, Rhodes House Library, Mss. Brit. Emp. s. 283 Fraser.

[35] Report of the Achimota Third Educational Conference held on 20 and 21 December 1928, Accra, Gold Coast: Government Printing Office, 1929 p. 30, Achimota School Library.

[36] An interviewee who was at Achimota between 1927 and 1940 was tutored in violin by Mrs Grace, the wife of the second principal. Interview in summer 2002.

[37] Report of the Achimota Third Educational Conference held on 20 and 21 December 1928, Accra, Gold Coast: Government Printing Office, 1929.

[38] Minutes of Conference on the Education of African Women, 21 July 1925, CBMS-IMC Box 207.

[39] Notes from a meeting on the education of women and girls in Africa, 5 January 1927 at Edinburgh House Gold Coast, CBMS-IMC Box 207.

[40] According to the 1932 Achimota Inspectors' Report, female students' fees for secondary school were 40 pound, whereas male students' fees were 50 pound. (Newlands, et al 1932: 28).

The female interviewees the author met enrolled at Achimota for reasons such as their brother(s) was/were already schooled at Achimota or their parents had personal ties with Aggrey, one of the founders. They are either from elite families in the coastal area or are the relatives of traditional chiefs. Table 8-4 will reveal that, even though the enrolment of female students had changed unstably, about 40 per cent of middle school students and a quarter of secondary school students were female. There was a Wesleyan girls' school established in 1836, but even at this school, the number of students at the middle and secondary school levels were few. Together with Achimota students, the total female middle and secondary school students added up to only about one fiftieth the number of their male counterparts (Table 6-1).

[41] Interview with George, an old Achimotan, in 2002.

[42] Interview in 2002 with K.B., who was teaching at Achimota in the periods of 1945–48 and 1953–57.

[43] Until the University College of the Gold Coast was established in 1948, an education at secondary schools and teacher training colleges was the highest available in the colony, although a number of people had already acquired degrees from British institutions.

[44] The number of students for each school in 1934 was as follows: Mfantsipim – 206; SPG (Adisadel) – 183; Achimota (116 Boys and 18 girls), CBMS-IMC Box 263.

[45] Interview with Francis, Emmanuel and John in 2002.

[46] Interview with Dave in 2002.

[47] Interview with Cathleen in 2002.
[48] Interview with Jane in 2002.
[49] Gaitskell reports that the girls' vocational classes in colonial South Africa transmitted the Victorian–Christian notion of the good family life (2002). For a similar analysis of girls' education in French Africa, see Barthel 1985.
[50] Interview with Jane and Malerine in 2002.
[51] Report on Achimota College 1932, 14, cited in Setse 1974: 42.

Part IV
Post-history and conclusion

Chapter 9

Educational adaptation and public response in Ghana after independence

The argument to adapt education to students' socio-economic and cultural background was not peculiar to the colonial period. However, as I have discussed in the introduction to this book, the meanings attached to 'adaptation' or 'Africanisation' of education have been constantly in flux. The term 'adaptation' does not specify which part of education should be 'adapted' to what. It could mean either the adaptation of curricular contents to the labour market demand or the revision of teaching materials to be culturally relevant. It could also mean the usage of the vernacular as the language of instruction. The interpretations would also vary according to the analysis of the current situation in the country. When there was consensus among policy makers that the country lacked university degree holders, 'adapting' to the labour demand could mean increasing the budget allocation to higher education, which looks very different from an educational policy 'adapted' to the demand for manual workers. At the time of independence, the cultural relevance of the curriculum gained increased attention as an issue related to the development of national identity. The terms 'adaptation' and 'Africanisation' were always there in the educational discourse of colonial and post-colonial Ghana but their meanings have been too diverse to determine a single definition of 'adaptation'.

This chapter will turn to 'adaptation' in post-colonial Ghana in relation to the changing trends of policies and enrolment at the level of secondary education. Here, I will maintain the consistent stance of this book to examine the impact of the global discourse and local responses to it, seen in the policies and practices of education in Ghana. While the post-colonial period is not the main focus of this book, it is important to demonstrate some consistent undercurrent of educational discourse across different time periods.

As I argued in Chapter 2, in the centre of policy debates on education, there always had been the tug-of-war between more literary and more vocational education. Therefore, despite that such debates are not labelled so much as the matter of 'adaptation' anymore, the fundamental nature of the discourse and the key concerns of the stakeholders have persisted. There is no clear-cut division between the two models, but what has been ceaselessly discussed was how to strike the balance along the continuum between the two extremes. For this balancing act, the historically developed system, the political, cultural and social context of the country, has exercised a significant influence.

Based on this consideration, in this chapter, I will first overview the global trends in policy priorities and their justifications on secondary education, particularly vocational education since the 1950s. With those as the background, changes to Ghanaian secondary education policies will be discussed. While Ghanaian education policies have been under strong influence of global trends, there have been some significant divergences. As I did in other parts of this book, this chapter will try to demonstrate the ways in which both international and domestic forces contributed to shape the policies. Then, the policy changes will be matched with the data of resource allocation and enrolment in different time periods, which will indicate how the policies were implemented and received by the general public. I will also try to cite public opinion on education policies when possible. Throughout my twenty years' research on education in Ghana, I have interviewed policy makers, teachers, parents and students for different purposes. Since these interviews were conducted for other research, they will not serve as systematic evidence for this chapter's argument. Still, I consider they would help readers to grasp the feeling among Ghanaian stakeholders.

9-1 External influences on the vocational secondary education policies

9-1-1 The 1950s and 1960s

Globally, there have been rises and falls of vocationalism with different justifications. Continuing from the late colonial period, there was a global enthusiasm to invest in vocational education in the 1950s and 60s. The theory of trusteeship brought about the education model to emphasise developing the professionals and leaders in respective fields to gradually replace Europeans and to be able to rule themselves independently. With the strong trust in the 'scientific' manpower planning, external aid providers have concentrated resources on higher education and technical and vocational education.

The late 1950s and early 1960s, the period when many African colonies achieved independence, saw the establishment of international organisations with their attendant goal setting. In 1963, for example, the World Bank launched a massive loan programme for vocational education in developing countries. Between 1964 and 1969, secondary-level vocational education was the Bank's second most significant area of educational loans, for which 20 per cent of all funds were allocated (World Bank Priorities and strategies for education (1995), cited in Atchoarena and Caillods 1999: 69).[1] On the other hand, provision for general secondary education was gradually curtailed. Comparing World Bank funds allocated for various educational sub-sectors in the periods 1963–68 and 1969–80, one can see that the fund for sub-professional training (technical, vocational and agricultural education) rose from 26 to 32 per cent, while secondary and higher education declined from 70 to 31 per cent (Jones 1992:125).

Support for this shift in funding from general secondary and higher education to vocational secondary education was provided by the economic theory of 'human capital'. This theory is based on the rates of return on investment in education. The difference between the wages of graduates and the cost expended by individuals (tuition, transportation to school, forgone opportunities for earning, etc.) and by society (tax revenue spent on education) are calculated as the private and social rates of return, respectively. The higher the rates of return, the more effective the education is considered to be in preparing the workforce. Until the 1970s, the reports of international organisations stated that the rate of return from vocational secondary education was high (World Bank 1963).

9-1-2 From the 1970s to early 1980s

Then, in the 1970s, the priorities of educational development programmes shifted away from secondary and tertiary education altogether, including the vocational track. During this period, there arose a global norm that the goal of development programmes should be to fulfil basic human needs, particularly for the impoverished population, such as rural subsistence farmers. The promotion of the support for basic human needs caused a reorientation of policies in various fields. In the case of education, it meant to redirect resources away from tertiary and secondary (both vocational and academic tracks) to primary and adult literacy education.

During this period, in many developing countries, quality of facilities and equipment in secondary and higher education institutions were devastated. For example, Balme Library of the University of Ghana, a beautiful colonial building erected in 1948, has a good collection of books published before the 1970s, but has limited addition of books for the few decades afterwards. It is only after the turn of the century, partly because of the development of the Ghanaian economy itself and partly of the return of donors' attention to higher education, that the library building was renovated and shelves started to contain recently published books. Also, during the era of the Cold War, Africa became the site of proxy war between the Eastern and the Western blocks. With conflicting external back-ups, many African countries, including Ghana, experienced frequent changes of regimes which led to inconsistency of public administration and financial management. Against such background, social services such as education suffered in general, but particularly at the middle to higher levels.

In the late 1970s and early 1980s the World Bank initiated a series of research projects on the rate of return from vocational secondary education in Tanzania and Colombia. The report of the projects stated that while the cost of introducing vocational subjects is higher than conventional academic education, graduates from vocational secondary schools neither find employment more quickly nor earn higher wages than graduates of conventional schools (Psacharopoulos 1988: 275). Also at this time, segregated vocational secondary education began to be criticised from the viewpoint of egalitarianism (Benavot 1983: 73). It has been pointed out that vocational graduates often experience economic and social inequality, largely due to the general perception that vocational school students are academically less qualified than those in general secondary schools. Given the criticism from the egalitarian perspective and the lack of convincing evidence of the cost-effectiveness of vocational secondary education, since the 1980s international educational discourse has headed towards blurring the boundary between general and vocational secondary curricula (vocationalisation). Vocational school students were to learn more academic subjects and general secondary schools have diversified the elective subjects to include more practical subjects. The international trend in vocational education of this period was to entrust non-formal bodies of education with specific skills training and to make formal education, either vocational or academic, more general preparation for the world of work. By utilising this non-formal channel, it is hoped that vocational preparation will be more flexible and reflective of workforce demand (Atchoarena and Caillods 1999: 76–80; Fluitman 1992: 5; McGrath & King 1999: 216).

9-1-3 The 1980s: the age of structural adjustment

Globally, the 1980s is known as the period of structural adjustment. The World Bank and the International Monetary Fund (IMF) introduced a loan programme to relieve heavily indebted countries at lower interests. To qualify for this additional support, there was a set of conditions for developing country governments to fulfil. To reduce the fiscal imbalance, the structural adjustment programmes (SAPs) required the borrowing countries to reduce public expense and promote a free market economy. To improve macro-economic performance of the country, trade barriers such as tariffs and import licences were restricted. At the same time, massive privatisation and deregulation were introduced to reduce governmental intervention in the domestic market. The effects of SAPs on education surfaced immediately. Education started to be considered as the service to purchase, instead of public goods, and school fees were introduced even at the level of primary education.

Those who could not afford it were excluded from access to education altogether. In contrast to the 1950s and 60s, when there was a strong governmental initiative to 'plan' based on 'scientific' examination of manpower needs, the *laissez-faire* approach of the 1980s did not promote any form or level of education, unless the demands naturally lead some services to be more popular than others. Technical and vocational education, a form of education which has always been seen with dubious eyes by the public since the colonial period, was left largely unattended in this period. Meanwhile, education above high school remained a luxury of a small population with financial means and exposure to elite culture at home.

9-1-4 From the 1990s to the mid-2000s: the dominance of 'education for all'

After a decade of neoliberal policies of SAPs, systems of social services were damaged in many developing countries, and the gap between the privileged and the poor disadvantaged population had enlarged. Seeing this situation, the global trend swung to another extreme: the welfare state approach to ensure basic services for the lower level of the social pyramid. 'Poverty reduction' became the fundamental norm to be shared across global initiatives for social development. Accordingly, in the field of education, the governments resumed their commitment to the provision of schooling opportunities, instead of leaving it to the market mechanism. At the same time, priority was given to the lower level of education rather than to medium to higher levels (Yamada 2010).

In 1990, the World Conference on Education for All was held in Jomtien, Thailand, jointly convened by UNESCO, UNICEF, World Ban, and UNDP, attended by the delegates from 155 countries and representatives of some 150 governmental, non-governmental and intergovernmental organisations. The Declaration adopted at this conference was considered as the collective commitment of the global 'education community' and constituted the normative framework in the following decade. While there were six goals under EFA, including adult literacy, vocational and general secondary and tertiary education, the main focus of funding assistance has shifted dramatically to primary education.

The shift of global educational ideologies is directly linked to a shift in international organisations' financial focus. The World Bank's investment in vocational education declined by half from the 1960s to 1990 (Table 9-1). Within this sub-sector, the secondary level showed the sharpest decline. In 1992, the Bank decided to further reduce loans to this sector to only 6 per cent of the total amount for the education programme (World Bank 1991). Within general education, funding increases were mostly at the primary level.

Table 9-1: Distribution of Project Investments, by Education Sub-sector, FY 1963–90

	1963-76		1977-86		1990	
	US$M	Percentage	US$M	Percentage	US$M	Percentage
General education	963	42	6,171	52	1,222	64
Primary	134	6	2,580	22	456	24
Secondary	461	20	1,176	10	163	8
Post-secondary	89	4	1,615	14	323	17
Non-formal (literacy)	30	1	48	0		0
Teacher education	251	11	752	6	280	15
Vocational education	1,150	51	5,220	44	489	25
Secondary	511	23	706	6	69	4
Post-secondary	367	16	2,810	24	302	16
Non-formal	249	11	1,579	13	45	2
Teacher education	23	1	124	1	73	4
Non-allocated	153	7	368	3	207	11
Total	2,266	100	11,759	100	1,918	100

Source: Jones 1992: 182

Throughout the 1990s, the disproportionate emphasis on primary education continued. In the early 2000s, in the most of African lower developing countries, the proportion of the budget allocated to primary education was more than half of the total education budget. It was not rare that it reached as much as 70 per cent (Yamada 2005a). Figure 9-1 shows the composition of overseas development aid for education provided by DAC member countries. In 2004, almost 60 per cent of educational ODA was for basic (primary and lower secondary) education. During this period, the major efforts of both the developing country governments and donors were focused on increasing primary school enrolment. The number of students in school was considered as the indicator of the degree that the society reached the population who has missed the opportunity to enjoy 'human rights on education'. In this sense, the discussion on the contents of education subsided, even in primary education. Needless to say, the attention to (senior) secondary education, both in general and vocational categories was limited.

Figure 9-1: DAC Member Countries' Education ODA by Sub-sectors, 2004 and 2008

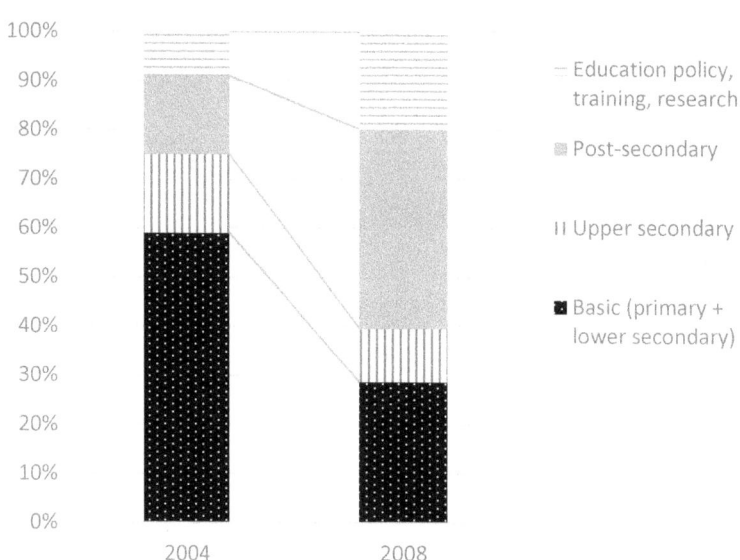

Source: OECD 2005 and 2009

The extreme concentration on basic education had started to reduce in the mid-2000s. As Figure 9-1 shows, only in four years from 2004 to 2008, the composition of educational ODA changed greatly. After a decade and half of effort to increase access to basic education, gross enrolment rates in most developing countries reached close to 100 per cent or even higher.[2] Facing this situation, educational issues to be discussed and picked up for development projects became diversified. While basic education has continued to be a major focus, this time on quality improvement, technical and vocational education at the secondary level and higher education came back to the main stage.

9-1-5 Recent revival of vocationalism and promotion of competency-based training

Despite its rather simple underlying assumption – that expanded school access would lead to poverty reduction – the universal basic education policy did not demonstrate a visible contribution to either better learning outcomes or increased employment, which would be the condition for schooling to contribute to reduce poverty. To get a decent job and a stable life, knowledge and skills are preconditions. However, they cannot necessarily be gained by sitting in the classroom or swallowing the curricular contents that Ministry of Education experts consider important. In the last several years there has been a revival of the logic, which would have become familiar to the readers of this book, that a smooth transition from school to work would require enhanced relevance of knowledge and skills taught at school to the actual work, reflecting the voices of the private sector in decisions on educational contents (King & Palmer 2013; UNESCO 2012).

The aid community has promoted competency-based training (CBT) in developing countries as the ideal way to develop such 'relevant' vocational skills. The recent idea of industrial skills development has broadened the scope of training from formal technical and vocational education (TVET) institutions to apprenticeship, non-formal education, and firm-based training. As mentioned in Chapter Two, a large part of the African workforce is employed in the informal sector. The major part of their training also takes place informally as the apprenticeship. Recognising such situation, the recent CBT reforms also highlight the importance of skills formation for workers in the informal sector with a lower and unstable income, unlike the conventional bias toward the training of mid- to high-level technicians and engineers. Another feature is promotion of various forms of public–private partnership in training. Adapting neoliberalism, the recent trend is to reduce the direct involvement of the government in training itself, while emphasising its role in facilitating the process of enhancing the relevance of training. As I have reviewed, one of the major criticisms against formal vocational education was the cost inefficiency, where the price of equipment and trainers was expensive. The CBT is supposed to minimise the cost of formal training by involving private enterprises and workshops as the training providers, while at the same time, improving the responsiveness of training to the actual needs of the skilled workers. To achieve these goals, expatriate advisors encourage governments to establish an independent agency to coordinate among training providers, industries that employ graduates of training institutions and the various ministries involved. Another popular measure is to establish a pooled fund for skills development, which is used for subsidising firms that send their workers to training programmes or institutions that, in turn, develop new programmes in response to the skills demanded by the industries. In these arrangements, the role of the government is envisaged as more of catalyst than a direct training provider, with the private sector expected to drive the competitive training market (Eichhorst et al 2012: 4–9; Yamada & Mazda 2009: 130–135).

9-1-6 *Longitudinal patterns of debates on vocational education*

As summarised in Table 9-2, the trends to promote vocational education in the history of global education discourse have recurred. There have been the shifts of emphasis along an axle, one end of which is complete vocational education, while another end is exclusive literary education. It is not a zero-sum game, but rather a matter of a fulcrum to balance vocational and literary education. Sometimes the centre of gravity has shifted to more general education, while it has always shifted back to the side of vocational education. This is a cyclical dynamics of ideas, which, in the case of Africa, has its root in the colonial period, but has persisted and will continue.

There has been recurring discussion that education has to be relevant ('adapted') to the needs of the learners and their background. Skills and knowledge learned at school has to be linked closely with the work the learners are going to do after graduation. Also, from an egalitarian perspective, vocational education would make the opportunity of schooling more equitable, while access to general secondary education cannot be expanded much without a prospect of labour market demand and of capacity at higher education institutions. At the same time, there has been as frequent criticism that vocational programmes of secondary education would rather contribute to confirm the class and gender gap. Vocational education was also criticised for the lack of flexibility to meet the fast changing demands from the labour market. While the financial investment in vocational education is large, the rate of return and the employment rate of the vocational graduates are not high. Such logic for or against vocational education has not changed much since the colonial period.

At the same time, it would be important to recognise the forces that drive the global discourse on education and set the standard for the policies of various countries. The policies and practices of the Gold Coast Colony and Ghana cannot be understood in isolation from global trends, regardless that the local power politics and socio-economic contexts cannot be reduced to minor variations. By situating the case of the Gold Coast Colony and post-colonial Ghana in this broad history of transferring educational ideas, it would be possible to examine the relationship between the contemporary global influence, longitudinal trends of such ideas and local realities.

Table 9-2: Global Trends of Education Policies and Vocationalism

	Colonial period	1950s – 60s	70s – early 80s	80s – early 90s	90s – mid-2000s	Mid-2000s– present
Goals	Formation of colonial subjects	Economic growth	Fulfillment of Basic Human Needs (BHN)	Rehabilitation of macro-economic policies	Universal access to basic social services	Sustainable development
Foci of education programs	Incorporation of mission education Establishment of education system	Tertiary Technical and vocational secondary	Non-formal education Adult literacy program Rural education	Reduced governmental commitment to education	Access to primary and lower secondary Girls education	Learning outcomes Life skills Skills for decent work
Key terms	Trusteeship Scientific planning Trickle-down	Manpower planning Human capital Trickle-down	BHN Redistribution Rural development	Structural adjustment Neo-liberalism Efficiency Privatization Cost-sharing	Equity Poverty reduction Bottom-up Welfare state	Sustainability Relevance Inclusiveness
Models of vocational education	American Black industrial education	Planned development of professionals	Lack of attention ⇦	Vocationalization of secondary education	Lack of attention ⇦	Competency-based training

Source: author

9-2 Education policies in the post-colonial Ghana and the changing focus on vocational education

In this section, I will discuss education policies initiated by successive Ghanaian regimes after independence, with particular focus on vocational secondary education in relation to general secondary education.

9-2-1 System development in the 1960s

Kwame Nkrumah, the first prime minister and president of independent Ghana, highlighted the importance of education as a means to promote economic growth by expanding the literacy and scientific knowledge among its population (Adu-Gyamfi et al 2016: 162). Accordingly, he paid particular attention to technical and engineering education.

The recognised necessity of professionals in science and technology in these early years of independent Ghana was inherited from the colonial period. Kumasi College of Technology (KCT), which was established in 1951, six years before the independence, was upgraded to Kwame Nkrumah University of Science and Technology. The fact that the first batch of students of KCT was transferred from Achimota suggests the continuum of the vocationalism in elite education before and after independence. Meanwhile, for the training of medium-level technicians, Kumasi Technical Institute was founded in 1956, which was followed by technical institutes in major cities of Ghana. The Technical Teacher Training Centre was also established in Kumasi in 1960.

Given the well-established apprenticeship mechanism, it is a unique characteristic of Ghanaian discourse on vocational secondary education that the policy makers attempted to bring about a mechanism to partner with artisans, who train and employ prospective workers through traditional informal channels. As such, in 1961, the Convention People's Party (CPP), the ruling party of Ghana then, passed the Apprentice Act, and created a general Apprenticeship Board along with committees for each industry (Hazel 1992: 53–5).

9-2-2 Turmoils in the 1970s

Nkrumah's regime was overthrown by a military coup in 1966, but the commitment of the government to promote basic and secondary education persisted. As soon as it grasped the office in 1966, the Government of National Liberation Council appointed an Education Review Committee. Among widely-ranged proposals provided by the Committee, there was also a proposal that 'middle school (current junior high school) pupils should attend two years pre-vocational continuation classes', which are 'patterned on the industrial and farming needs of the country' (Great Pola Africa Foundation 2017). However, the drive to increase the years of schooling and contents of the curriculum became clearer than in Nkrumah's period, which meant schools became more academic and less open to the public. As Figure 9-2 indicates, the increase in the number of enrolments in secondary education had been marginal throughout the 1970s, while primary education also did not expand much.

In the context of political instability and financial breakdown of short-lived governments which appeared one after another, it was difficult to see any consistent development of systematically designed public systems in any field. Therefore, until the second coup d'état of Jerry Rawlings succeeded and led to his long-lasting regime of nearly 20 years, a large part of secondary schools continued to be elitist institutions, which were accessible only to the rich and privileged class.

Figure 9-2: Trend of Enrolment in Primary and Secondary Education in Ghana (1971–2016)

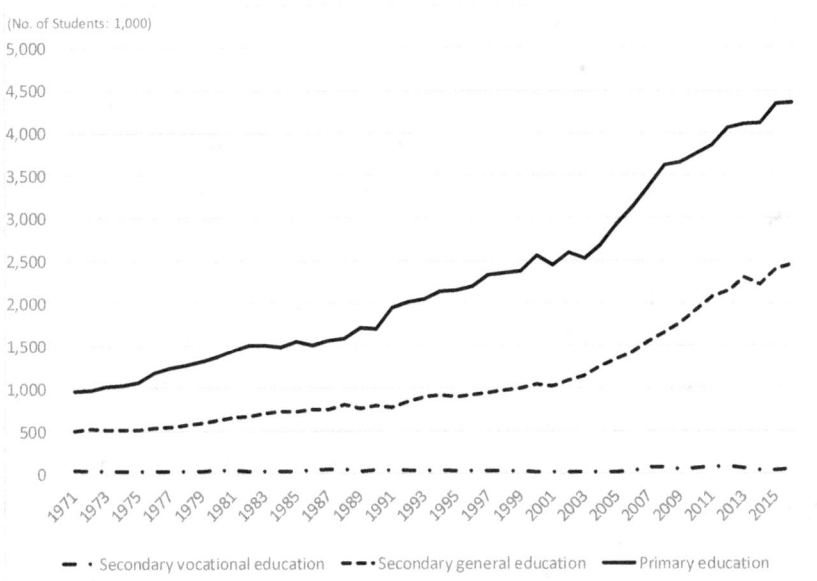

Source: World Bank 2017

9-2-3 1987 Education reform: socio-moralist vocationalism

The Educational Reform Program (ERP) of 1987 introduced a 6-3-3-4 school system, which simplified and shortened the length of pre-university education from 17 to 12 years. This occurred during the government of Jerry Rawlings, who seized power by means of military coups supported by the masses. Given the origins of the government, it had a strong populist orientation. Therefore, in the field of education, it announced its intention to provide universal access to education, while, at the same time, seeing education as a means of providing skills to live, including vocational skills. Academic education was condemned as elitist, while highly-educated leaders in various fields – especially those who were politically active – were purged from their positions. The extreme populism of the Rawlings government was replaced by the centrist liberalism of the Kufor government, which took office in 2000. But the vocationalising policy of secondary education was basically maintained by the succeeding governments.

According to the ERP 1987, vocationalisation of the lower cycle of secondary education (junior secondary school, or JSS)[3] was meant to provide vocational orientation to students, rather than to train them in specific employment skills, while at the upper secondary level (senior secondary school, or SSS), the vocational subjects were meant to provide skills for paid- or self-employment (Akyeampong 2002: iv–12). Similar to the vocational subjects introduced in Achimota and other secondary schools during the colonial period, the vocationalism in JSS aimed to eliminate the distaste for manual work and plant a work ethic and attitude in the minds of students that was to orient students' minds rather than transmit specific skills.

As a part of ERP 1987, Integrated Community Centers for Employable Skills were built all around the country. Also, for the sake of coordination between the labour market and the education and training institutions, the National Coordinating Committee on Technical and Vocational Education and Training (NACVET) was established, which initiated various measures to improve the relevance of TVET to labour market needs (Akyeampong 2002: 25).

As I discussed elsewhere (Yamada 2005b), vocationalisation started in the late 1980s was not unique to Ghana but a global phenomenon. It aimed to diversify the general school curriculum so that students could take vocational subjects as electives. Globally, it was said to be a more cost efficient and egalitarian approach to developing the workforce, meeting the changing labour demand more flexibly while avoiding tracking students between vocational and general courses. Meanwhile, in Ghana, the justification for vocationalism was made in more moralistic terms, namely that it would prepare the minds of students to appreciate the work available to them and make a smooth transition. As I reviewed in Chapter Two, justifications for vocational education can be economic, social and moralistic. In terms of vocationalisation under ERP 1987, while it converged with the global trend of vocationalisation, its local context added more socio-moralist flavour to the practice.

9-2-4 Popularisation of basic education: sidelined (vocational and general) secondary education

As I mentioned earlier in this chapter, after the World Conference on Education for All in 1990, the international education community concentrated its efforts on expanding access to basic (primary and lower secondary (JSS)) education. Ghana was no exception. In accordance with the global compact of EFA, in 1996 in Ghana, the World Bank and other international donors active in the field of education launched a large scale programme named 'Free Compulsory Universal Basic Education' (FCUBE), aiming to achieve a hundred per cent enrolment in primary education by 2005.

Accordingly, prioritisation of basic education in the Ghanaian Ministry of Education became clearer as time went by. Ghanaian total education discretionary budget as a percentage of GDP increased from 3.7 per cent to 5.1 per cent between 1999 and 2006, nearly half of it (49.7 per cent) being allocated to basic education (Ministry of Education, Science and Sports 2007a). During this period, other educational subsectors, particularly senior secondary and vocational education were sacrificed. The budgetary allocation to senior secondary education had been below 15 per cent for several years, and was planned to be kept low under the Ghana Poverty Reduction Strategy (Republic of Ghana 2003).

In Ghana, the gross enrolment rate at the primary level was 93.7 per cent in 2006/07, while it was 35.8 per cent at the senior secondary level (including both vocational and general tracks) (Ministry of Education, Science and Sports 2007b), and the transition rate from basic to senior secondary education has been kept at around 30 per cent consistently (Ministry of Education and Sports 1999). As basic education expands, the demand for post-basic education for basic school leavers also expands. The number of teachers required at the basic schools was growing, though the intake of teacher training institutions could not dramatically increase unless senior secondary education expanded. After all, the lack of financial and strategic attention to senior secondary education had negative implications for the education system as a whole.

There was widespread anxiety among politicians, educational administrators and the public about how to handle the mass of students who finish basic education but are not absorbed into the labour market. Social unrest and unemployment of JSS-leavers – a recognised social problem – continued to provide justification for the old policy of vocationalisation, which was reinforced in 1987. In interviews, I often heard that the JSS's programme of vocational orientation would help students to find employment locally, instead of aspiring to white-collar jobs which are not available (Yamada 2009).

9-2-5   2007 New education reform

Toward the adoption of the bill for 2007 Education Reform, Ghanaian governmental policy shifted slightly toward promoting post-primary education, the share of senior secondary education in the education budget having increased to 21.2 per cent in 2006 (Ministry of Education, Science and Sports 2007a). Still, compared with basic education, the financial resources the government could allocate were not enough to cover the cost of senior secondary education. The subsidy per student pledged by the government would have added up to a quarter of the total budget allocated to senior secondary education, but in reality, 92 per cent of the budget was spent on personnel emolument (Ministry of Education and Sports 2005).

The education reform of 2007 turned out to be the largest scale after the one in 1987. Partly as a reaction to the excessive emphasis on basic education, the 2007 reform is characterised by increased emphasis on secondary and higher education, including technical and vocational education and training (TVET) at secondary and post-secondary levels. Abandoning the long lasting ceiling of senior secondary enrolment rate at around 35 per cent, the number of SHS intakes increased greatly (see Figure 9-2).

In terms of TVET, a large part of the reform arrangements and their justifications seem to reiterate what had already been done. A characteristic of the reform in the 2000s is the emphasis placed on the competencies of problem solving in the actual settings of work and life. Because of its emphasis on 'competency' in real life contexts, it is called 'competency-based training (CBT)'. With this emphasis on competencies in the work context, the focus of examining the effectiveness of education has shifted from the school system to the acquired knowledge and skills of learners.

It was South Africa that first adopted CBT in Africa, and Ghana is in the first group of sub-Saharan African countries which followed suit, with growing support from donor organisations (Allais 2007; Mahomed 1996). Following the prescription to establish an independent coordination agency, the national parliament of Ghana passed the Council for TVET (COTVET) Act in 2007, and the comprehensive reform of the formal and informal skills development system has been in progress under the initiative of COTVET.[4] The COTVET has also led the process of developing occupation standards for respective vocational skills, National TVET Qualification Framework and Accreditation Standard for the providers of education and training (Darvas & Palmer 2014: 5; Government of Ghana 2014: ix; COTVET 2012). With the support of donors such as the World Bank, Africa Development Bank and bilateral aid agencies of Germany, Belgium and Denmark, the skills development fund was established in 2012 to implement CBT.

Reflecting the global trend, curriculums in secondary TVET institutions increased the required hours of practical training in school and at private sector companies. Also, certification for vocational skills is to be provided based on the assessment of practical skills rather than by the completion of the school curriculum. Therefore, theoretically, it is possible for apprentices without a TVET diploma to get the skills certificate at the same level as those from TVET. Because of its massive scale, the reform process has caused a lot of confusion and it still needs time to take root in daily practices at school (Kumasi Technical Institute 2011; Acheampong et al 2014).

9-3 Dialectics between the global and the national

9-3-1 Convergences and divergences of Ghanaian policies and global trends

Comparing the Ghanaian education reforms and global trends of education policies shown in Table 9-2, one must admit that the rises and falls of secondary and vocational education in Ghana are closely linked with shifting global trends.

The glory of manpower planning and scientific planning from the late colonial period to the 1960s in the international scene was matched by Nkrumah's and CPP's policy to promote development of scientific literacy and highly skilled professionals by strengthening secondary and higher education. During this period, both vocational and general secondary education was highlighted at least in the policy. Such emphasis on higher levels of education was based on the assumption that the benefit of narrow-based elite education would trickle down to the masses eventually.

The downfall of secondary education and vocationalism in the 1970s was a global phenomenon. In Ghana also, the period between the regimes of Nkrumah and Rawlings did not see much progress in education. Such situation in Ghana may not be much related to the global normative trend, however. It was rather the matter of discontinuity of political leadership and lack of consistent plans. Also, before Ghana accepted the Structural Adjustment Program proposed by the World Bank and IMF in the 1980s, financial and normative influences from external bodies were limited. In this sense, despite the outlook of convergence, Ghanaian education policies in the 1970s were determined more by domestic factors than international.

Vocationalisation of secondary education, which was started under the 1987 Education Reform Program, echoes ideas promoted globally. The neo-liberal conception of education under the Structural Adjustment Program had an affinity with education policies which are linked with labour market needs and desires of parents and students, who are the customers of education services, for better and higher education. At the same time, as I argued in the earlier part of this chapter, vocationalisation in Ghana was not so much promoted according to the economic justification. While it did not abandon the logic of supplying a skilled workforce to the market, more emphasis was placed on the potential benefit of vocationalisation for reducing social delinquency caused by inequality, and for moral preparation of students before employment. Here again, we see significant reinterpretation of the globally promoted model to the national context and demands.

After the wholesale neglect of secondary and higher education under the Education for All and Millennium Development Goals from the 1990s, in the recent decade, the idea of competency-based education has been mainstreamed in the global discourse. As I mentioned in the introduction, Ghana is one of the first African countries which adopted the fundamental reform of the skills development mechanism and TVET. Financially, the governmental resources allocated to higher education has increased much, which is also followed by the increase in TVET.

Despite the massive effort to revise the curriculum, assessment framework and partnership mechanism with private sector enterprises, school-level practices are slow to change. While promoting vocationalisation, the 2007 education reform increased the years of senior secondary education from three to four years. The reason for this extension was that three years are not enough to cover the academic contents for Ghanaian students to be competitive in the global knowledge economy. This argument suggests that regardless of the commitment to the globally accepted prescription of competency-based vocational education, deep in the minds of educational policy makers, there is a persistent belief that more academic content will lead to national strength. Parents are willing to devote resources and energy for providing the best education for their children, which means, almost without exception, ensuring entrance to top academic schools. Such equivocation of stated principles and personal views is often caused by the historical background of the education system and cultural and social background of the education discourse in the country. Then, such inherent contradiction will result in practices which seem to divert from principles raised in the policy.

Based on this consideration, it is not enough to examine the similarities and differences between the global discourse and national policies. It is also important to see how the announced national policies were practised and how the public reacted to them. Therefore, in the next section, I will briefly overview the actual patterns of enrolment referring to government-provided statistics.

9-3-2 Practices of secondary education in Ghana: persistent distrust in the vocational track

In Ghana, while it is always a hot issue how to strike a balance between vocational and general secondary education, and there have been rises and falls of vocational focus in policy debates, in reality, school-based vocational education occupies only a small part of educational provision. For those people who have chances to access post-basic education, general secondary education is the first and predominant choice.

Ghana has had a relatively high level of educational achievements among African countries, having been an educational centre of British West Africa. As of 1971, the gross enrolment rate of primary education was already 67.2 per cent, reached 83.4 per cent in 2005 and 108.5 per cent in 2014. Also the promotion rate of primary school students to junior high school (JHS) – the level to which education is compulsory – is 93.8 per cent. Meanwhile, the promotion rate from JHS to senior high school (SHS) remains as low as 45.8 per cent. Even though it improved much from around 35 per cent in the mid-2000s, still there is a significant bottleneck of academic education between JHS and SHS, and many JHS graduates choose other career tracks than SHS (Ghana Education Service 2015, 2006). Therefore, it is still less than half of the cohort who proceed beyond JHS. Among those privileged youths who are promoted to post-basic (beyond JHS) education, those absorbed in the TVET track are strikingly limited in Ghana (Figure 9-2). TVET students increased 1.34 times, from 39,630 in 1971 to 53,171 in 2016, while general secondary students increased 4.86 times (505,784 to 2,458,694) during the same period. Of course, post-basic TVET institutions are not only secondary schools, but also include Technical Institutes. Still, adding all post-basic channels, students in this category constitute only 12 per cent and nearly 90 per cent are in general secondary schools. There are no accurate data of other youths who terminate schooling after JHS. However, it is assumed that they are either in apprenticeship, informal employment, household work or idle (Government of Ghana 2014: 2–11). According to estimation, more than 440,000 youths are learning skills in informal apprenticeship. If this is true, the ratio of apprentices against TVET students is 4:1 (Darvas & Palmer 2014: 6; Palmer 2009: 32).

Such unpopularity of formal vocational education is seen not only in Ghana but in Africa as a whole. As shown in Table 9-3, in sub-Saharan Africa, the distinct vocational track at the secondary level shrunk from 15.40 per cent at senior secondary education in 1960 to 5.30 per cent in 1996. In most other regions, vocational education has rather expanded. The rate of increase in the 'Far East and Oceania' region is a remarkable contrast to Africa (4.10 per cent in 1980 to 13.60 per cent in 1996) (Atchoarena & Caillods 1999). This consistent downward trend does not make sense in the light of the influence of global trends.

At the epistemic level, globally, vocationalism rose in the 1960s, 1980s and mid-2000s. However, the patterns of enrolment demonstrate clear regional differences, which suggest strong historical and cultural backgrounds of vocational education in respective regions. In Latin America and the Caribbean and in Europe, the patterns are pretty consistent in that about a quarter of secondary level students were in vocational and technical programmes. This fact suggests that the career prospects of the graduates from vocational programmes are relatively good in these regions, backed by the tradition of appreciating technical experts who are trained in special programmes.

Meanwhile, in Africa, as I argued earlier, the perceived inferiority of vocational education is deeply rooted in its history of colonialism (Yamada 2005b). The school was a place to prepare Africans to be clerks and lower-order colonial officials with minimal literacy and numeracy in English. As preparation for the world of work, such academic education was already 'vocational' (Foster 1966). Despite the tight link between schooling and white-collar employment, selection for such limited job opportunities did not depend much on the contents the candidate learned at school, but which level of school certificate he/she possessed. The consistent preference of modern-sector employers for holders of academic school certificates degraded vocational education to second-class status (Dore & Oxenham 1984:27; Foster 1966).[5]

Table 9-3: The Proportion of Secondary-level Pupils in Vocational and Technical Education by Region and by Category of Country

	1960	1970	1980	1990	1996	Average 1960-96	Average 1980-96
Sub-Saharan Africa	15.40	10.70	6.40	5.80	5.30	8.72	5.83
Arab countries	17.00	11.10	10.70	12.00	15.30	13.22	12.67
Far East and Oceania			4.10	11.50	13.60	9.73	9.73
South Asia			1.70	1.70	1.50	1.63	1.63
Latin America and the Caribbean	24.00	22.40	24.10	23.40	26.30	24.04	24.60
Europe	24.30	26.40	24.60	25.60	26.70	25.52	25.63
World	13.80	14.60	10.50	12.00	13.00	12.78	11.83
Developing countries	9.80	9.10	6.70	9.50	10.60	9.14	8.93
Less advanced countries			4.20	5.30	5.10	4.87	4.87
Developed countries	15.70	19.10	16.20	17.00	18.50	17.30	17.23

Source: Atchoarena & Caillods 1999: 71, based on UNESCO statistics, 1998

Such unconditional trust in academic education and its certificates, shared among the general public, intensifies the competition for access to good schools. Although academic competition to enter university has long been tough, in the last couple of decades, competition has descended to the level of junior high school. To enable their children to go to a good SHS (one which sends many students to university), parents make sure their children attend an academically well-performing private JHS. In the academic year 1999/2000, 75 per cent of entrants to the University of Ghana and Kwame Nkrumah University of Science and Technology came from the top fifty SSSs (out of 504 schools) and 46 per cent were from the top eighteen schools (Addae-Mensah 2000:6–14). Private universities are mushrooming to meet the pressing demand for higher education. Regardless, while the promotion ratio from JHS to

SHS is less than 50 per cent, still out of those who managed to go to SHS, the majority cannot proceed any further.

The gap between high- and low-status schools is widening at both the JHS and SHS level. In Ghana, high-status SHSs are all public schools and the fees are basically the same regardless of status. However, it is extremely difficult for a student from a public JHS to enter a top SHS, and the average basic fees of private JHSs is one hundred times more expensive than its public counterpart (Addae-Mensah 2000:18–9). Moreover, private JSSs are mostly in urban areas. The implication is clear: children of poor rural families are mostly excluded from the chance of climbing the social ladder through education. As I discussed in Chapter Eight, Achimota provided chances of social mobility for students from remote areas with scholarships. However, such mobility existed only at the transitional period when the vacuum of power caused by the submission of traditional chiefs to the colonial authority was yet to be filled by the elite produced by the School. Later generations of such educated elite rather maintained their status and reproduced their class. Still, the shared memory of dramatic social promotion of such an educated elite has upheld the desire for academic education among the masses in Ghana and many other sub-Saharan African countries.

Because of such a historical background, ironically, debates over vocational and general education in Ghana tend to scratch at the surface but do not go deeper into the contents and objectives of respective subjects and programmes. There has been a constant divide between normative discourse and practices regarding secondary education in Ghana. On the one hand, there has been high-level discussion on principles about the design of the education system for achieving better and relevant learning outcomes of students. At this level, vocational education has been given certain degree of attention and the differential roles of academic and core subjects in gaining desired results are discussed. Reforms have been initiated, partly following the fashionable models and prescriptions brought from overseas, but also based on the assessment of local needs for educated human resources. On the other hand, when it came to the practices, idealism of reform had often been watered down. Public pressure for expanding access to the academic track of education affected parliamentary decisions on budgetary allocations and authorisation of implementation programmes. Within the Ministry of Education too, vocational education tends to have weaker support for implementation than academic secondary education. Because of the existence of stumbling blocks and the lack of driving forces in the course of translating the policies into practices, it is difficult to see a secondary education reform (both vocational and academic) which drastically changes the curricular contents and objectives for teaching respective subjects.

Notes

[1] According to 'Proposed Bank/IDA Policies in the Field of Education', published in 1963, two urgent needs were (1) vocational and technical education, and (2) secondary education, cited in Jones 1992:55.

[2] Gross enrolment rate uses total population within the range of standard enrolment ages as the denominator to actual enrolment. Therefore, when there are enrolees who are outside of the standard ages, the gross enrolment rate may exceed 100 per cent.

[3] After the 2007 education reform, JSS was renamed Junior High School (JHS) and SSS became Senior High School (SHS).

[4] The idea of COTVET is similar to NACVET, which was established in 1990. However, because of the lack of political will and administrative support, NACVET had been left ineffective. Establishment of COTVET was along the effort to boost ideas promoted in the 1987 Education Reform Program.

[5] In 2002, King and Martin re-examined the thesis that the school functions as the credential mechanism and educational content does not matter. They modified it, demonstrating that there are some cases in which curricular effect and individual school character affect students' occupational choices (King & Martin 2002). However, the findings of King and Martin did not overthrow the thesis of the 1960s and it is still valid in Africa in the 2000s.

Chapter 10

Conclusion

This book has analysed the discourse on education for African colonial subjects in the metropole and in the Gold Coast Colony (present-day Ghana). The time period I focused on was roughly between the 1910s and 30s, when the British government increased control over its colonies in Africa and formalised its administration, including in the field of education. The increased interest of colonial officials in developing the character of colonial subjects and the advancement of Western educated Africans brought the issue of education to the centre of political discourse. I described the process in which education policy for British Africa was formulated in the imperial capital of London, African responses in the Gold Coast Colony to such London-initiated policy and educational ideas, and the way such policy and ideas were transformed in local negotiation and through the course of implementation. The analysis of Achimota School, a model secondary school established by the colonial government of the Gold Coast in 1927, was highlighted as a case to illustrate how people discussed 'good' education for Africans, how it was actualised and how students experienced it.

In Part II, the book considered the role played by British colonial officials, mission educators and American philanthropists in the discourse on education in Africa. To establish a collaborative relationship with the government in the field of education and to protect the place of religious education from government intervention, mission societies attempted to exercise their influence in the formation of colonial education policy in British Africa. At the same time, American philanthropists actively promoted their own black industrial education model in Africa. The idea of agricultural and industrial education itself was not new to the British. Even so, the British valued American policy input because of their experience in linking agricultural and industrial education with the management of racial issues. In practice some actors questioned how much the experience of educating American blacks in the US was relevant for

Africa. What made the whole exchange of ideas possible were the racial preconceptions and the collective desire to believe in their relevance at this point in time. Colonial officials and missionaries were in need of some authoritative assurance with respect to what they were doing. In such a situation, the skills of negotiation and presentation held by the key figures in the discourse, like Thomas Jesse Jones and J.H. Oldham, were important factors in giving British education policy a seal of authorisation by 'American specialists'. In analysing this political discourse, the book has paid attention to the motivations and psychology of these key figures. This actor-oriented approach helps to reveal the true nature of the discourse, putting aside the imagined influence which was somewhat strategically showed up by actors.

What I intended in this book was to capture the inter-related constructs of the discourse, namely, structure, actors, norms and context. The politics of transferring foreign educational ideas to Africa was closely linked but treated in this book as separate dynamics from the spread of educational philosophies across continents. Philosophies and theories were employed to justify policies which were developed as a result of the political negotiation process. Such references to ideas were done by discretionarily picking pieces from different sources to make a patchwork of fashionable norms. Therefore, compared to the meanings in the original philosophies of American progressives or British moralist education, some popular terms like 'learning by doing' or 'character development' were drastically reinterpreted or combined with contradictory terms in the process of exchanging ideas. Such reinterpretations and changes of ideas happened in response to the political, social and economic context both in the metropole and in the colonies. As significant contextual variables, I have examined the impact of the economic conditions of the inter-war period, which were fragile but demonstrated an outlook of positive recovery, trust in scientific planning, heightening nationalism in colonies and solidarity among Pan-Africanists across continents.

The British education system, on which those of African colonies were modelled, segregated students on the basis of social class. The notion that a liberal education is for the elite and a vocational education is for the working class originated in 19th century Britain when the mass education system was developed (Green 1994: 84; Young 1984: 4).

When the British education system was transplanted to colonies, in addition to class, another dimension of segregation was introduced, namely 'race'. Accordingly, orientations of the educational adaptation policy for Africans have a twofold explanation: Africanisation and vocationalisation. Africanisation suggested modifying the education programmes to fit to the African 'race' which was considered to be less advanced than Caucasians. To Africanise, even in the elite schools, some vocational elements were to be included. That was a general pattern, particularly in the government schools, while mission schools looked at education as a channel of religious exposure and had different approaches to vocational education. Further, the British culture of the Victorian and post-Victorian era was not only class conscious but also gender conscious, which was strongly reflected in the differential 'character training' for girls and boys, of different classes (Gaitskell 2002; Barthel 1985). In sum, the discourse on colonial education in Africa has to be understood in such intricately intertwined notions of race, class and gender.

It has often been said that British colonialism was adaptation, in contrast to the French model of assimilation. However, the term 'adaptation', which was frequently used, did not indicate the direct application of any fashionable educational model to schools in Africa. The practices on the ground did not necessarily reflect what was discussed at the point of policy making.

Also, adaptation and assimilation were both sides of a coin, which happened simultaneously. In Part III of this book, the analysis of Achimota School reveals that both efforts were made within a single school. While the School tried to assimilate Africans to English public school norms and European civilization, it stated its purpose as adapting its education to the African 'tradition', and many vocational subjects were introduced for students to learn the 'dignity of labour' from experience. Despite these serious efforts to strike the balance between assimilation and adaptation, I demonstrated in this book that what happened was, in fact, the *creation* of a new culture.

In its early days Achimota School was a site of cultural production. The School's students were from diverse social backgrounds. Achimota had several scholarship schemes and as many as 40 per cent of the students were on some type of scholarship. Further, Achimota was one of very few co-educational secondary institutions in Africa at the time. Therefore, Achimota students of both genders came from families of different socio-economic status, from various parts of the country, and from different ethnic groups. Achimota provided a gate for socially upward mobility. Students from various backgrounds were exposed to the Achimota founders' idea of new African leaders through classroom learning and various other aspects of school life. In this situation, the education of Achimota played a significant role not only in defining the character of individual students, but in creating a class of people who shared the cultural traits learned at Achimota. They were inevitably influenced by their contact at the School with Western values in such matters as styles of living, married life, music and literature.

After the analysis of the discourse during the colonial period, in Chapter Nine of Part III, I presented an overview of the dialectics between global trends of educational development planning and Ghanaian education policies since independence. The fundamental approach of analysis was the same as other parts of the book, namely to untangle the relationships between the global and local discourses on educational policy making, while attempting to pin down the changing norms which characterised the policy options proposed in different time periods. The policy priorities shifted between different levels of education from higher to primary, and the fulcrum of balance between the vocational and general curriculum has constantly moved. Ghanaian national education policies reacted to the global trends of recommended models, except for the period from the 1970s to the early 80s, when the country was ruled by the series of short-lived military regimes and was rather disconnected from the Western donor community. Regardless of such fluctuation in policies both at the global and national levels, I demonstrated that the public reactions to education and patterns of enrolment at different levels of education were consistent. Despite recurring promotion of vocationalisation of secondary education, such policies

have repeatedly turned ineffectual. The reasons for such public responses could be rooted in the colonial period and the way formal education was introduced. The academic track of education provided access to white-collar jobs, while vocationalism was linked with racial and class segregation. Also, social mobility created by colonial elite schools like Achimota did not last for long. Achimota created the culture of the new elite by exposing them to Western values and the identity of African leaders. The students who experienced dramatic upward mobility of social status maintained it and transmitted it to their children. For such reproduction of class, access to and a certificate of academic education, rather than vocational, have contributed.

In terms of analytical approaches, this book contributes to the academic discussions in two ways. First, as a policy study of a historical case, I have attempted to untangle the discourse in a more nuanced manner than conventionally done by the scholars of world culturalism and multilateralism. The formation of British colonial education policy in the inter-war period has caught the attention of scholars and many analyses have been done. One group of such works highlights the influence of the American black industrial education model promoted by philanthropists. Another group has predominantly focused on the negotiation of missionary interests in the face of the governmental move to formalise colonial rule. Using the interpretivist approach, I reconstructed the political discourse on African education from subjective perspectives of individual and collective actors involved in policy making in London and the Gold Coast, and in practices at Achimota. I also examined the discourse as the process of interaction among actors with different motivations and power, which were expressed in response to specific contexts and demands. In doing so, I illustrated several flaws in the conventional analytical framework of educational transfer. One of the theoretical contributions of this book is, therefore, to revise and add to the framework of educational policy analysis.

While this work is a policy study, it also draws upon African historiography. Formal education has been a relatively unattended topic in African historiography. Education was an important aspect of colonial African life, and it has gained some attention from social and cultural historians – who are interested in topics like Christianity, modernity or sexuality – as well as from political historians. However, the works that focused primarily on education or viewed the issues of Christianity, women or politics from the perspective of educational philosophy and policy are few. The educationist perspective – especially the philosophical aspect of it, which I brought into my analysis – is a contribution to African historiography.

10-1 Framework of policy analysis

My basic attitude of analysis has been that policy making was not simply the enforcement of the intentions of bureaucrats or politicians, but the process of negotiating different interests introduced by the various actors, both in the metropole and in the Gold Coast Colony. I have given considerable attention, therefore, to who participated in the discourse and with what kind of interests, and how each set of actors interacted with others of differing interests. Policy documents which were announced are important in the sense that they standardised and legitimised certain orientations of educational practices, but more important was the process by which they were formulated. Policy documents, albeit nicely phrased, are the results of the process of compromise and negotiation, and obscure the differences of views involved in their formation. Therefore, the sources on which I relied more for my analysis than official policy documents were correspondence, minutes of meetings and articles published in newspapers and journals, in which people expressed their opinions, not the cut-and-dry outcome of political negotiation.

As the clue for the analysis of discourse, frequently used terms were important. Despite their appearance of commonalities, these terms were used with various different connotations by actors with different motivations for participating in the discourse. For example, 'adaptation' and 'character training' were two of the most popular terms. In Chapter Six, I presented five different categories of definition of 'character' to be developed through education on the Gold Coast, namely, efficient workmanship, leadership, Christian character, holder of a sense of citizenship and follower of African tradition. These different ideas were expressed using the same term 'character development'. This very multiplicity of meanings suggests the complex nature of the negotiation, on the one hand, and the ambiguity and inclusiveness of the catchy words which enabled the temporal agreement, on the other hand.

Based on the consideration that the policy was the product of compromise, this book did not try to judge if the policy achieved its goal or not. Such a judgment would necessarily imply the adoption of a single perspective of determining the success of implementation. Instead of assuming the perspectives of colonial officials and accepting their evaluations of educational practices as given, I attempted to see how policies formulated away from the field were digested and experienced by local policy makers, the public, teachers and students. In this very sense, the case of Achimota School was useful. It provided a window to glance at the ways that teachers and students experienced and reinterpreted the educational ideas and policies emanating from distant places through their daily practices at school. As it was a model school intended to provide the best education possible according to the latest ideas of the time, the discourse on Achimota reveals the perceptions of colonial administrators, British and American educationists and missionaries about the African race and education suited to them. The case of the early days at Achimota is a study of the appropriation process of the most progressive educational ideas of the early 20th century.

The second point I would like to make is that of the theoretical framework of educational transfer. As I presented in Chapter Two, there have been various scholarly efforts by world culturalists, world system theorists and multilateralists to theorise the mechanism of global discourses and practices of international educational development since the colonial period to the present. However, they tend to assume the transfer of educational model as the process that one dominant model to be transplanted to other locations. They do not assume a multipolar power structure, which may influence actors from different directions at different levels, causing intermingling of diverse sources of influence.

The analysis of this book shows that there was no single exporter of educational policy or idea in the discourse on colonial education in British Africa. It was a new creation by people involved in the discourse both at the metropole and in colonies. Actors picked pieces of ideas from different sources and created their own package to justify the programme they wanted to promote. In the sense that there was no straightforward transfer of any single educational model or idea, any scholarly work which focuses solely on American or British influence is not comprehensive or accurate. There were many scholars who wrote about the role played by American philanthropists, especially the Phelps-Stokes Fund (Berman 1971; King 1971; Steiner-Khamsi and Quist 2000). The American involvement in the discourse on the British colonial education tended to be considered as a plain case of educational transfer, in which outsiders have imposed an educational model motivated by arrogance and racial prejudice against African descendants, without soliciting the opinions of the Africans. The role played by American philanthropists has caught so much scholarly attention that the African perspective has been neglected, as well as the influence of the colonial masters themselves, the British. On the other hand, a few scholars who studied the dynamics of policy formation in Britain itself made little mention of American involvement (For example, Sivonen 1995). In sum, there has been virtually no study which pays attention to the fact that the ideas for the policy were not from one source but was moulded by mixing ideas from different sources.

With enhanced globalisation, nowadays, it is getting even more difficult to analyse policy adaptation without considering the constant cross-feeding of ideas. The resultant hybrid ideas, which often occur unconsciously, are adapted by the respective participants to their own societies and sometimes brought back to the global discourse after a fundamental metamorphosis. In this sense, the analysis of the global mechanism of international educational development requires a new step to theorise the changing landscape through a multipolar structure among actors who constantly cross-feed and hybridise ideas.

In this book, I have examined the discourse of educational transfer by capturing it as the dynamic correlations among several categories of variables, namely actors, structure, norms and contexts. Their correlations were also considered as the mutual enforcement between the global and local processes. This approach frees us from the restriction inherent in the effort of grasping the influence of a readily packaged policy or model. The 'influence' is rendered by the will of involved actors, who actually pick pieces from different sources. Often these actors wish to declare the models they adopt are from a specific source. That was the case with actors involved in the colonial education discourse, who liked to show up the influence of American black industrial education. Such political show is one layer of the process, but at the layer of normative exchange, in reality, ideas were hybridised to a large extent. The outlook of 'transferred model' was a kind of nice wrapping paper to cover the real intentions and practices to appeal to the stakeholders who are concerned about the issue.

10-2 Educational philosophies in colonial Africa

My contribution to African historiography is the analysis of educational philosophies which were employed in the discourse on African education and were at the basis of educational practices. Many scholars have revealed the political aspects of educational development. In colonial Africa, schools were rarely established purely for the sake of intellectual satisfaction. To put it roughly, for missionaries, the school was a tool for Christianisation. For colonial administrations, it was a means of control and feeding manpower to the colonial mechanism. For Africans, it was a channel to access European culture and salaried jobs and to gain political advancement. The access to and the control of schooling were political issues for both Africans and Europeans. And this is why many historians have written about the political aspects of education as a part of their larger research projects. The debates over vocational education and adaptation have caught the eye of some scholars, as they were at the core of power conflicts over education. Also, there have been scholars who saw education as a cultural project in which European culture and Christian values were transmitted. Through education, traditional culture was broken down, and a new space and identity of educated Africans was created divorced from either European settler communities or African societies. I myself have also devoted a large portion of this book to the political and cultural aspects of education in Africa.

What lacked in earlier scholarly works is the perspective that the school was a site designed to educate people according to certain educational philosophies. To put it differently, historical works on African education have tended to overlook the black box of classrooms – teacher–student interaction, overt and covert messages transmitted at schools, peer influences, etc. – which are the processes for students to experience and internalise the philosophies of schools or educational decision makers. Therefore, as an educationist, my contribution is to analyse education according to the *intended* objectives of colonial officials and Achimota founders, and to demonstrate why those were intended in contrast to the experience of students and teachers at Achimota, a model school for cultivating African leaders. In other words, my main focus is the perceived goals and forms of education, not the *unintended* effect of schools and their graduates on African society, whether it is political, economic or cultural.

There has been no critical study on the jargon of colonial education, 'adaptation' and 'character training', from the perspective of educational philosophies. What did it mean to adapt education to an African social and economic background in terms of moulding certain character traits among students? The analysis of British and American educational philosophies in the early 20th century reveals that this was the era when schools were delegated the tremendous responsibility of forming student character. Educational theorists of the time did not hesitate to state that character training was of greater importance than transmission of knowledge or skills. Thus, an analysis which does not look at moralistic messages the schools transmitted is only partially satisfactory. This book illuminates the different perceptions among African and European participants in the discourse on education about the 'character' to be developed at school and, by extension, about the role of education for national development in general.

Bibliography

Archives

Ghana
National Archives of Ghana
Central Regional Archives, Cape Coast
School records – Achimota School, Mfantsipim School, Adisadel College

England
Public Record Office (PRO)
- CO 96 Gold Coast Correspondence.
- CO 98 Gold Coast Sessional Papers and Reports.
- CO 323 General Correspondence.
- CO 554 West Africa Correspondence.
- CO 847 General Africa Correspondence.
- CO 1045 Sir Cox Collection.

Rhodes House Library, Oxford University
- Oxford Project on the Development of Education in Pre-independent Africa.

School of Oriental and African Studies (SOAS), University of London
- The Conference of British Missionary Society and the International Missionary Council Archives (CBMS-IMC), Box 207-230, 263-267.
- Wesley Methodist Missionary Society Archives (WMMS), Synod Minutes.
- WMMS, West Africa Correspondence.

United States
Phelps-Stokes Fund
- Minutes of Board Meetings.
- "Twenty-Five Years of Thomas Jesse Jones and the Phelps-Stokes Fund" unpublished volume.

Rockefeller Archive Center (RAC)
- General Education Board Series 1-2.
- International Education Board, Series 1.

- Rockefeller Foundation Archives No. 26, Series 1.

Journals
- Africa
- Crisis
- International Review of Missions
- Journal of Royal Society of Africa
- Overseas Education
- Southern Workman

Newspapers
- African Times and Orient Review
- Gold Coast Independent
- Gold Coast Leader
- Gold Coast Nation
- Gold Coast Spectator
- Gold Coast Times
- Vox Populi
- West Africa Times

Published Primary and Secondary Works

Acheampong, E.O., Williams, A.A., and Azu, T.D. (2014) 'Industrial Attachment: Perspectives, Conceptions and Misconceptions of Students at Cape Coast Polytechnic, Ghana', *Journal of Education and Practice,* Vol. 5, No. 37, pp. 63–67.

Addae-Mensah, I. (2000) *Education in Ghana: A Tool for Social Mobility or Social Stratification?,* J.B. Danquah Memorial Lectures, Ghana Academy of Arts and Sciences, Accra: Institute for Scientific and Technological Information.

Adeyemi, M. B., and Adeyinka, A. A. (2003). 'The Principles and Content of African Traditional Education', *Educational Philosophy and Theory,* Vol. 35, No. 4, pp. 425–440.

Adu-Gyamfi, S., W.J., and Addo, A.A. (2016) 'Educational Reforms in Ghana: Past and Present', *Journal of Education and Human Development,* Vol. 5, No. 3, pp. 158–172.

Agbodeka, F. (1977) *Achimota in the National Setting: A Unique Educational Experiment in West Africa*, Accra: Afram Publicaton Ltd.

———(2002) 'Education in Ghana: Yesterday and Today', *Ghana Studies* No. 5, 1–25.

Agelasto, M. (1996) 'Educational Transfer of Sorts: The American Credit System with Chinese Characteristics'. {Incomplete ref}

Akyeampong, A.K. (2002) V*ocationalization of secondary education in Ghana: A case study*, Washington, D.C.: Human Development, Africa Region, the World Bank.

Aldcroft, D.H. (2013) *The European Economy Since 1914*, London: Routledge.

Allais, S.M. (2007) 'Understanding the Failures of the South African National Qualifications Framework as the Driver of Educational Reform in Post-Apartheid South Africa', *Paper presented at UKFIET Conference*, 2007.

Amu, E. (1940) 'The Position of Christianity in Modern Africa', *International Review of Missions* Vol. 29, p. 483.

Amissah, S.H. (1947) *A Thesis on Educational Adaptation and Teacher Training in the Gold Coast*, unpublished thesis, University of London.

Anderson, B. (1991) *Imagined communities: reflections on the origin and spread of nationalism* (revised and extended ed.), London: Verso.

Anderson, J.D. (1988) *The Education of Blacks in the South, 1860–1935*, Chapel Hill: The University of North Carolina Press.

Anderson, J. (1970) *The Struggle for the School: The Interaction of Missionary, Colonial Government and Nationalist Enterprise in the Development of Formal Education in Kenya*, London: Longman.

Anderson-Levitt, K.M., and Alimasi, N-I. (2001) 'Are Pedagogical Ideas Embraced or Imposed? The Case of Reading Instruction in the Republic of Guinea', in Margaret Sutton and A.U. Bradley Levinson (eds), *Policy as Practice: Toward a Comparative Sociocultural Analysis of Educational Policy*, pp. 25–58, Westport, Connecticut: Ablex Publishing.

Ania, L. (2005) *Colonialism/Postcolonialism: The New Critical Idiom*, 2 ed., Oxford: Routledge.

Anim, N.O. (1966) 'Ghana', in David G. Scanlon (ed.), *Church, State, and Education in Africa*, pp. 167–96, New York: Teachers College Press.

Anokye, P.A., Afrane, S.A., and Oduro-Ofori, E. (2014) 'The Informal Apprenticeship System in Ghana: Post Graduation Job Integration and Its Implications for the Management of Urban Space', *Journal of Environment and Earth Science*, Vol. 4, No. 18, pp. 84–93.

Antwi, M.K. (1992) *Education, Society and Development in Ghana*, Accra: Unimax Publisher Ltd.

Armstrong, C.W. (1926) 'Progress in West Africa', *The Southern Workman* May, pp. 215–7.

Arnove, R.F. (1980) 'Comparative Education and World-Systems Analysis', *Comparative Education Review*, February. {page numbers missing}

———(1999) 'Reframing Comparative Education: The Dialectic of the Global and the Local', in Robert F. Arnove, and Carlos Alberto Torres (eds), *Comparative Education: The Dialectic of the Global and the Local*, pp. 1–23, Oxford: Rowman & Littlefield Publishers, Inc.

Ashby, E., in association with Anderson, M., (1966) *Universities: British, Indian, African – a Study in the Ecology of Higher Education*, London: Weidenfeld and Nicolson, 1966.

Atchoarena, D., and Caillods, F. (1999) 'Technical Education: A Dead End or Adapting to Change?', *Prospects*, Vol. 29, No. 1, pp. 67–87.

Author unknown (1927) 'James E. Kwegwir Aggrey', *The Southern Workman*, September, pp. 11-30.

Author unknown (1922) 'Washington's Atlanta Speech, Delivered on 18 September, 1895', *The Southern Workman*, May, pp. 209–12.

Bacchus, K. (1988) 'The Political Context of Vocationalization of Education in the Developing Countries', in Jon Lauglo and Kevin Lillis (eds), *Vocationalizing Education: An International Perspective*, pp. 31–44, Oxford: Pergamon Books, Ltd.

Baker, M.C. (1955) *Foundations of John Dewey's Educational Theory*, New York: Atherton Press, 1955.

Baker, D.P., and LeTendre, G.K. (2005) *National differences, global similarities: World culture and the future of schooling*, Stanford, CA: Stanford University Press.

Ball, S.J. (1983) 'Imperialism, Social Control and the Colonial Curriculum in Africa', *Journal of Curriculum Studies* Vol. 15, No. 3, pp. 237–63.

Barthel, D. (1985) 'Women's Educational Experience under Colonialism: Toward a Diachronic Model', *Journal of Women in Culture and Society* Vol. 11, No. 1, pp. 137–54.

Bassett, T.J. (1994) 'Cartography and Empire Building in Nineteenth-Century West Africa', *Geographical Review*, Vol. 84, No. 3, pp. 316–335.

Becker, G.S. (1964) *Human capital: A theoretical and empirical analysis, with special reference to education*, Chicago: University of Chicago Press.

Benavot, A. (1983) 'The Rise and Decline of Vocational Education', *Sociology of Education*, Vol. 56, Apri, pp. 63–76.

Benavot, A., Cha, Y.-K., Kamens, D., Meyer, J.W., & Wong, S.-Y. (1991) 'Knowledge for the masses: World models and national curricula, 1920–1986', *American Sociological Review*, Vol. 56, pp. 85–100.

Berman, E. (1971) 'American Influence on African Education: The Role of the Phelps-Stokes Fund's Education Commission', *Comparative Education Review* June, pp. 132–45.

——— (1975a) 'Christian Missions in Africa', in Edward Berman (ed.), *African Reactions to Missionary Education*, pp. 1–53, New York: Teachers College Press.

——— (1975b) 'Commonalities and the Continuing Christian Presence', in Edward Berman (ed.), *African Reactions to Missionary Education*, pp. 206–17, New York: Teachers College Press.

——— (1975c) 'Introduction', in Edward Berman (ed.), *African Reactions to Missionary Education*, pp. xi–xvii, New York: Teachers College Press.

——— (1972) 'Tuskegee-in-Africa', *Journal of Negro Education* 41, no. 2: 99–112.

Bhabha, H.K. (1994) *The Location of Culture*, London: Routledge, 1994.

Bhola, H.S. (1995) 'Functional Literacy, Workplace Literacy and Technical and Vocational Education: Interfaces and Policy Perspectives', Paris: UNESCO.

Bibby, J. and Peil, M. (1974) 'Secondary Education in Ghana: Private Enterprise and Social Selection', *Sociology of Education* Vol. 47, No. 3, pp. 399–418.

Blyden, E.W. (1903) 'West Africa before Europe', *Journal of the African Society*, Vol. 2, July.

Boahen, A.A. (1987) *African Perspectives on Colonialism*, Baltimore: The Johns Hopkins University.

——— (1996) *Mfantsipim and the Making of Ghana: A Centenary History, 1876–1976*, Accra, Ghana: Sankofa Educational Publishers, 1996.

Boateng, E.A. (1996) *Crisis, Change and Revolution in Ghanaian Education, Armstrong-Amissah Memorial Lectures*, Accra: Wesley College Past Students' Association.

Boateng, F. (1983) 'African Traditional Education: A Method of Disseminating Cultural Values', *Journal of Black Studies*, Vol.13, No. 3, pp. 321–336.

——— (1975) 'The Catechism and the Rod: Presbyterian Education in Ghana', in Edward Berman (ed.), *African Reactions to Missionary Education*, pp. 75–91, New York: Teachers College Press.

Boli, J., Ramirez, F., and Meyer, J.W. (1985) 'Explaining the origins and expansion of mass education', *Comparative Education Review*, Vol. 29, pp. 145–70.

Bourdieu, P. (2000) *The social structures of the economy*, London: Polity Press.

——— (1974) 'The School as a Conservative Force', in J. Eggleston (ed.), *Contemporary Research in the Sociology of Education*, London: Methuen.

Bowles, S., and Gintis, H. (1975) 'The Problem with Human Capital Theory – a Marxian Critique', *The American Economic Review*, Vol. 65, No. 2, pp. 74–82.

Briggs, A. (1968) 'The world economy: Interdependence and planning', in C. L. Mowat (ed.), *The Shifting Balance of World Forces, 1898–1945*, The New Cambridge Modern History, Vol. 12, pp. 37–86.

Brock-Utne, B., and Hopson, R.K. (eds) (2005) *Languages of instruction for African emancipation: Focus on postcolonial contexts and considerations*, East Lansing: State University of Michigan Press.

Brock-Utne, B. (2000) 'Whose Education for All? The Recolonization of the African Mind', in Mark B. Ginsberg (ed.), *Studies in Education/Politics*, Vol. 6, New York: Falmer Press.

Brown, I. (1989) *The Economies of Africa and Asia in the Inter-war Depression*, London: Routledge.

Brown, G.N. (1964) 'British Educational Policy in West and Central Africa', *The Journal of Modern African Studies*, Vol. 2, No. 3, pp. 365–77.

Brown, G.N., and Hiskett, M., (eds), (1976) *Conflict and Harmony in Education in Tropical Africa*, Rutherford: Fairleigh Dickinson University Press.

Bruner, J. (1990) *Acts of Meaning*, Cambridge, MA: Harvard UP.

Bude, U. (1983) 'The Adaptation Concept in British Colonial Education', *Comparative Education*, Vol. 19, No. 3, pp. 341–55.

Carmody, B.P. (1991) 'Conversion and Jesuit Schooling in Zambia', in Marc R. Spindler (ed.), *Studies in Christian Mission*, Vol. 4, Leiden: E.J. Brill.

Casely Hayford, J.E. (1968) *Ethiopia Unbound: Studies in Race Emancipation*. London: Frank Cass (reprint).

———(1903) *Gold Coast Native Institutions*, London: Frank Cass.

Casey, K. (1995) 'The new narrative research in education', *Review of Research in Education*, No. 21, pp. 211–253.

Chabbott, C. (2003) *Education for development: International organizations and Education for All*, New York: Routledge Falmer.

———(1998) 'Constructing educational consensus: International development professionals and the World Conference on Education for All', *International Journal of Educational Development*, Vol. 18, No. 3, pp. 207–218.

Clatworthy, F.J.(1969) *The Formation of British Colonial Education Policy, 1929–1961. Final Report*, Washington, DC: Office of Education, US Department of Health, Education and Welfare.

Cole, R.W. (1960) *Kossoh Town Boy*, Cambridge: Cambridge University Press.

Colonna, F. (1997) 'Educating Conformity in French Colonial Algeria', in Frederick Cooper and Ann Laura Stoler (eds), *Tensions of Empire*, Berkeley: University of California Press.

Comaroff, J.L., and Comaroff, J. (1997) *Of Revelation and Revolution: The Dialectics of Modernity on a South African Frontier*, Vol. 2, Chicago: The University of Chicago Press.

Cooper, F. (1994) 'Conflict and Connection: Rethinking Colonial African History', *The American Historical Review*, Vol. 99, No. 5, pp. 151–45.

——(2005) *Colonialism in Question: Theory, Knowledge, History*, Oakland: University of California Press.

COTVET (2012) *COTVET* Brochure, Accra, Government of Ghana.

Cromwell, A.M. (1986) *An African Victorian Feminist; the Life and Times of Adelaide Smith Casely Hayford, 1868–1960*, London: Routledge.

Curti, M. (1978) *Social Ideas of American Educators*, New Jersey: Littlefield, Adams & Co., (first published in 1935).

Davin, A. (1996) *Growing up Poor: Home, School and Street in London 1870–1914*, London: Rivers Oram Press.

Darvas, P., and Palmer, R. (2014) *Demand and Supply of Skills in Ghana: How can training programs improve employment and productivity?*, Washington D.C., the World Bank.

Dolowitz, D., and Marsh, D. (1996) 'Who learns what from whom: A review of the policy transfer literature', *Political Studies*, Vol. 44, No. 2, pp. 343–357.

Dore, R. (1976) *The Diploma Disease: Education, Qualification and Development*, Berkeley: University of California Press.

Dore, R., and Oxenham, J. (1984) 'Educational Reform and Selection for Employment – an Overview', in John Oxenham (ed.), *Education Versus Qualifications? A Study of Relationships between Education, Selection for Employment and the Productivity of Labour*, pp. 3–40, London: George Allen & Unwin.

Dougall, J.W.C. (1938) 'The Case for and against Mission Schools', *Journal of the Royal African Society*, pp. 91–108.

——(1937) 'The Relationship of Church and School in Africa', *International Review of Missions*, Vol. 26, pp. 204–14.

———(1928) 'Training Visiting Teachers for African Village Schools', *The Southern Workman*, October. {page numbers missing}

———(1928) 'Training Visiting Teachers for African Village Schools', *The Southern Workman*, October, pp. 403–14.

D'Souza, H. (1975) 'External Influences on the Development of Educational Policy in British Tropical Africa from 1923 to 1939', *African Studies Review*, Vol. 18, No. 2, pp. 35–43.

Duckworth, F. (1912) *From a Pedagogue's Sketch Book*, London: Chatto and Windus.

Dunn, F. (1993) 'The Educational Philosophies of Washington, Dubois, and Houston: Laying the Foundations for Afrocentrism and Multiculturalism'. *The Journal of Negro Education*, Vol. 62, No. 1, pp. 24–34.

Edsman, B.M. (1979) *Lawyers in Gold Coast Politics 1900–1945, Studia Historica Upsaliensia Iii*, Stockholm, Sweden: Almqvist & Wiksell International.

Eichhorst, W., Rodriguez-Planas, N., Schmidl, R., and Zimmermann, K.F. (2012) *A Roadmap to Vocational Education and Training Systems Around the World*, IZA Discussion Paper Series, No. 7110, Bonn: IZA.

Emudong, C.P. (1997) 'The Gold Coast Nationalist Reaction to the Controversy over Higher Education in Anglophone West Africa and Its Impact on Decision Making in the Colonial Office, 1945–47', *Journal of Negro Education*, Vol. 66, No. 2, pp. 137–46.

Engels, D., and Marks, S. (1994) 'Introduction: Hegemony in a Colonial Context', in Dagmar Engels and Shula Marks (eds), *Contesting Colonial Hegemony: State and Society in Africa and India*, London: British Academic Press.

Engs, R.F. (1999) *Educating the Disfranchised and Disinherited: Samuel Chapman Armstrong and Hampton Institute, 1839–1893*, Knoxville: University of Tennessee Press.

Escobar, A. (1995) *Encountering Development: The Making and Unmaking of the Third World*, New Jersey: Princeton University Press.

Fanon, F. (1967) *Black Skin, White Masks*, New York: Grove Press.

Feierman, S. (1993) 'African Histories and the Dissolution of World History', in Robert H. Bates, V.Y. Mudimbe and Jean O'Barr *(eds)*,

Africa and the Disciplines: The Contributions of Research in Africa to the Social Sciences and Humanities, Chicago: The University of Chicago Press.

Ferguson, J. (1990) *The Anti-Politics Machine: 'Development,' Depoliticization, and Bureaucratic Power in Lesotho*, Cambridge: Cambridge University Press.

Finegold, D., McFarland, L., and Richardson, W., (1993) 'Introduction', in David Finegold, Laurel McFarland and William Richardson *(eds), Something Borrowed, Something Learned? The Transatlantic Market in Education and Training Reform*, Washington, D.C.: Brookings Institute.

Fleische, B.D. (1995) 'The Teachers College Club: American Educational Discourse and the Origins of Bantu Education in South Africa, 1914–1951', Ph.D. Dissertation, Columbia University.

Fluitman, F. (1992) 'Traditional Apprenticeship in West Africa: Recent Evidence and Policy Options', *Discussion Paper* 34. {incomplete}

Forsyth, M. (2014) *Collins English Dictionary*, 12 ed., Glasgow: HarperCollins UK.

Fosdick, R.B. (1962) *Adventure in Giving: The Story of the General Education Board, a Foundation Established by John D. Rockefeller*, New York: Harper & Row Publishers.

Foster, P.J. (1965) *Education and Social Change in Ghana*, Chicago: University of Chicago Press.

——— (1963) 'Secondary Schooling and Social Mobility in a West African Nation', *Sociology of Education*, Vol. 37, No. 2, pp. 150–71.

——— (1966) 'The Vocational School Fallacy in Development Planning', in C. Arnold Anderson, and Mary Jean Bowman (eds),*Education and Economic Development*, Chicago, Illinois: ALDINE Publishing Company, pp. 142–66.

Foucault, M.L.H., Gutman, H., and Hutton, P.H. (1988) *Technologies of the Self: A Seminar with Michel Foucault*, London: Tavistock Publications.

Foucault, M. (1972) 'Two Lectures', in Colin Gordon (ed.), *Power/Knowledge: Selected Interviews and Other Writings 1972–1977*, New York: Pantheon Books.

Fraser, A.G. (1925) 'Aims of African Education', *International Review of Missions*, Vol. 14, pp. 514–22.

Gaitskell, D. (2002) 'Ploughs & Needles: State & Mission Approaches to African Girls' Education in South Africa', in Holger Bernt Hansen and Michael Twaddle (eds), *Christian Missionaries & the State in the Third World*, Athens, Ohio: Ohio University Press, pp. 98–120.

——— (1984) 'Upward All and Play the Game: The Girl Wayfarers' Association in the Transvaal 1925–1975', in Peter Kallaway (ed.), *Apartheid and Education: The Education of Black South Africans*, Johannesburg: Ravan Press.

Gardner, B.T. (1975) 'The Educational Contribution of Booker T. Washington', *Journal of Negro Education*, Vol. 44, No. 4, pp. 502–18.

Ghana Education Service (2015) *Report on Basic Statistics and Planning Parameters for Education in Ghana 2014–5 Academic Year*, Accra, Government of Ghana.

——— (2006) *Report on Basic Statistics and Planning Parameters for Education in Ghana 2005-6 Academic Year*, Accra, Government of Ghana.

Gill, I, and Fruitman, F. (2000) *Skills and Change: A Synthesis of Findings of a Multi-Country Study of Vocational Education and Training Reforms ILO and the World Bank, 2000*.

Ginsburg, M.B., Cooper, S., Raghu, R.R., and Zgarra, H. (1991) 'Educational Reform: Social Struggle, the State and the World Economic System', in Mark B. Ginsberg (ed.), *Understanding Educational Reform in Global Context: Economy, Ideology, and the State*, New York: Garland publishing, Inc..

Government of Ghana (2014) *How to improve, through skills development and job creation, access of Africa's youth to the world of work*, unpublished conference paper, Ghana Country Report for the 2014 Ministerial Conference on Youth Employment, Abidjan, Cote d'Ivoire, 21–23 July.

——— (2010) 'Population and Housing Census 2010: Demographic, Social, Economic and Housing Characteristics Report', Accra, Ghana Statistical Service.

Government of the Gold Coast (1921) 'Report of Committee of Enquiry on the Native Civil Service", Accra.

———(1920) 'Report of the Educationists' Committee Appointed by His Excellency the Governor'," Accra.

Grabb, E.G. (1990) *Theories of Social Inequality: Classical and Contemporary Perspectives*, 2nd edition, Toronto: Holt, Rinehart and Winston.

Graham, C.K. (1971) *The History of Education in Ghana*, London: Frank Cass and Company Ltd.

Gray, R. (1990) 'Christianity', in Andrew Roberts (ed.), *The Colonial Moment in Africa: Essays on the Movement of Minds and Materials 1900–1940*, Cambridge: Cambridge University Press, pp. 140–90.

Great Pola Africa Foundation (2017) *History of Education in Ghana*, http://politicalpola.wikifoundry.com/page/HISTORY+OF+EDUCATION+IN+GHANA (last accessed 10 October2017).

Green, A. (1994) 'Technical Education and State Formation in Nineteenth-Century England and France', in Anja Heikkinen (ed.), *Vocational Education and Culture – European Prospects from History and Life-History*, Hameenlinna.{not sure about publisher}

Greene, S.E. (2001) *Sacred Sites and the Colonial Encounter: A History of Meaning and Memory in Ghana*, Bloomington: Indiana University Press.

Guggisberg, G. (1927) *The Gold Coast: A Review of the Events of 1920–26 and the Prospects of 1927–28*, Accra: Government Printing Works.

Gupta, A. (1998) *Postcolonial Developments: Agriculture in the Making of Modern India*, Durham: Duke University Press.

Gyang-Duah, C. (1996) *The Scottish Mission Factor in the Development of the Presbyterian Church of Ghana: 1917–1957*, University of Edinburgh.

Hailey, L. (1938) *An African Survey*, London: Oxford University Press.

Halpin, D., and Troyna, B. (1995) 'The Politics of Education Policy Borrowing', *Comparative Education*, Vol. 31, No. 3.{page numbers}

Hammond, S.A. (1928) 'Biology and African Education', *International Review of Missions*, Vol. 17, pp. 495–504.

Hart K. (1970) 'Small scale entrepreneurs in Ghana and development planning', *Journal of Development Studies*, Vol. 6, No. 4, pp.104-120.

Hazel, E.A. (1992) 'Education in Ghana, 1951–1966', in Kwame Arhin (ed.), *The Life and Work of Kwame Nkrumah: papers of a symposium organized by the Institute of African Studies, University of Ghana, Legon*, African World Press, pp. 55–75.

Hetherington, P. (1978) *British Paternalism and Africa 1920–1940*, London: Frank Cass and Company Ltd.

Hillard, F.H. (1957) *A Short History of Education in British West Africa*, London: Thomas Nelson and Sons Ltd.

Holmes, A.B. (1972) 'Economic and Political Organizations in the Gold Coast 1920–45', Ph.D. Dissertation, University of Chicago.

Honig, B. (1993) 'Research Perspectives on African Education and the Informal Sector', in *Paper presented at the annual meeting of the American Education Research Association. Atlanta*, 1993.

Honny, L.A. (1999) 'Reshaping Vocational Training: Hopeful Signs from a Ghanaian Experience', in Kenneth James King and Simon McGrath (eds), *Enterprise in Africa: Between Poverty and Growth*, London: Intermediate Technology Publications, Ltd.

Horowitz, A., and Schenzler, C. (1999) 'Returns to General, Technical, and Vocational Education in Developing Countries: Recent Evidence from Suriname', *Education Economics*, Vol. 7, No. 1, pp. 5–19.

Howard, V.A. and Scheffler, I.. (1995) *Work, Education & Leadership: Essays in the Philosophy of Education*. New York: Peter Lang Publishing.

Hubbard, J.P. (2000) *Education under Colonial Rule: A History of Katsina College: 1921–1942*, Lanham: University Press of America, Inc.

Hughes, T. (1857 and 1971) *Tom Brown's Schooldays*, Harmondsworth: Penguin.

Hunt, R.D. Jr. (1984) 'Charles T. Loram and the American Model for African Education in South Africa', in Peter Kallaway (ed.), *Apartheid and Education: The Education of Black South Africans*, Johannesburg: Ravan Press.

Hurd, G.E., and Johnson, T.J. (1967) 'Education and Social Mobility in Ghana', *Sociology of Education*, Vol. 40, No. 1, pp. 55–79.

Hurt, J.S. (1977) 'Drill, Discipline and the Elementary School Ethos', in Phillip McCann (ed.), *Popular Education and Socialization in the Nineteenth Century*, London: Methuen & Co, Ltd.

Ikejiani, O. (1964) *Nigerian Education*, Ikeja: Longman Nigeria.

International Labor Organization (ILO) (1950) 'Asian conference of experts on vocational and technical training', in *Report IV, Organization of Manpower, Asian REgional Conference of the ILO*, Montreal: ILO.

———(1946) 'Vocational training', in *Report II, Third Conference of American States Members of the ILO*, Montreal: ILO.

Ipaye, B. (1969) 'Philosophies of Education in Colonial West Africa: A Comparative Study of the British and French Systems', *West African Journal of Education*, June, pp. 93–97.

Irvine, F.R. (1995) 'Co-Operation for Africa', *The Southern Workman*, January, pp. 34–36.

Jacobs, S.M. (1995) 'The Impact of African American Education on 19th Century Colonial West Africa: Livingstone College Graduates in the Gold Coast', *Negro History Bulletin*, Vol. 58, No. 1/2, pp. 5–13.

Jones, P.W. (1999) 'Globalisation and the UNESCO mandate: Multilateral prospects for educational development', *International Journal of Educational Development*, Vol. 19, pp. 17–25.

———(1992) *World Bank Financing of Education: Lending, Learning and Development*, New York: Routledge.

Jones, T.J. (1925) 'East Africa and Education', *The Southern Workman*, June, pp. 239–53.

———(1924) *Education in Africa: A Study of West, South, and Equatorial Africa by the African Education Commission, under the Auspices of the Phelps-Stokes Fund and Foreign Mission Societies of North America and Europe*, New York: Phelps Stokes Fund.

———(1906) *Social Studies in the Hampton Curriculum*, Humpton: Humpton Institute Press.

Kallaway, P. (2012) 'Science and policy: anthropology and education in British colonial Africa during the inter-war years', *Paedagogica Historica*, Vol. 48, No. 3, pp. 411–430.

———(1996) 'Fred Clarke and the Politics of Vocational Education in South Africa, 1911–2', *History of Education*, Vol. 25, No. 4, pp. 353–62.

———(1984) 'An Introduction to the Study of Education for Blacks in South Africa', in Peter Kallaway (ed.), *Apartheid and Education*, Johannesburg: Ravan Press, pp. 1–44.

Kay, G.B. (ed.), (1972) *The Political Economy of Colonialism in Ghana: A Collection of Documents and Statistics 1900–1960*, Cambridge: Cambridge University Press.

Keller, E.J. (1983) 'Development Policy and the Evaluation of Community Self-help: the Harambee School Movement in Kenya', *Studies in Comparative International Development*, Winter, pp. 53–75.

Kelly, G.P. (1983) 'Interwar Schools and the Development of African History in French West Africa', in David H. Kelly (ed.), *French Colonial Education: Essays on Vietnam and West Africa by Gail Paradise Kelly*, ew York: AMS Press, Inc., pp. 209–34.

———(1986) 'Learning to Be Marginal: Schooling in Interwar French West Africa', in David H. Kelly (ed.), *French Colonial Education: Essays on Vietnam and West Africa by Gail Paradise Kelly*, New York: AMS Press, Inc., pp. 189-208.

Kerre, B.W. (1999) 'The Role and Potential of Technical and Vocational Education in Formal Education System in Africa' in Kenneth James King and Simon McGrath (eds), *Enterprise in Africa: Between Poverty and Growth*, London: Intermediate Technology Publications, Ltd. pp. 202-210.

Kimble, D. (1963) *A Political History of Ghana: The Rise of Gold Coast Nationalism 1850–1928*, Oxford: Clarendon Press.

King, K.J. (1971) *Pan-Africanism and Education: A Study of Race, Philanthropy and Education in the Southern States of America and East Africa*, Oxford: Clarendon Press.

King, K., and Martin, C. (2002) 'The vocational school fallacy revisited: Education, aspiration and work in Ghana 1959–2000', *International Journal of Educational Development*, Vol. 22, pp. 5–26.

King, K. and Palmer, R. (2013) *Education and Skills Post 2015: What Evidence, Whose Perspectives?* NORRAG Discussion Paper No. 6., Geneva: NORRAG.

Kolli, R. (2016) *Identifying Informal Sector and Informal Employment*, Paper presented at the Expert Group Meeting on Statistics for SDGs: Accounting for Informal Sector in National Accounts, 11–14 January 2016, Addis Ababa, Ethiopia.

Komba, W. (1998) 'Choices in Liberal and Non-liberal Political and Educational Thought', *Journal of Philosophy of Education*, Vol. 32, No. 2, pp. 195–207.

Krige, S. (1997) 'Segregation, Science and Commissions of Enquiry: The Contestation over Native Education Policy in South Africa, 1930–36', *Journal of South African Studies*, Vol. 23, No. 3, pp. 491–506.

Kumasi Technical Institute (2011) *Tracer Study of Industrial Attachment by KTI students,* unpublished report.

Lauglo, J., and Lillis, K. (1988) '"Vocationalization" in International Perspective', in Jon Lauglo and Kevin Lillis (eds), *Vocationalizing Education: An International Perspective*, Oxford: Pergamon Books, Ltd., pp. 3–26.

Levinson, B.A.U., and Holland, D.C. (1996) 'The Cultural Production of the Educated Person: An Introduction', in Bradley A.U. Levinson, Douglas E. Foley and Dorothy C. Hollan (eds), *The Cultural Production of the Educated Person: Critical Ethnographies of Schooling and Local Practice*, Alberny: State University of New York Press, pp. 1–54.

Lewis, J (1982) 'Parents, Children, School Fees and the London School Board 1870–1890', *History of Education*, Vol. 11, No. 4, pp. 291–312.

Lewis, L.J. (1954) *Educational Policy and Practice in British Tropical Areas*, Osprey: Nelson.

———(1971) 'The Evolution of Educational Policy in English-Speaking African Countries', *West African Journal of Education*, Vol. 15, No. 1, pp. 35–39.

Little, A. (1984) 'Education, earnings and productivity: The eternal triangle', in J. Oxenham (ed.), *Education versus qualification? A study of relationships between education, selection for employment and the productivity of labour*, London: George Allen & Unwin, pp. 220-241.

Lillis, K.M., and Lowe, J. (1987) 'The Rise and Fall of the Schools Science Project in East Africa', *Compare*, Vol. 17, No. 2, pp. 167–79.

Livingston, T.W. (1975) *Education and Race: A Biography of Edward Wilmot Blyden*, San Francisco: The Glendessary Press.

———(1976) 'The Exportation of American Higher Education to West Africa: Liberia College, 1850–1900', *The Journal of Negro Education*, Vol. 45, No. 3, pp. 246–62.

Ludlow, H.W. (1904) 'The Overtoun Institute: A Hampton in Africa', *The Southern Workman*, December, pp. 669–76.

Lowden, F.Y. (2000). *Kindezi: A Distinctively Africentric Perspective on Early Childhood Education*, unpublished manuscript.

Lugard, F.D. (1922) *The Dual Mandate in British Tropical Africa*, London: William Blackwood and Sons.

———(1933) 'Education and Race Relations', *Journal of the African Society*, Vol. 32, No. 126, pp. 1–11.

———. "Education in Tropical Africa." *The Edinburgh Review* July (1925).

Mackenzie, C.G. (1993) 'Demythologising the Missionaries: A Reassessment of the Functions and Relationships of Christian Missionary Education under Colonialism;, *Comparative Education*, Vol. 29, No. 1, pp. 45–66.

Madeira, A.I. (2005) 'Portuguese, French and British Discourses on Colonial Education: Church–State Relations, School Expansion and Missionary Competition in Africa, 1890–1930', *Paedagogica Historica*, Vol. 41, Nos. 1&2, pp. 31–60.

Mahomed, N. (1996) *The Integration of Education and Training in South Africa within the Context of Labour Market Theories and Globalisation*, Durban, South Africa: Education Policy Unit, University of Natal.

Mak, G.C.J. (1997) 'Reconstructing Schooling Process: A Review of Gail Kelly's Works on Colonial Education in Indochina and French West Africa, 1918–193', *Comparative Education Review*, May, pp. 210–12.

Mangan, J.A. (1982) 'Darwinism, Sport and Upper Class Education', *Stadion*, Vol. 8, Autumn, pp. 92–115.

———(1987) 'Ethics and Ethnocentricity: Imperial Education in British Tropical Africa', in William J. Baker and James A. Mangan (eds), *Sport in Africa: Essays in Social History*, New York: Africana Publishing Company, pp. 138–71.

———(1986) *The Games Ethic and Imperialism: Aspects of the Diffusion of an Ideal*, Middlesex: Viking.

Marah, J.K. (1987) 'Educational Adaptation and Pan-Africanism: Developmental Trends in Africa', *Journal of Black Studies*, Vol. 17, No. 4, pp. 460–81.

Martel, G. (2005). (1976) *A Companion to Europe 1900–1945*, Hoboken: Wiley-Blackwell.

Martin, C.A. (1976) 'Significant Trends in the Development of Ghanaian Education', *The Journal of Negro Education*, Vol. 45, No. 1, pp. 46–60.

Martin, S.M. (1988) *Palm Oil and Protest: An Economic History of the Ngwa Region, South-Eastern Nigeria, 1800–1980*, Cambridge: Cambridge University Press.

Mayer, J.W., Nagel, J., and Snyder, C.W. Jr. (1993) 'The Expansion of Mass Education in Botswana: Local and World Society Perspectives', *Comparative Education Review*, Vol. 37, No. 4, pp. 454–75.

Meyer, J.W., and Ramirez, F.O. (2000) 'The world institutionalization of education', in J. Schriever (ed.), *Discourse formation in comparative education*, New York, NY: Peter Lang, pp. 111-32.

Mazrui, A. (1997) 'The World Bank, the Language Question and the Future of African Education', *Race & Class*, Vol. 38, No. 3, pp. 35–48.

McCann, P. (1977) 'Popular Education, Socialization and Social Control: Spitalfields 1812–1824', in Phillip McCann (ed.), *Popular Education and Socialization in the Nineteenth Century*, London: Methuen & Co, Ltd, pp. 5-72.

McClellan, B. E. (1992) *Schools and the Shaping of Character: Moral Education in America, 1607 – Present*, Bloomington, Indiana: ERIC Clearninghouse for Social Studies, Social Science Education and the Social Studies Development Center, Indiana University.

McClure, A.F., Riley, C.J., and Mock. P. (1985) *Education for Work: The Historical Evolution of Vocational and Distributive Education in America*, New Jeursy: Associated University Presses.

McGrath, S., and King, K.J. (1999) 'Enterprise in Africa: New Contexts Renewed Challenges', in Kenneth James King and Simon McGrath (eds), *Enterprise in Africa: Between Poverty and Growth*, London: Intermediate Technology Publications, Ltd., pp. 1-12.

———(1999) 'Learning to Grow? The Importance of Education and Training for Small and Micro-Enterprise Development', in Kenneth James King and Simon McGrath (eds), *Enterprise in Africa: Between Poverty and Growth*, London: Intermediate Technology Publications, Ltd., pp. pp. 211-222.

McMahon, W.W., Jung, J.H., and Boediono. (1992) 'Vocational and Technical Education in Development: Theoretical Analysis of Strategic Effects on Rates of Return', *Economics of Education Review*, Vol. 11, No. 3, pp. 181–94.

McWilliam, H.O.A., and Kwamena-Poh, M.A. (1959 and 1975) *The Development of Education in Ghana*, London: Longman.

Memmi, A. (1965) *The Colonizer and the Colonized*, Boston: Beacon Press.

Meyhew, A. (1939) *Education in the Colonial Empire*, London: Longman, Green, and Co.

Miescher, S.F. (1997) 'Becoming a Man in Kwawu: Gender, Law, Personhood, and the Construction of Masculinities in Colonial Ghana, 1875-1957', Ph.D. Dissertation, Northwestern University.

Mills, C.W. (1940) 'Situated Actions and Vocabularies of Motive', *American Sociological Review*, No. 5, pp. 904–13.

Ministry of Education and Sports, Republic of Ghana (1999) *Ghana National Report*. Paris: International Bureau of Education, UNESCO.

———(2005) *Preliminary Education Sector Performance Report 2005*, unpublished manuscript, Accra.

Ministry of Education, Science and Sports, Republic of Ghana (2007a) *Report on the National Education Sector Annual Review 2007*, Accra.

———(2007b) *Education Sector Performance Report 2007*, Accra.

Mobley, H.W. (1970) *The Ghanaian's Image of the Missionary*, Leiden: E.J. Brill.

Molteno, F. (1984) 'The Historical Foundations of the Schooling of Black South Africans', in Peter Kallaway (ed.), *Apartheid and Education: The Education of Black South Africans*, Johannesburg: Ravan Press, pp. 45–107.

Mullins, B.K., Fordjor, P.K., Kotoh, A.M., Kpeli, K.K., Kwamefio, A., Mensa, Q.B., and Owusu, E. (2003) 'A Review of Traditional Ghanaian and Western Philosophies of Adult Education', *International Journal of Lifelong Education*, Vol. 22, No. 2, pp. 182–199.

Mundy, K. (2007) 'Global governance, educational change', *Comparative Education*, Vol. 43, pp. 339–357.

——— (1999) 'Educational multilateralism in a changing world order: UNESCO and the limits of the possible', *International Journal of Educational Development*, Vol. 19, pp. 27–52.

Murray, A.V. (1929) *The School in the Bush: A Critical Study of the Theory and Practice of Native Education in Africa*, London: Longman, Green and Co.

Nagel, J., and Conrad W.S. Jr. (1989) 'International Funding of Educational Development: External Agendas and Internal Adaptations – the Case of Liberia', *Comparative Education Review*, Vol. 33, No. 1, pp. 3–20.

Newlands, H.S., E.R.J. Hussey, E.R.J., and Vaughan, W.W. (1932) 'Report of the Committee Appointed in 1932 by the Governor of the Gold Coast Colony to Inspect the Prince of Wale's College and School, Achimota', London: The Crown Agents for the Colonies.

Ngũgĩ, wa T. (1986) *Decolonising the Mind: the Politics of Language in African Literature*, Portsmouth: Heinemann.

Noah, H.J. (1984) 'The Use and Abuse of Comparative Education', *Comparative Education Review*, Vol. 28, No. 4, pp. 550-562.

Noah, H.J., and Eckstein, M.A. (1969) *Toward a Science of Comparative Education*, London: Macmillan.

Ocaya-Lakidi, D., and Mazrui, A.M. (1976) 'Secular Skills and Sacred Values in Uganda Schools: Problems of Technical and Moral Acculturation', in Godfery N. Brown and Mervyn Hiskett (eds), *Conflict and Harmony in Education in Tropical Africa*, Rutherford: Fairleigh Dickinson University Press, pp. 278–95.

Ofosu-Appiah, L.H. (1975) *The Life of Dr. J.E.K. Aggrey*, Accra: Waterville Publishing House.

Okunor, S. (1991) *Politics, Misunderstandings, Misconceptions: The History of Colonial Universities*, American University Studies, New York: Peter Lang.

Oldham, J.H. (1934) 'The Educational Work of Missionary Societies', *Africa*, Vol. 7, pp. 47–59.

Oldham, J.H., and Gibson, B.D. (1931) *The Remaking of Man in Africa*, London: Oxford University Press.

Optimist (1923) 'Missionaries and Education in Pagan Africa', *Journal of African Society*, Vol. 23, pp. 44–47.

Organization for Economic Co-operation and Development (OECD) (2009), *Development Aid at a Glance 2009*, Paris: OECD.

——— (2005) *Development Aid at a Glance 2005*, Paris: OECD.

Palmer, R. (2009) 'Skills Development, Employment, and Sustained Growth in Ghana: Sustainability Challenges', *International Journal of Educational Development*, Vol. 29, pp. 133–139.

Pearce, R. (1988) 'Missionary Education in Colonial Africa: The Critique of Mary Kingsley', *History of Education*, Vol. 17, No. 4, pp. 283–94.

Peil, M. (1965) 'Ghanaian University Students: The Broadening Base', *British Journal of Sociology*, Vol. 16, pp. 19–28.

Persianis, P. (1996) 'The British Colonial Education "Lending" Policy in Cyprus (1878-1960): An Intriguing Example of an Elusive "Adapted Education" Policy', *Comparative Education*, Vol. 32, No. 1, pp. 45–68.

Parsons, T. (1968) 'On the Concept of Value-Commitments', *Sociological Inquiry*, Vol. 38, Issue 2, pp. 135–160.

Peterson, P.M. (1971) 'Colonialism and Education: The Case of the Afro-American', *Comparative Education Review*, June, pp. 146–57.

Phillips, D. (1993) 'Borrowing Education Policy', in David Finegold, Laurel McFarland and William Richardson (eds), *Something Borrowed, Something Learned? The Transatlantic Market in Education and Training Reform*, Washington, D.C.: the Brookings Institute.

——— (1989) ;Neither a Borrower nor a Lender Be? The Problems of Cross-National Attraction in Education', *Comparative Education*, Vol. 25, No. 3, pp. 267-274.

Phillips, D., and Ochs, K. (2003) *Processes of policy borrowing in education: Some explanatory and analytical devices*, Comparative Education, Vol. 39, No. 4, pp. 451–461.

Povey, J. (1966) 'Education through the Eyes of African Writers', *The Educational Forum*, Vol. 31, No. 1, pp. 95–102.

Price, T. (1938) 'The Task of Mission Schools in Africa', *International Review of Missions*, Vol. 27, pp. 233–8.

Proctor, T.M. (2000) '"A Separate Path": Scouting and Guiding in Interwar South Africa', *Comparative Studies in Society and History*, Vol. 42, No. 3, pp. 605–31.

Psacharopoulos, G. (1997) 'Child Labour Versus Educational Attainment: Some Eviddence from Latin America', *Journal of Population Economics*, Vol. 10, No. 4, pp. 377–386.

——— (1994) 'Earnings and Education in Latin America', *Education Economics*, Vol. 2, No. 2, pp. 1–29.

——— (1988) 'Curriculum Diversification, Cognitive Achievement and Economic Performance: Evidence from Tanzania and Colombia', in Jon Lauglo and Kevin Lillis (eds), *Vocationalizing Education: An International Perspective*, Oxford: Pergamon Press.

Ranger, T. (1965) 'African Attempts to Control Education in East and Central Africa 1900–1939', *Past and Present*, No. 32, pp. 57–85.

——— (1983) 'The Invention of Tradition in Colonial Africa', in Eric Hobsbawm and Terence Ranger (eds), *The Invention of Tradition*, Cambridge: Cambridge University Press.

Rathbone, R. (1994) *The Conservative Nationalist Tradition in Ghana*, African Studies Center Working Papers, No 183, Boston: African Studies Center, Boston University.

——— (1993) *Murder and Politics in Colonial Ghana*, New Haven: Yale University Press.

Read, M. (1955) *Education and Social Change in Tropical Areas*, Osprey: Nelson.

Republic of Ghana (2003) *Ghana Poverty Reduction Strategy (2003–2005): An Agenda for Growth and Prosperity*, Accra.

Rich, P.J. (1991) *Chains of Empire: English Public Schools, Masonic Cabalism, Historical Causality, and Imperial Clubdom*, London: Regency Press.

Robertson, D.B., and Waltman, J.L. (1993) 'The Politics of Policy Borrowing', in David Finegold, Laurel McFarland and William Richardson (eds), *Something Borrowed, Something Learned? The Transatlantic Market in Education and Training Reform*, Washington, D.C.: The Brookings Institute.

Rosenthal, M. (1986) *The Character Factory: Baden-Powell and the Origins of the Boy Scout Movement*, New York: Pantheon Books.

Rubinstein, D. (1969) 'School Attendance in London, 1870–1904: A Social History', in John Saville (ed.), *Occasional Papers in Economic and Social History*, No. 1, Hull, England: Hull Publishers Ltd.

Ruggie, J.G. (1992) 'Multilateralism: The anatomy of an institution', *International Organization*, Vol. 46, pp. 561–98.

Said, E. (1978 and 1995) *Orientalism*, Harmondsworth: Penguin.

Samoff, J. (1999) 'Institutionalizing International Influence', in Robert F. Arnove, and Carlos Alberto Torres (eds), *Comparative Education: The Dialectic of the Global and the Local*, Oxford: Rowman & Littlefield Publishers, Inc.

Sampson, M.J. (1969) *West African Leadership: Public Speeches Delivered by J.E. Casely Hayford*, London: Frank Cass& Co. Ltd.

Sarbah, J. M. (1897) *Fanti Customary Laws*, London: William Clowes and Sons.

——(1906) *Fanti National Constitutions*, London: Frank Cass.

Scanlon, D.G., (ed.) (1966) *Church, State, and Education in Africa*, New York: Teachers College Press.

Schultz, T.W. (1971) 'Investment in Human Capital', *American Economic Review*, Vol. 51, No. 1, pp. 1–17.

Scribner, S., and Cole, M. (1981) *The Psychology of Literacy*, Cambridge: Harvard University Press.

Semali, L. (1999) 'Community as Classroom: Dilemmas of Valuing African Indigenous Literacy in Education', *International Review of Education*, Vol. 45, No. 3/4, pp. 305–319.

Setse, T.K. (1974) 'Foundations of Nation-Building: The Case of Achimota School', Legon.

Sifuna, D.N. (1992) 'Diversifying the Secondary School Curriculum: The African Experience', *International Review of Education*.Vol. 38, No. 1, pp. 5-18.

Sivonen, S. (1995) *White-Collar or Hoe Handle: African Education under British Colonial Policy 1920–45*, Helsinki: Suomen Historiallinen Seura.

Smith, E.W. (1929) *Aggrey of Africa: A Study in Black and White*, London: Student Christian Movement.

Sonnenberg, K. (2012) 'Traditional Apprenticeship in Ghana and Senegal: Skills Development for Youth for the Informal Sector', *Journal of International Cooperation in Education*, Vol. 15, No. 2, pp. 93–105.

Spivak, G. (1987) *In Other Worlds: Essays in Cultural Politics*, Abington: Taylor & Francis.

Springhall, J. (1977) *Youth, Empire and Society: British Youth Movements, 1883–1940*, London: Croom Helm.

Stanley, B. (1990) *The Bible and the Flag: Protestant Missions & British Imperialism in the Nineteenth & Twentieth Centuries*, Leichester, UK: Apollos.

Steiner-Khamsi, G., and Quist, H.O. (2000) 'The Politics of Educational Borrowing: Reopening the Case of Achimota in British Ghana', *Comparative Education Review*, Vol. 44, No. 3.

Stoler, A.L., and Cooper, F. (1997) 'Between Metropole and Colony: Rethinking a Research Agenda', in Frederick Cooper and Ann Laura Stoler (eds), *Tensions of Empire: Colonial Cultures in a Bourgeois World*, Berkeley: University of California Press.

Summers, C. (1997) 'Demanding Schools: The Umchingwe Project and African Men's Struggles for Education in Southern Rhodesia, 1928–1934', *African Studies Review*, Vol. 40, No. 2, pp. 117–39.

——— (1999) 'Mission Boys, Civilized Men, and Marriage: Educated African Men in the Missions of Southern Rhodesia, 1920–1945", *The Journal of Religious History*, Vol. 23, No. 1 (February), pp. 75–91.

Tedla, E. (1995) *Sankofa: African Thought and Education*, New York: Peter Lang.

Trouillot, M.-R. (1995) *Silencing the Past: Power and Production of History*, Boston, Mass.: Beacon Press.

UNESCO Regional Office for Education in Africa (BREDA) (1995) 'Education Strategies for the 1990s: Orientations and

Achievements: Report on the State of Education in Africa 1995', Paris: UNESCO.

UNESCO (2012) *Youth and Skills: Global Monitoring Report 2012*, Paris: UNESCO.

———(1961) *Report on the Conference of African States on the Development of Education in Africa, Addis Ababa*, Paris: UNESCO.

Verner, D. (1999) 'Wage and Productivity Gaps: Evidence from Ghana', Washington, D.C.: The World Bank.

Wallbank, T.W. (1935) 'Achimota College and Educational Objectives in Africa', *Journal of Negro Education*, Vol. 4, No. 2, pp. 230-245.

Wallerstein, I. (1974) *The Modern World-System*, New York: Academic Press.

Ward, W.E.F. (1959) *Educating young nations*, London: George Allen & Unwin.

———(1965) 'The Early Days of Achimota', *West African Journal of Education*, Vol. 9, No. 3, pp. 125–8.

———(1965) *Fraser of Trinity and Achimota*, Accra: Ghana University Press.

———(1991) *My Africa*, Accra: Ghana University Press.

Weis, L. (1979) 'Education and the Reproduction of Inequality: The Case of Ghana', *Comparative Education Review*, February, pp. 41–51.

Welldon, J.E.C. (1915) *Recollections and Reflections*, London: Cassell.

White, Bob W. (1996) 'Talk about School: Education and the Colonial Project in French and British Africa, (1860-1960)', *Comparative Education*, Vol. 32, No. 1, pp. 9–25.

Whitehead, C. (2003) 'Overseas Education and British colonial education 1929–63', *History of Education*, Vol. 32, No. 5, pp. 561–575.

——— (1995) 'The medium of instruction in British Colonial education: a case of cultural imperialism or enlightened paternalism', *History of Education*, Vol 24, No. 1, pp. 1–15.

———(1989) 'The Impact of the Second World War on British Colonial Education Policy', *History of Education*, Vol. 18, No. 3, pp. 267–93.

———(1981) 'Education in British Colonial Dependencies, 1919–39: A Re-Appraisal', *Comparative Education*, Vol. 17, No. 1, pp. 71–80.

Williams, C. K. (1962) *Achimota: The Early Years 1924–1948*, Accra: Longmans,

Williams, T. D. (1964) 'Sir Gordon Guggisberg and Educational Reform in the Gold Coast, 1919–1927', *Comparative Education Review*, December, pp. 290–306.

Wise, C.G. (1956) *A History of Education in British West Africa*, London: Longmans, Green and Co.

World Bank (2017) *World Development Indicators*, https://data.worldbank.org/ (last accessed 17 September 2017).

———(1995) *Priorities and strategies for education*, Washington, D.C.: The World Bank.

——— (1991). *Vocational and Technical Education and Training: A World Bank Policy Paper*. Washington, D.C.: World Bank.

———(1963) *Proposed Bank/IDA policies in the field of education*, Washington, D.C.: The World Bank.

Wyllie, R.W. (1976) 'Some Contradictions in Missionizing', *Africa*, Vol. 46, No. 2, pp. 196–204.

Yamada, S., and Mazda, N. (2009) 'TVET as viewed from the education sector in Ghana, Uganda and Malawi', in S. Krishna (ed.), *Vocational education and training: Issues and perspectives*, Hyderabad, India: Institute of Chartered Financial Analysts of India University Press, pp. 121–150.

Yamada, S. (ed.) (2016) *Post-Education-For-All and Sustainable Development Paradigm: Structural change and diversifying actors and norms*, London: Emerald Publishing, p. 392.

———(2010) *Multiple Conceptions of Education for All and EFA Development Goals: The processes of adopting a global agenda in the policies of Kenya, Tanzania, and Ethiopia*, VDM Publisher, p. 255.

———(2009) 'Who is the true bearer? The visible and hidden private cost of senior secondary education and equity in Ghana', *Africa Today*, Vol. 55, No. 3. pp. 63–82, Indiana University Press.

———(2005a) *Educational Finance and Poverty Reduction: The cases of Tanzania, Kenya, and Ethiopia*, GRIPS Development Forum Discussion Paper Series, No. 9. p. 26.

———(2005b) 'Socio-Moralist Vocationalism and Public Aspirations: Secondary Education Policies in Colonial and Present-day Ghana', *Africa Today*, Vol. 52, No. 1, pp. 71–94, Indiana University Press.

Yates, B.A. (1971) 'African Reactions to Education: The Congolese Case', *Comparative Education Review*, June, pp. 158–71.

———(1984) 'Comparative Education and the Third World: The Nineteenth Century Revisited', *Comparative Education Review*, Vol. 28, No. 4.

———(1976) 'The Triumph and Failure of Mission Vocational Education in Zaire 1879–1908', *Comparative Education Review*, January, pp. 193–208.

Young, A. (1976) 'The Educational Philosophy of Booker T. Washington, a Perspective for Black Liberation', *Phylon*, Vol. 37, No. 3, pp. 224–35.

Young, D. (1984) 'Knowing How and Knowing That: A Philosophy of the Vocational', London: Birkbeck College, University of London.

Ziderman, A. (1997) 'National Programmes in Technical and Vocational Education: Economic and Education Relationships', *Journal of Vocational Education and Training*, Vol. 49, No. 3, pp. 351–66.

Zimmerman, A. (2012) *Alabama in Africa: Booker T. Washington, the German Empire and the Globalization of the New South*, Princeton: Princeton University Press.

Appendix: List of Interviewees

No.	Name (some are pseudonym)	School	Sex	Year of entrance	Year of graduation	Place of origin	Occupations after graduation, parents' occupation
1	Ekim	Achimota	Male	1927 (Kindergarten)	1940 (Secondary school)	Central Region	High school teacher (was on duty at the time of interview). His father knew Aggrey, one of Achimota founders.
2	Francis	Achimota	Male	1930s		Volta Region	After serving Achimota as a teacher, university professor (History).
3	Dave	Achimota	Male	1927 (Kindergarten)	1938 (Secondary school)	Saltpond (Central Region)	Business executive, former chairman of Ghana Chamber of Commerce. His father knew Aggrey, one of Achimota founders.
4	Emmanuel	Achimota	Male	1935 (Secondary school)	1939 (Secondary school)	Akuwapim (Central Region)	Funded by scholarship to Achimota. Medical doctor from Edinburgh University. First dean of Department of Medicine, University of Cape Coast.
5	George	Achimota	Male	Late 1950s		Accra (Capital)	Lawyer
6	K.B.	Achimota	Male	1938 (Middle school)	1945? (Secondary school)	Accra (Capital)	After serving Achimota as a teacher, foreign service official. One of policy advisors to first president Nkrumah.
7	Robert	Achimota	Male	1946 (Middle school)	Early 1950s? (University intermediate)	Keta (Volta Region)	Achimota teacher (retired after served as school master)

309

8	John	Achimota	Male	1947 (Middle school)	Early 1950s? (University intermediate)	Keta (Volta Region)	Business executive
9	Mareline	Achimota	Female	1933 (Middle school)	1945? (Teacher training college)	Mampong (Eastern Region)	Achimota student teacher, teacher of a girls' high school, before marrying to Dave
10	Rebecca	Achimota	Female	1937 (Primary school)	1949 (Secondary school)	Kumasi (Ashanti Region)	Relative of a chief of Ashanti tribe. Her husband was a registrar at University of Ghana.
11	Cathleen	Achimota	Female	1931 (Kinder-garten)	Finished primary to Secondary school at other place. 1937-40 Achimota teacher training college	Accra (Capital)	Her father was an accountant of Government Treasury. After serving as a teacher for a short period, married to an Achimota teacher, who got advanced degree in the UK and became economist.
12	Mary	Achimota	Female	1933 (Middle school)		Accra (Capital)	After Achimota, learned phermacy in the Gold Coast and nursing in the UK. Her father was a rich land-owned farmer. Her husband was also Achimota graduate and Cathleen's brother.
13	Jane	Achimota	Female	1934 (Middle school)	1941 (Teacher training college)	Akyim-Oda (Eastern Region)	Her father was a spokesman of a traditional chief. After Achimota, served as a teacher before marriage. Her husband got advanced degree in history at Oxford and was a high official at Nkrumah's

							time (went in exile after the coup).
14	Sydney	Mfantsipim*	Male	1947	1951	Nsawam (Eastern Region)	His father was a cocoa buyer. After Mfantsipim, went to Achimota Teacher Training College. After serving as a teacher, got an advanced degree in stock farming.
15	John	Mfantsipim	Male	1928		Cape Coast (Central Region)	His father was a master tailor. Worked for the Ministry of Health for years and the last position before retirement was principal pharmacist.
16	Kofi	Mfantsipim	Male	1930s		Sekondi (Central Region)	Entered Achimota Kindergarten, but lost his father at the age of 9 and quit. During the years at Mfantsipim, non-payment of fees often caused discontinuation of his education. After years of service at government postal office, counsellor of the Ghana Methodist Church.
17	Earnest	Mfantsipim	Male	1941	1946	Shama (Central Region)	Went to Mfantsipim with the scholarship of Anglican Church. One of the first students at the University of Gold Coast. His father was a pastor of Seventh Adventist Church. Got a

							Ph.D. in Physics from a British university. After years of service for the government, he is a reverend now.
18	Kwame	Mfantsipim	Male	1939		Kumasi (Ashanti Region)	After working for the government audit department, got civil servant scholarship to be one of first students of University of Gold Coast. Served as the secretary to the cabinet (head of the civil service) before his retirement.
19	Albert	Mfantsipim	Male	1944	1948	Tarkwa (Central Region)	His father was a master goldsmith. He taught at Achimota and University of Ghana. Politician and once Minister of Education. Ph.D. from SOAS, University of London.
20	Brew	Mfantsipim	Male	1944	1949	Cape Coast (Central Region)	His father was a teacher. M.A. in education from University of Ghana. Ph.D. in Theology from Yale University. Once Director General of Ghana Education Service. Currently, Secretary General of Ghana Methodist Church.

21	James	Mfantsipim	Male	1935	1939	Cape Coast (Central Region)	Mixed-blood of Dutch, British, and Fanti. After studying at Cambridge on scholarship, senior government official. Served for Ministry of Land and Mineral Resources, Ministry of Finance, Ministry of Industry, and Ministry of Labor, before serving for Volta River Land Company as the Chairman of the Board. Retired in 1998.
22	Kwesi	Mfantsipim	Male	1943	1948	Cape Coast (Central Region)	His father was a pastor. After graduating University of Ghana, learned theology in the UK. Former professor of University of Ghana.
23	Joe	Mfantsipim	Male	Late 1950s		Accra (Capital)	Director of an economic research institute

*Mfantsipim had secondary school only.

INDEX

A

Aborigines Right Protection Society 163, 165, 168, 191, 195
Accra 150, 151, 209
　Technical School 191
Achimota education 22, 146-147, 201, 213–219, 223–225
　experiencing 229–237
Achimota Educational Conference 209
Achimota School 3–9, 18, 21–23, 34, 37, 42, 50, 67, 73, 77, 89, 107, 143, 145, 190, 193, 195, 271, 273–274, 277
　emblem 217–218
　as an experiment 199–241
　founders 15, 23, 42, 188, 191, 215, 225–237, 274, 280
　song 220
　teaching staff 145, 188, 219–220
ACNEBTA *see* Advisory Committee on Native Education in British Tropical Africa
actors 4–9, 21–25, 30, 48–49, 66–67, 80, 83, 85, 88–94, 109–111, 115, 145–146, 155, 168, 171, 192–194, 201, 271–272, 275–279
adaptation 4–5, 12, 23–25, 31–40, 49–51, 62, 86–98, 105–129, 143–153, 171–175, 185–188, 199–207, 211–212, 273, 276, 278–280
　to African tradition 222–223
　cultural production under the name of 235–237
　educational adaptation 245–270
　of educational ideas 43–45
　interchangeable concepts for educational 136–138
　public response in Ghana after independence to educational 245–270
　theories of borrowing and 43–45
　Thomas Jesse Jones's theory 142
Adisadel 15, 18, 184, 190–191, 230
Advisory Committee on Education in the Colonies 17
Advisory Committee on Native Education in British Tropical Africa 3, 6, 95, 216
African cultural activities 233
African demands for more and better education 182–187
African historiography 24–25, 34,

275–276, 279
African intellectuals 3, 27, 34, 38, 78, 81, 84–85, 124, 155, 184, 187, 193–194, 202–203, 206, 208, 215–216, 222
African leader 3, 5–6, 10, 34, 43, 50, 72, 82, 141, 145, 186
secondary schools as sites for producing 187–192, 195, 206, 211, 213, 221, 230, 236–237, 274–275, 280
African tradition 8, 10, 12, 23, 38, 75, 146, 161, 167, 186, 194, 201, 203, 206, 236, 276
adaptation to 222–223
definition of 213–219
follower of 211–213
Africanisation 11, 186, 214, 245, 273
age of structural adjustment 249
agencies 9, 31, 48, 263
of the key individuals: 'good' mediators of interests 97–111
Aggrey, James 21, 95, 107–112, 188, 204, 216–218, 225–226, 236
agriculture 56, 73, 92, 100, 125, 134–136, 153, 188, 190, 204–205, 225
Akim Abakwa 164, 185
Akropong 150
all-round education 188, 190, 232

ambivalence 110, 194, 199, 213
among actors 192–195
American influence 83, 111
on colonial education 31–34
American philanthropists 3, 8, 21, 34, 66, 84, 96, 103, 111, 125, 142, 218, 271, 278
American progressive educationists 199
Amfom, Emmanuel 230
Amissah, Samuel Hanson 18
Amu, Ephraim 158
analysis 14, 21, 23–25, 27–29, 31–32, 34–35, 37–38, 40, 42, 45, 49, 62–63, 171, 182, 212, 235–236, 245, 271–276, 279–280
data used for 14–20
of discourse 65–144
framework of 4–9, 276–279
Angola 92, 100
Asante K.B. 230
assimilation 205, 235, 273
Asuom 157

B

Baden Powell 42, 133
Balme Library 248
Banda, Hastings 13
Bannerman, James 162
Basel Missionary Society 124, 149–151, 157, 177–178, 180

Beetham, T.A. 181
Belgian Congo 92
Blyden, E.W. 10, 113, 185–186
boarding school life 231–233
boarding system 231
bourgeois women 134–135
Boy Scout movement 41, 138–139
  elitist moralism translated to a mass programme 133–134
Brass 124
Bremen Missionary Society 124, 150–151, 177–178, 226
British Africa 3, 9, 18, 21, 30, 41, 45, 49, 70, 85–97, 100, 102–103, 111, 155, 271, 277
British colonial education 4, 24, 29–31, 34, 66, 80, 175, 275, 278
  policies 85–115
British Colonial Office 3, 4, 8, 17, 30, 34, 66, 87, 91, 94
British colonial subjects 209
British policies and planning on colonial education 29–31
British South Africa 92
British Victorian moralism 67, 120, 129–136
British West Africa 3, 27, 32, 153, 155, 163, 168, 193–194, 227, 226
British working-class education 203
Brown, E.J.P. 163, 190, 214

Busia, K.A. 230

C

Cambridge Certificate Examination 190,
Cape Coast 15, 18, 149, 151, 190, 231
capitalist economic hierarchy 199
Carnegie Corporation 16, 97
Casely Hayford *see* Hayford
cash-cropping 204, 205
Castle schools 28, 149
character
  development 67, 134, 200–213, 237, 272, 277
  training 4–5, 22–25, 28, 41–42, 92, 127–143, 146, 174–175, 180, 199–212, 218–224, 229–236, 273, 276, 280
chiefs' authority 205
Christian character 200–203, 207–209, 212, 219, 276
Christianity 36, 122, 134, 156, 158, 160, 183–186, 208, 276
Christiansburg 150
chronology 28, 66
  of education in British West Africa 27–28
civilized family life 226
civilising mission 76, 156–159
clerks 211–212, 231 fig 8-1, 267

Clifford, Hugh 160, 172, 187, 193
cocoa 70 fig 3-1, 71 fig 3-2, 72, 159, 165, 172, 204
co-education 174, 201, 225-228, 233–235
colonial Africa 15, 21, 33, 37, 56, 275
 educational philosophies in 279–280
colonial education 3–11, 21, 24–25, 145–147, 171, 179, 199, 201, 205, 271, 273, 275, 277–280
 American influence on 31–34
  development 172–176
 global discourse 65–144
 history 27–43
  reflection on the British policies and planning on 29–31
colonial elite schools 275
**Colonial Office 3–4, 6, 8, 17–18, 21, 29–30, 34, 65–66, 74–77, 83–84, 87–88, 91–94, 102–105, 112, 163, 187, 193, 206
Colonial School 149
Colombia 53, 248
Columbia University 33, 91, 106–107, 120
community transformation 128, 156
Company of Merchants 149
competency-based training (CBT) 253–254, 262–263

Conference of Missionary Societies in Great Britain and Northern Ireland (CBMS-IMC) 17–18, 77, 93, 101
context which conditioned the discourse 69–84
Convention People's Party (CPP) 257, 264
convergence of interests 88–97
convergences and divergences of Ghanaian policies and global trends 263–265
coordination 21, 75, 88, 106, 110, 260, 263
Council for TVET (COTVET) Act 263
criticism 31, 39, 48, 51, 85, 109, 155, 168, 210–211, 227, 249, 254–255
 against mission schools 156–159
 of tracking and the vocationalisation of the general secondary curriculum 57–60
cultural influence 43, 232–233, 274
cultural nationalism 171, 186, 194, 199
cultural production 37, 43, 62
 under the name of 'adaptation' 235–237
curriculum 12, 16, 38, 41–43, 50, 55, 83, 121–123, 131, 138, 145, 150,

161, 177, 185–186, 190–191, 194, 199, 205, 207, 213–215, 218, 224, 245, 258, 260, 263, 265, 274

    general secondary 57–60

customary laws 168, 199, 214

D

Damas, Léon 82
Data used for the analysis 14–20
Davis, Jackson 16, 96
De Richelieu 150
demands from the general public 182–184
denominational rivalry 177
   and increasing control by the government 181–182
denominational segregation 236
development of the colonial education system during the governorship of Guggisberg 172–176
developmental stages 127
Dewey, John 7, 67, 120–122
dialectics between the global and the national 263–270
dignity of labour 127, 136, 219, 234, 236, 273
    handwork 223–225
Dillard, J.H. 96, 108
Diploma Disease 12
documentary research 15–19

Donohugh, Thomas 100
Du Bois, W.E.B. 13, 78–83, 109, 112, 115, 187
Dutch West India Company 149

E

economic justification for vocational education 52–54, 264
educated elite 155, 161–168, 193, 195, 199, 206, 211, 269
education for Africans 4, 14, 22–23, 75, 78, 110, 135, 184, 186, 219, 271
education for all
education in Africa 3, 7, 50, 57, 59, 61, 175, 207–273, 280
   global discourse 65–144
   history of colonial education and 27–43
education in the systemic web of colonialism 74–77
Education Ordinance, 1925 173, 179–182
education policies 3, 24, 29–30, 43, 45, 51, 77, 84, 246, 264, 274
   external influences on the vocational secondary 246–256
   genesis of British colonial 85–117
   in the post-colonial Ghana and the changing focus on vocational education 257–263

education reform 263–265, 270
  new 262–263
  socio-moralist vocationalism 259–260
educational adaptation 32, 45, 105, 110, 125, 142, 212, 273
  interchangeable concepts for 136–138
  and public response in Ghana after independence 245–270
educational administration 21, 27, 65, 83, 88, 94, 112, 153, 171, 174–176, 179
educational discourse 22–23, 32, 36, 102, 140, 199, 245, 249
  and Guggisberg's administration 171–197
Educational Ordinance of 1882 153
Educational Ordinance of 1887 153
educational philosophies 22, 29, 40, 42, 105, 115, 119–122, 126, 129, 136, 142–143, 236, 272
  in colonial Africa 279–280
educational practice 9, 44, 86, 89–90, 94, 97, 99, 102, 115, 138, 142, 173, 175, 177–178, 191, 199, 202, 276–277, 279
  and experience of schooling 39–43
educational transfer 16, 24, 46, 49–50

and politics of discourse 111–115, 119, 142, 275, 277–278
efficient workmanship 201–205, 212, 276
egalitarian perspective 249, 255
Elementary Education Act, 1870 123, 181
elite education 123, 139, 257, 264
  'Public school': masculinity in 129–132
Elmina 149
Empire's Day 209
ethnic background 213, 219
European civilization 156, 185, 235, 273
European culture 13, 36–37, 134, 155, 194, 208, 232, 279
Ewe 150, 222, 232
experiencing Achimota education 229–237
external influences on the vocational secondary education policies 246–256
  1950s and 1960s 246–247
  1970s to early 1980s 248–249
  1980s 249–250
  1990s to the mid-2000s 250–253

F

Fia Sri II 213, 215
First World War 69–70, 72, 83, 151
follower of African traditions and customs 201, 203, 211–213, 276
formulating the Alliance of Mission Societies 71, 88–89
framework of policy analysis 276–279
Fraser, A.G. 18, 42, 89, 188–189, 202, 205–206, 219, 225–226
Free Compulsory Universal Basic Education (FCUBE) 261
Freetown 124

G

Ga 150, 214 table 8-1, 222–223, 232
games 6, 131, 139–141, 174–175
genesis of British colonial education policies 85–117
Ghana Poverty Reduction Strategy 261
Girl Guide 41, 134, 139
girls' boarding schools 226
girls' education 28, 110
    wives of the classed men 134–136, 175, 226–227, 235
global discourse 24, 146, 171, 245, 255, 265, 277–278
    on colonial education in Africa and its constructs 65–144
    perspectives on 43–50
global mechanism
    for developing a common policy framework 47–48
    of international educational development 49, 278
global trends 51, 246, 255, 267, 274
    convergences and divergences 263–265
Gold Coast Board of Education 17
Gold Coast Education Ordinance of 1925 179
government–mission relationship 171
    forces for alignment 177–182
grants-in-aid 94, 153, 177
Great Depression 71–72, 146
Greaves, Lionel Bruce 18
Greek 127, 183, 185, 190
Guggisberg, Frederick Gordon 21–22, 27–28, 72–73, 92, 140–141, 146, 155, 160, 162, 213, 216, 226
Guggisberg's administration 171–197
Gurvey, Marcus 13

H

habitus 6
Hampton Institute 19, 80, 98, 108, 113, 126, 186

Hampton University 15–16
Hampton-Tuskegee 105, 111, 122, 127–129, 142, 222–223
handwork 127, 188, 223–225, 232, 235
harambee schools 10
Hardaker 101–102
Hausa kingdoms 164
Hayford, Adelaide 194
Hayford, J.E. Casely 10, 113–114, 158, 163, 167–168, 178, 185–186, 190, 193–195, 199, 206, 214–215
Hillard, F.H. 27
holder of a sense of citizenship 201, 203, 209–210, 276
Hood, J.E.W. 206
humility 233

I

implication of vocationalism in Africa 60–62
Indonesia 13, 54
industrial schools 122, 124
informal sector 60, 253
intelligentsia 13, 80, 178
interchangeable concepts for educational adaptation 136–138
International Missionary Council 17, 19, 30, 77, 87, 90, 96, 102
interventionism 72–73
interventionist government and scientific planning 72–74
interview 14, 19–20, 23, 98, 104, 108, 147, 165, 201, 215, 229, 233, 262
inter-war period 6, 22, 65, 73, 83, 171, 272, 275
    political economy of 69–72
inviting the American experts 89–92
involvement of the colonial government in education 152–153
issues of political debates and actors in the early 20th century 155–166

J

Jeanes
    Fund 96, 108, 114, 128
    School 97, 128, 142
jointly moulding the global policy framework 93–97
Jomtien 250
**Jones, Thomas Jesse 21, 86–87, 90–96, 104–106, 108–110, 112, 125, 127, 142, 199, 223, 272
    salesperson of the American model 98–102
Jullien, Marc-Antoine 44
justifications for vocational education 52–57, 260

K

Katsina College 43
Keigwin 101
Kenya 10, 13, 35–36, 54, 56–57, 82, 97, 108
Kenyatta, Jomo 13, 82
Kikuyu 10
King Edward VII Memorial Scholarship 177
King, Martin Luther 83
Kohle Bu 73, 172
    Hospital 234
Kufor government 259
Kwapong A.A. 230

L

labour market demand 245, 255
laissez-faire approach 73, 250
Lands Bill 163, 166
Latin 25, 31, 127, 183–185, 190, 223
Latin America 31, 53–54, 267
Le Zoute 96
**leadership 3, 34, 37, 50, 72, 76, 78, 81–82, 110, 130, 132–133, 138, 141, 145, 155, 167, 172, 175, 186, 201, 203, 205–207, 212, 215, 218–219, 221, 223, 229, 264, 276
learning by doing 120–123, 136, 272
Liberia 16, 34, 92, 113
    College 185
limitations of conventional analytical framework 48–50
literary education 38–30, 77–78, 85, 127, 140, 161, 174, 176, 192, 205, 254
    controversy, mission schools: a root of vocational versus 149–151
    perennial debate over vocational versus 50–62
local politics of education in Africa 34–39
Lockhart, Rev. R.A. 178,
longitudinal patterns of debates on vocational education 254–255
Loram, C.T. 95–96
Lovedale Industrial School 124
Lugard, Lord 18, 74, 88, 95, 138–139, 163, 180, 205–207, 219

M

Mann, Horace 44
manual work 40, 56, 96, 121, 135, 137, 153, 160–161, 190, 205, 224, 260
Marshall, J.R. 18
masculinity 40
    in elite education 129–132
mass education 7, 37, 67, 100–111, 124, 135, 141
    system 273
mélange of fashionable ideas to legitimise colonial education 136–

Memorandum on Education Policy in British Tropical Africa 4, 87, 95, 145, 179

**metropole 3, 5–9, 13, 21, 29, 43, 47–48, 70, 72–73, 76, 86–88, 98, 102, 112, 145, 147, 166, 171, 201, 213, 271–272, 276, 278

Mfantsipim 15, 18–19, 38, 42–43, 178, 183–184, 192, 194, 201–202, 215, 230–231

   other secondary schools 190–192

military drill 131, 140

Millennium Development Goals (MDGs) 14

Mills, Hutton 167

mission boys 86, 112, 160, 168

mission education 35, 86, 90, 159, 168, 171, 176, 199, 207–208

   saturating the labour market and scepticism of 159–161

mission schools 85, 101, 153, 162, 166, 177, 183, 192, 208, 273

   Basel and Bremen 178

   civilising mission and rising criticism against 156–159

   a root of vocational versus literary education controversy 149–151

*mission societies 21, 30–31, 75–77, 86–90, 93–96, 102–103, 106, 112, 157, 171, 184, 192, 271

mission societies' dilemma 176–182

mixed model for the African colonies 138–143

model school 145, 188, 190, 201, 213, 277, 280

motivations for transferring educational ideas 45–47

Murray, Victor 39, 74, 106

N

National Association for the Advancement of Colored People (NAACP) 82, 115

National Congress of British West Africa 163, 168, 193–194

national discourse 31

   on education and struggle over hegemony 145–241

National TVET Qualification Framework and Accreditation Standard 263

nationalists' demands for higher education 184–187

needlework 41, 153

neoliberalism 254

Nigeria 18, 43, 74, 88, 92, 106, 129, 138–139, 155, 163–164

Nkrumah, Kwame 13, 82, 187, 230,

257–258, 264, 268
    University of Science 257
norms 4–9, 21, 25, 48, 67, 73, 130, 146–147, 200–201, 212, 221, 235, 272–274, 278
Nyerere, Julius 12, 82

O

Oettli, Rev. 180
Office of Special Inquiries and Reports of the English Board of Education 44
Ofori Atta I, Nana 157, 164–168, 185, 195, 213–215
Oldham, J.H. 17–18, 21, 30, 77, 87–90, 93–95, 100–102, 110, 112, 272
    the spider of the missionary web 102–106
Omanhin Ababio II 211
Onitsha 124
Ormsby-Gore 93, 95, 104–105
overlapping spaces of global influence 83–84
Oxford
    Rhodes House Library 15, 17
    University 18, 129

P

Pan-African Congress 13, 82, 112
Pan-Africanism 83, 187
    and inspirations for nationalism in Africa 78–83
paternalism 33, 72, 133, 139
Peki Blengo 226
perennial debate over vocational versus literary education 50–62
persistent distrust in the vocational track 266–280
perspectives on global discourse and transfer of educational models 43–50
**Phelps-Stokes Commission 32, 66, 74, 86, 90–91, 95, 97–98, 101–103, 105, 107, 109, 124
**Phelps-Stokes Fund 3, 7, 15–16, 31–32, 66–67, 86–87, 89–90, 94, 96–98, 100, 108, 114, 125, 141, 278
philosophical sources of inspiration for African education 119–144
policy documents 87, 142, 276
political context 65, 176
    on the Gold Coast 149–170
political economy 21, 127, 146
    of the inter-war period in Europe 69–72
political rivalry 193
    and accusation for 'denationalisation' 167–169
popularisation of basic education 261–262
post-colonial Africa 14
    attention to education in the

colonial and 10–14

post-history and conclusion 243–270

practices of secondary education in Ghana 266–280

prehistory: education until early 20th century 149–154

Prince of Wales College and School at Achimota 173, 187–190, 193

progressive education 121

    philosophies 22, 39, 120

    philosophies: learning by doing 120–123

progressive educationists 121–123, 199

progressive philosophers 120

Project on the Development of Education in Pre-independent Africa 18

Public Record Office 15, 17

public school 7, 41–42, 67, 124, 128, 132–142, 205, 235–236, 269, 273

    in Africa 218–228

    masculinity in elite education 129–132

Q

Quaque, Philip 149

R

racial evolutionism 156, 160

racial preconceptions 156, 185, 272

Rawlings, Jerry 258–259, 264

recent revival of vocationalism and promotion of competency-based training 253–254

reflection on the British policies and planning on colonial education 29–31

religious education 77, 86, 92–93, 96, 111–112, 160, 179–181, 192, 202, 207, 271

Riis, Andreas 150

Rockefeller Archive Center (RAC) 15–16

Rodger, Sir John 160

role of education 43, 128, 201, 280

S

Sadler, Michael 44–45

Salems 157

Armstrong, Samuel 114, 126–127

Sarbah, John Mensah 10, 163, 166, 168, 190–191, 199, 201, 206, 214

saturating the labour market and scepticism of mission education 159–161

scholarship 13, 78, 162, 229–230, 234–235, 269, 274

Schomburg Center Library 16
School of Oriental and African Studies (SOAS) 15, 17–18
Second World War *see* World War II
**secondary school 14, 18–20, 38, 43, 52–53, 57–59, 172, 174, 178, 185, 193, 205, 215, 220–221, 230, 235, 237, 248–249, 258, 260, 266, 271

    other 190–192

    as the sites for producing African leaders 187–192

Senghor, Léopold Sédar 82
Sierra Leone 149, 155, 163, 183
Sixteen Principles 173, 175, 192
skills training 40–41, 56, 60–62, 150, 177, 249
Slater Fund 96, 114
social mobility 211, 223, 229–231, 269, 275
social services 14, 75–76, 86, 221, 234, 248, 250
social welfare 71, 73, 76, 221
socially upward mobility 236, 274
socio-economic status, 229, 236, 274
socio-moralist vocationalism
    education reform 259–260
Southern blacks 66, 114
Structural Adjustment Program 264
structural adjustment

    the age of 249–250

structure of the book 21–25
struggle for political representation 161–166
sustainable development goals (SDGs) 14
system development in the 1960s 257

T

Takoradi 73, 172
Tanzania 12, 53, 56–57, 82, 248
teaching materials 23, 245
team sports 41, 131, 219
technical and vocational education (TVET) 61, 96, 247, 250, 253, 262
theories on borrowing and adaptation of educational ideas 43–45
three R's 151, 153, 160, 212
thriftiness 200, 233
Togo 151
Touré, Sékou 12
traditional chiefs 3, 23, 75, 146, 155, 163–166, 173, 185, 193, 195, 205, 211–214, 231, 269
transfer of educational models 43–50
turmoils in the 1970s 258
Tuskegee Institute 34, 79, 113–114, 121–122, 140

Twi 150, 216, 222–223, 232

type of character 41

    to be developed at school 200–213

V

Vischer, Hanns 88, 94–96, 102

vocational education 21, 24, 32, 38–39, 45, 50–52, 57–62, 78–79, 82–84, 110–111, 121–123, 176–179, 192, 246–254, 260–270, 273, 279

    in Britain and America 123–129

    education policies in the post-colonial Ghana

    and the changing focus on 257

    justifications for 52–57

    longitudinal patterns of debates on 254–255

vocationalisation 39, 51, 54–55, 249, 260–265, 274

    Criticism of tracking and the 57–60

vocationalism 24, 56, 246, 257, 264, 267, 275

    implication of 60–62

    recent revival of 253–254

    socio-moralist 259–260

W

Ward, W.E.F. 18, 29, 42, 216

Washington, Booker T. 80–82, 109, 112–113, 122, 126, 204, 217–218

Wesley Methodist Mission Society (WMMS) 17

Wesleyan High School 151, 190–191

Westernisation 155, 168, 194, 213

Wilkie, Rev. 90

Williams, Garfield 95

World Bank 49, 53, 55, 247–251, 261–264

World Conference on Education for All 250, 261

World Missionary Conference 3, 66, 86, 89, 93

World War II 11, 15, 52, 65

world-system theorists 47–48

worldview 5, 13, 158

www.ingramcontent.com/pod-product-compliance
Lightning Source LLC
Chambersburg PA
CBHW051349290426
44108CB00015B/1941